NATU

Natural Law

A Jewish, Christian, and Islamic Trialogue

ANVER M. EMON, MATTHEW LEVERING, AND
DAVID NOVAK

OXFORD
UNIVERSITY PRESS

OXFORD

UNIVERSITY PRESS

Great Clarendon Street, Oxford, OX2 6DP,
United Kingdom

Oxford University Press is a department of the University of Oxford.
It furthers the University's objective of excellence in research, scholarship,
and education by publishing worldwide. Oxford is a registered trade mark of
Oxford University Press in the UK and in certain other countries

First published 2014
First published in paperback 2015

Published in the United States of America by Oxford University Press
198 Madison Avenue, New York, NY 10016, United States of America

British Library Cataloguing in Publication Data
Data available

Library of Congress Cataloguing in Publication Data
Data available

ISBN 978-0-19-870660-1 (Hbk.)
ISBN 978-0-19-874500-6 (Pbk.)

*To Allyssa J. Case, Joy Levering, and Melva Novak:
our beloved wives*

Acknowledgments

Each of us came to this project from different scholarly traditions and communities, all of which helped us individually to reflect on our own traditions as we collectively sought to do something together. We want to take this moment to thank them for all they have offered.

ANVER M. EMON

I wish to thank my dean, Mayo Moran, for creating a supportive and encouraging interdisciplinary environment in which the all-too-neat divides between the medieval and the modern, the legal and the historical, the religious and the secular can be called into question. My colleagues at the University of Toronto and other leading institutions in North America and Europe have been steady interlocutors over the years. Many of them have been directly engaged in the ideas I explore in this book, though none of them are responsible for the limitations of the argument herein. Many thanks are due to Nicholas Adams, Rumee Ahmed, Alan Brudner, Ayesha Chaudhry, Yasmin Dawood, Robert Gibbs, Bernard Haykel, Audrey Macklin, Andrew March, Nadia Marzouki, Muhammad Khalid Masud, Ziba Mir-Hosseini, Walid Saleh, David Schneiderman, Adam Seligman, Adel Omar Sherif, Denise Spellberg, Mairaj Syed, James Tully, Robert Wisnovsky, and Muhammad Qasim Zaman. Also, many thanks go to Marianne Constable of UC Berkeley who organized a workshop at the Rhetoric Department where an earlier version of this essay was presented. The participants at that workshop offered numerous comments that helped improve this essay. Much of the research for my section was undertaken with the generous support of a grant from Canada's Social Sciences and Humanities Research Council (SSHRC).

MATTHEW LEVERING

I gratefully acknowledge J. Budziszewski, Jana Bennett, and John Berkman. They read my essay and offered helpful corrections and resources. Paul Benson and Sandra Yocum generously encouraged the project from the beginning, and supported our 2011 meeting at the University of Dayton. Doctoral students in theology at the University of Dayton helped out extensively in coordinating that meeting, above all Jason Heron, Alan Mostrom, and Matthew Archer. David B. Burrell, CSC merits particular thanks for inspiring me many years ago to dream of undertaking this kind of work. As this book was completed, I moved to Mundelein Seminary to the newly established Perry Family Foundation Professor of Theology. I wish to thank James and Mary Perry for their wonderful generosity and encouraging welcome. Let me also especially thank Mundelein's extraordinary Rector, Robert Barron, along with Melanie Barrett, Thomas Baima, Emery de Gaal, John Lehocky, the late Edward Oakes, S.J., and all others who so graciously welcomed my family and me to the Chicago area.

DAVID NOVAK

I thank my "Doktorvater," Germain Grisez, who guided my initial efforts to work out my own natural law theory at Georgetown University, and the late Leo Strauss who first stimulated my interest in natural right at the University of Chicago. Like all theorists, natural law theorists best develop their own perspective by conversing with others who have important things to teach them from both similar and dissimilar perspectives. Among those with whom I have been in sustained conversation over the years on this and related topics are: Hadley Arkes, Leora Batnitzky, Joseph Boyle, the late Boaz Cohen, the late Ze'ev Falk, the late Marvin Fox, Robert George, Mary Ann Glendon, Lenn Goodman, Eric Gregory, Russell Hittinger, Bernard Jackson, Martin Kavka, Paul Nahme, the late Richard John Neuhaus, Oliver O'Donovan, Randi Rashkover, Kurt Richardson, Abdulaziz Sachedina, Gregor Scherzinger, Robert Tuttle, Michael Walzer, John Witte, and Alan Yuter. Finally, I want to thank the Faculty of Arts and Science at the University of Toronto for providing me with an academic environment in which the pursuit of truth is expected and thus comes naturally.

The authors are most grateful to Cole Sadler, a doctoral student in the Department for the Study of Religion at the University of Toronto. Cole did us outstanding service by recording our consultation at the University of Toronto in September 2012, and in preparing the bibliography and the index. The authors also wish to express appreciation to Tom Perridge of Oxford University Press for skillfully guiding the manuscript to publication.

Contents

Introduction

Anver Emon, Matthew Levering, David Novak

This book had its origins in early Fall 2010, when Matthew Levering invited Anver M. Emon and David Novak to participate in a symposium devoted to "Natural Law: Jewish, Christian, and Islamic Perspectives." The goal of the symposium was to produce the present book, consisting in programmatic essays by each of us and responses by each of us to the essays of the other two. In Fall 2010, Levering had just published a book engaging Novak's theology. In the course of researching that book, he had noted that although Novak had devoted much time to Jewish–Christian dialogue, Novak had also said important things in the area of Jewish–Muslim dialogue—a fact that some Christian reviewers had overlooked about his work. Levering was also reading Emon's then newly published *Islamic Natural Law Theories*, and was intrigued to find that in defining "natural law" for his audience, Emon had recourse to Christian natural law theorists such as Thomas Aquinas, John Finnis, and Anthony Lisska. In these thinkers, and in the Muslim thinkers whom he studies, Emon finds a "focus on reason and its authority for normatively ordering the world," and his book probes deeply into this topic through close readings of pre-modern Islamic legal texts.[1] Since Novak had authored notable works on natural law, including *Natural Law in Judaism*, and since Levering had studied natural law doctrine from a Christian theological perspective in his *Biblical Natural Law*, a collaborative project on natural law doctrine seemed a fruitful next step. That is the purpose of the

---

[1] Anver M. Emon, *Islamic Natural Law Theories* (Oxford: Oxford University Press, 2010), 8.

present book. The book aims to stimulate reflection on natural law and to encourage further discussions and friendships among Jewish, Christian, and Muslim scholars and communities.

In addition to the fact that the three authors are Jewish, Christian, and Muslim respectively, certain creative differences were present from the outset that gave further impetus to the project. Foremost among these were the differences in our specific areas of expertise. Novak is a Jewish philosopher and theologian, deeply trained not only in classical Jewish sources but also in the tradition of Western philosophy. Levering is a Catholic theologian whose dialogue partners are generally biblical scholars and theologians. Emon is an expert on the tradition of Islamic jurisprudence and a lawyer, and he teaches not philosophy or theology but law. We hope that these different emphases and intellectual backgrounds come across in the present book in creative and interesting ways.

The original symposium took place on November 9–10, 2011. During the presentations and the panel discussion that followed, the authors benefited from the insights of numerous participants, including Gregor Scherzinger, John Inglis, Myrna Gabbe, Jason Heron, Brad Kallenberg, and Jana Bennett. A second symposium followed on September 20–21, 2012 at the University of Toronto Law School. Instead of public presentations, here we shared our drafts with a select group of scholars and friends, including Cole Sadler, Walid Saleh, John Berkman, Abraham Rothstein, Alan Brudner, Shayna Kravetz, Matthew LaGrone, and Kurt Richardson. We revised our essays and responses extensively in light of their criticisms and suggestions.

Books like the present might be expected to have concrete political ramifications: to promote peace and justice; to overcome intolerance and hatred; to heal tensions that exist around the world and in our own societies. We did not write this book for such purposes, although we hope that the book will indeed make a contribution to these goals. Instead we wrote the book in the hopes of better understanding natural law thinking and its sources in our respective traditions. In a comparable way, in the medieval period philosophical and theological discussions were carried forward by Jewish, Christian, and Muslim scholars—despite polemics and oppression—in the interest of better appreciating the realities that were under discussion, such as God, providence, the human soul, and so forth. The quest for insights in our own traditions—which have been and remain in community with each other—and not a pragmatic or political platform, is what brings us together.

Thus it should not surprise that for our main interlocutors in our essays, each of us chose figures whose prominence in and influence on our respective traditions is indisputable. Novak's essay engages critically and constructively not merely with philosophers such as Plato, Aristotle, and Immanuel Kant, but also with the Bible, the *Mishnah Torah*, the Talmud, Maimonides, Menahem ha-Meiri, and various contemporary scholars, not least Leo Strauss. Levering's essay focuses on Paul's letter to the Romans as seen through the eyes of patristic commentators including Origen of Alexandria, John Chrysostom, Ambrosiaster, Pelagius, and Augustine. He also has in view the writings of Thomas Aquinas, as well as more recent Christian thinkers such as Karl Barth, Paul Ramsey, Stanley Hauerwas, Germain Grisez, Russell Hittinger, Servais Pinckaers, and Alasdair MacIntyre. Emon, too, engages numerous contemporary thinkers, including John Rawls and Nasr Hamid Abu Zayd, but he grounds his study in the work of medieval Muslim theologians, philosophers, and legal scholars, such as Ibn Sina, Ibn Hazm, Abu Ishaq al-Shirazi, Abu Hamid al-Ghazali, Ibn Rushd, and Abu Ishaq al-Shatibi. The resulting trialogue is deeply rooted, therefore, in classical Jewish, Christian, and Islamic sources, while at the same time being shaped by contemporary concerns and aiming to contribute to contemporary conversations about natural law.

A co-authored trialogue requires an order of essays, even though this order cannot be taken to indicate a judgment of value. We have chosen to follow a historical ordering: Judaism, Christianity, Islam. Our responses to each other's essays then reverse this ordering. Thus Novak's essay on natural law and Judaism opens the volume, followed by the responses of Emon and Levering. Levering's essay on natural law and Christianity is followed by the responses of Emon and Novak. Lastly, Emon's essay on natural law and Islam is followed by the responses of Levering and Novak.

These essays and responses were not meant to produce a synthetic "conclusion" to the volume in which the three of us speak with one voice, even though we certainly do think that we have demonstrated numerous shared concerns and values. Instead, in the process of probing our own traditions, engaging critically with each other, and learning from each other, we aim to practice the kind of hospitable intellectual and interreligious engagement that, arguably, natural law itself requires.

1

Natural Law and Judaism

David Novak

For over thirty years I have been formulating and reformulating a theory of natural law, primarily drawing from texts in the biblical-rabbinic tradition (and, secondarily, from general philosophical texts) in three main works: *The Image of the Non-Jew in Judaism*[1]; *Natural Law in Judaism*[2]; and *Covenantal Rights*.[3] In addition, the theory has been developed in a number of articles.[4] Discussions of some more practical aspects of natural law have appeared in my *The Jewish Social Contract*[5]; *The Sanctity of Human Life*[6]; and *In Defense of Religious Liberty*.[7] This essay attempts to summarize the conclusions of these previously published works. It is also hoped that it might add something new to their conclusions. Here I propose and expound eleven propositions about natural law and Judaism. All eleven propositions are controversial and have been disputed by both Jewish and non-Jewish thinkers.

---

[1] New York and Toronto: Edwin Mellen Press, 1983; 2nd ed., ed. M. LaGrone (Oxford: Littman Library of Jewish Civilization, 2011).

[2] Cambridge: Cambridge University Press, 1998. For a condensed version of the conclusions of this book, see David Novak, "Judaism and Natural Law," *The American Journal of Jurisprudence* (1998), 43:117–34.

[3] Princeton, NJ: Princeton University Press, 2000.

[4] For some of these articles, see David Novak, *Talking with Christians: Musings of a Jewish Theologian* (Grand Rapids, MI: Eerdmans Publishing Co., 2005); *Tradition in the Public Square: A David Novak Reader*, eds. R. Rashkover and M. Kavka (Grand Rapids, MI: Eerdmans Publishing Co., 2008).

[5] Princeton, NJ: Princeton University Press, 2005.

[6] Washington, DC: Georgetown University Press, 2007.

[7] Wilmington, DE: ISI Books, 2009.

There are those who presume coherent natural law thinking presupposes the type of *natural* ontology developed by classical Greek philosophers, especially Plato, Aristotle, and the Stoics.[8] Some of those who hold this opinion reject any attempt to see the idea of "nature" that supplies the "natural" in *natural* law as being consistent with the doctrine of revelation that supplies the "revealed" in *revealed law*. (Needless to say, the doctrine of "Torah from God," i.e., divine revelation, lies at the very core of Judaism.[9]) In this view, any attempt to "do" natural law theory or praxis within the normative Jewish tradition is disingenuous, being based on a fundamental mistake. This view was boldly put forth by the late Leo Strauss (d. 1973), who wrote:

> The idea of natural right must be unknown as long as the idea of nature is unknown. The discovery of nature is the work of philosophy. Where there is no philosophy, there is no knowledge of natural right as such. The Old Testament, whose basic premise may be said to be the implicit rejection of philosophy, does not know "nature."[10]

[8] See, e.g., A. P. d'Entrèves, *Natural Law* (New York: Harper and Row, 1965), 17ff.; Heinrich A. Rommen, *The Natural Law*, trans. T. R. Hanley (Indianapolis, IN: Liberty Fund, 1998), 3ff.

[9] On this whole topic, see the magisterial work of my late revered teacher, Abraham Joshua Heschel, *Heavenly Torah*, trans. G. Tucker (New York: Continuum, 2005).

[10] *Natural Right and History* (Chicago: University of Chicago Press, 1953), 81. Strauss uses the term "natural right" in the sense of the German *Naturrecht*, viz., a normative order (e.g., *Rechtsordnung*) as distinct from explicitly prescribed specific norms. For Strauss, "Right" is thus *ius* rather than *lex* or *nomos* or *Gesetz*; it is *ius naturale* rather than *lex naturalis*. As such, Strauss's notion of Right is most akin to the older Greek idea of *dikē* or "cosmic justice" (see, e.g., Sophocles, *Antigone*, 365; Aristotle, *Nicomachean Ethics*, 5.7/1134b30). In fact, Strauss' oldest disciple, Harry V. Jaffa, argued that for the Greek philosophers the very term "natural law" (*nomos physeos*) would be an oxymoron, since "law" (*nomos*) is made (sometimes by gods, more frequently by humans), whereas "nature" (*physis*) is unmade, thus eternally present (see his "Natural Law" in *The International Encyclopedia of the Social Sciences*, 11:80). For the argument that the concept of natural *law* (as distinct from *Naturrecht* as "natural justice") has its origin in Hellenistic Judaism, however, beginning with Philo in the first century CE (who saw Nature to be a creation of God, and God to be the Lawgiver), see Helmut Koester, "νόμος φύσεως: The Concept of Natural Law in Greek Thought," in *Religions in Antiquity: Essays in Memory of Erwin Ramsdell Goodenough*, ed. J. Neusner (Leiden: E. J. Brill, 1968), 521ff. For two critiques of Strauss' notion that philosophy (which teaches natural right) and theology (which teaches natural law) are antithetical, see David Novak, *Jewish Social Ethics* (New York: Oxford University Press, 1992), 29–43; David Novak, "Philosophy and the Possibility of Revelation: A Theological Response to the Challenge of Leo Strauss" in *Leo Strauss and Judaism*, ed. D. Novak (Lanham, MD: Rowman and Littlefield, 1996), 173ff. Strauss was also distinguishing his notion of "classical natural right" from the individual "natural rights" proposed by modern social contract theorists such as Hobbes (see *Natural Right and History*, 165ff.). Nevertheless, for a powerful

Being a Jewish proponent of natural law, I must differ with Strauss by arguing for a different meaning of "nature" than his, and for a different meaning of "law" than his. Sorting out this essential difference is not easy; it must be done carefully.

No doubt, Strauss was deliberately avoiding a theistic formulation of natural law as a universal law promulgated by God, even when theology distinguishes between divine law revealed in history to a particular people and divine law all people can discover for themselves through ratiocination.[11] Like Strauss' characterizations of "classical natural right," theological formulations of this law also take it to be universal and rational, i.e., it applies to all humans and can be discovered by all humans through the exercise of their reason. Nevertheless, unlike Strauss' characterizations of "classical natural right," theologically formulated natural law is explicitly designated as God-given law or commandment (*mitsvah*).[12] In other words, its ontological foundation is God's creative commandment, not uncreated eternal Nature. Like anything created by God, even natural law is transcended by God.[13] Natural law is what God has wisely willed every human person to do, but it itself is not divine.[14] Like all creation natural law is *made* in time; it is not coequal with God, who has neither beginning nor end.[15] Like all creation, natural law's existence

---

argument that the idea of natural rights comes out of an idea of natural law heavily influenced by the Judeo-Christian religious tradition long before Hobbes, see Brian Tierney, *The Idea of Natural Rights* (Atlanta, GA: Scholars Press, 1997), 33ff., 214f., 343; also, Otto Gierke, *Natural Law and the Theory of Society*, sec. 14, trans. E. Barker (Boston: Beacon Press, 1957), 39.

[11] See *Natural Right and History*, 7; also, Strauss, *The Rebirth of Classical Political Rationalism*, ed. T. L. Pangle (Chicago: University of Chicago Press, 2007), 21ff. Cf. Thomas Aquinas, *Summa theologiae*, I-II, q. 90, a. 4, ad 1.

[12] See *Mishnah Torah* [hereafter "MT"]: Kings, 8.11–9.1; also, Rashi, *Commentary on the Torah*: Gen. 26:5.

[13] See I Kings 8:27.

[14] See MT: Kings, 8.12.

[15] That is why I do not think natural law stems from God's eternal nature or essence as Thomas Aquinas thought about *lex aeternae* being the ontological foundation of *lex naturalis*; cf. *Summa theologiae*, I-II, q. 91, a. 1, ad 3; also, Rémi Brague, *The Law of God*, trans. L. G. Cochrane (Chicago: University of Chicago Press, 2007), 221. For, if we cannot know *what* God is but only *that* God is (*Summa theologiae*, 1, q. 12, aa. 11–12, following Maimonides, *Guide of the Perplexed*, 1.52–53, 63–64), how then could what we do not know ground what we do know, viz., natural law? But natural law, which is to govern inter-human relations, is grounded in *what God does*, i.e., what God commands (see *Babylonian Talmud* [hereafter "B."]: Sanhedrin 56b re Gen. 2:16 and 18:19), which we can know; it is not grounded in *what God is* per se, which is beyond anything we could ever experience in this world and hence beyond anything we could ever know here. God's word functions immanently in the world; God's

is contingent not necessary; God remains God whether there are creatures or not for God to command.

Unlike Strauss' characterizations of "classical natural right," theistically formulated natural law is "natural," not because it conforms to some larger cosmic scheme called "Nature," but rather because this law is discovered by humans when reasoning about the indispensable requirements of *their created human nature*. And, this human nature is *a* nature or condition that defines humans as the unique creatures we truly are. It is unlike the nature of anything else in creation (even that of the universe taken as a whole). It is discovered *by* humans *through* their reason inasmuch as humans seem to be the only creatures *who* reason or deliberate about what they have to do in the world in order to act in their authentically natural (or essential) way, i.e., according to the way or plan by which God creates them to be. When one acts consistently with one's human nature, one is acting truthfully; when one acts in a way that is inconsistent with one's human nature, one is acting deceitfully. In fact, the very incoherence of living such a deceitful, unnatural life inevitably leads to one's becoming disoriented in the world. How long can one pretend to be what he or she is not? How long can one treat others as if they are what they are not?

As we shall see, conceptions of *nature* and *law* can worked out of the Hebrew Bible and the traditions built upon it. Other than supplying some useful conceptual terms, the larger theories of Plato, Aristotle, and the Stoics are not needed by Jews and Christians (or by Muslims who can work them out of the *Quran*) in order to formulate a theistically cogent natural law theory. The fact that such a Judaeo-Christian-Islamic natural law theory is not Platonic, not Aristotelian, and not Stoic should make it no less an attractive natural law theory than what has long been taken to be the only way to "do" natural law at all. In fact, I think theistically cogent natural law theory

---

essence or "quiddity" transcends the world. Conversely, the God of Aristotle, who is totally immanent within the natural world, is totally definable, which is why Aristotle can definitely say *what God is* (see *Metaphysics*, 12.7/1072b15ff.). Furthermore, the God of Aristotle, who doesn't engage in any transitive action, doesn't command or legislate (i.e., make law), "command" being a transitive verb that describes transitive action, i.e., God engaging in external relations. But "commanding" cannot be predicated of a God who could not be related to anything outside Himself. Aristotle's comparing God to a general, from whom an order (*taxin*) comes to the army under him (*Metaphysics*, 12.9/1075a15), or to a "ruler" (*koiranos—*, *Metaphysics*, 1076a4 à la Homer, *Iliad*, 2.204) is clearly a metaphor, not even an analogy. See W. D. Ross, *Aristotle* (New York: Meridian Books, 1959), 175ff. See n. 18 of this chapter.

can be shown to be more cogent than its ancient Greek or modern (especially Kantian) rivals are. This will be spelled out in the following eleven propositions.

1.1 NATURAL LAW IS DISCOVERED THROUGH THE EXERCISE OF PRACTICAL REASON

This active discovery of authentic human nature and its requirements comes when practical or moral reason is properly exercised. It is not discovered by contemplation of the beauty of the external world, nor by the contemplation of the beauty of mathematical or metaphysical propositions. Nor is it discovered by scientific reason that describes how non-human phenomena behave; nor is it discovered by technical reason that uses the descriptions of scientific reason in order to exercise more and more control over the external, non-human world (i.e., "nature" in the modern sense of the term). Thus humans have to discover by means of philosophical reflection what their nature is and how to act in accordance with it, and not just be moved by subrational impulses or inclinations like all other animals. So, one might say that in this theologically formulated view of nature, nature is not something in which humans participate (contra the ancients), nor is nature something simply there for humans to use at their will as *homo faber* (contra the moderns). Instead, human nature is what distinguishes humans from other creatures who have their own nature. The difference between the two types of nature is that humans have the choice whether to act according to their nature or not inasmuch as they are the subjects of laws qua commandments. Other creatures, though, are only the subjects of the intelligent directives of the Creator God, directives which they have no capacity to understand as such, and which they can neither accept nor reject, being felt as impulses rather than being experienced as commandments. Nevertheless, humans do share with the rest of nature certain subrational appetites or inclinations. (Here "nature" has the more modern meaning of the sum of all phenomena not made by humans, hence the subject matter of the "natural sciences."[16]) That might well be what is meant when Scripture

---

[16] In rabbinic texts, what moderns call "nature" is called that which is made "by God's hands," as distinct from what is made "by human hands," i.e., what moderns

states that "the Lord God formed humans [*adam*] from the dust of the soil [*min ha'adamah*]," and that they "became a living being [*le-nefesh hayyah*]" (Genesis 2:7).[17] But how is rational and free human nature related to subrational and compelling animal nature? Are these two natures subject to the same law or not? And, if not, how then are these two laws related to each other?

Subrational impulses or inclinations are the subject matter of what have been called "laws of nature" (*lex naturae*).[18] But these laws of nature are not really "laws" at all, since *laws* are *commands* that one free rational *person* addresses to another free rational *person*. [19] Calling them "laws"

call "artificial" (and what the Greeks called *technē*; see Aristotle, *Nicomachean Ethics*, 6.4/1140a1ff). See, *Mishnah* [hereafter "M."]: Kelim 9.8; *Tosefta:* Hullin 3.6; *Palestinian Talmud* [hereafter "Y."]: Sukkah 4.6/54d re Cant. 7:2; B. Hullin 55b; Maimonides, *Guide of the Perplexed*, 1.65 and 3.32.

[17] According to *Targum Onqelos* and Rashi thereon, human beings became human persons when God endowed them with the capacity for intelligent speech (*de'ah ve-dibbur*), which enables them to relate to one another in a distinctly human way.

[18] For Aristotle, the premier pre-modern philosopher of science, what we would call a "law of nature" is the "order" (*taxis*) that is rooted in cosmic Nature (*physis*). See *Physics*, 8.1/252a10; n. 15 of this chapter. It is clear, though, why he wouldn't call it *nomos*, because *nomos* denotes a rule made at a certain time, whereas *physis* and its *taxis* are eternal; they are always necessarily there. See *Nicomachean Ethics*, 5.5/1133a31 and 5.7/1134b20; also, Brague, *The Law of God*, 233ff., 241. Spinoza's view is quite similar. Like Aristotle's *taxis*, he defines "law" (*lex*) as what "depends upon natural necessity"; and like Aristotle's *nomos*, his other definition of "law" (*ius*) is what "depends upon human decision...that men prescribe to themselves and to others." (*Tractatus Theologico-Politicus*, chap. 4, trans. M. Silverthorne and J. Israel [Cambridge: Cambridge University Press, 2007], 57.) Unlike the Bible and Kant (see n.19 of this chapter) who privilege laws freely made over laws of necessity, both Aristotle and Spinoza privilege laws of necessity over laws freely made.

[19] See Kant, *Critique of Pure Reason*, A319, who privileges prescriptive moral laws over laws of nature (see, also, *Critique of Pure Reason*, B472ff.). The latter (see *Critique of Pure Reason*, A126) are made "for nature," i.e., they are an order or "rule" imposed upon the natural appearances humans experience by human understanding operating necessarily according to its own a priori criteria. Conversely, from the standpoint of a biblically based theology, the laws of nature are freely imposed upon the created entity called "nature" by the Creator God (see Job 38:33). Thus both kinds of law are essentially prescriptive. Nevertheless, human understanding finds the data with which it deals already there, and thus has no choice whether to deal with them or not, since they are necessarily correlative in the same world. But God's creative intelligence (God's "wisdom" or *hokhmah*; see Ps. 104:24) freely applies laws or order to what God has freely created; in fact, the creation of form or order and the creation of matter are simultaneous (see Gen. 1:31). Hence there is less of a difference between laws of nature and moral laws from this theological standpoint than there is from Kant's standpoint. The source of both kinds of law is the same; only the necessary recipients of the laws of nature differ from and are inferior to the free recipients of divine commandments (of which natural law is a kind thereof). See n. 20 of this chapter. In both kinds of law,

is at best metaphorical.[20] Such subrational instincts, libido being a prime example, only become the concern of natural law as moral law when they are involved in an interpersonal relationship between human persons. In other words, this happens when these inclinations become involved in human transactions and are, therefore, taken to be necessary for human survival and even for human flourishing.[21] As such, these activated inclinations are more than mere behavior. In the rabbinic tradition, such instincts are only called the *yester ha-ra* or "bad inclination" when they are allowed to dictate human behavior rather than being freely taken up into rational human interaction.[22] Moreover, by so doing, practical human reason needs to consider both the findings of scientific reason and the instruments invented by technology. Think of how the moral act of healing requires the healer to *learn* from biological science and *use* the techniques of the art of medicine, even though the actual commandment to heal the sick is derived neither from the science nor from the art.[23]

Such consideration means that subhuman nature is to be respected and not abused (i.e., used wisely and constructively), first as it is present within our own bodies, then with the bodies of animals separate from our own bodies in the world or earthly environment we share with them, and then with the plants and minerals upon which all

truth or justice is what corresponds to God's creative word/thought, a point well noted by Heidegger (see "On the Essence of Truth," trans. J. Sallis, in *Martin Heidegger: Basic Writings*, ed. D. F. Krell [New York: Harper and Row, 1977], 118ff.).

[20] Scripture does state: "He spoke and it came to be; He commanded [*tsivah*] and it endures" (Ps. 33:9; see Ibn Ezra's comment thereon), yet the statement is still metaphorical. Even though the One *speaking* the command is free to command otherwise or not at all, the "recipient" of the command, i.e., nature, is a created *thing* (not a person), whose "keeping" the command is *caused to be* by the utterance of the command itself. *It* could not "do" otherwise, which is not the case with the free recipient of a literal commandment or moral law. That is why, from our perspective, "laws of nature" are descriptive, but from God's perspective they are prescriptive in the sense that God freely chose to make them as the structure of His freely chosen creation (see Job 38:33). Nevertheless, an order is only literally a "law" when it is a prescription from both divine and human perspectives.

[21] See B. Yoma 69b.

[22] "Bad" (*ra*) actually means what is unintended per se rather than what is "wicked" per se (called *resh 'a*). It is to be ordered by the "good inclination" (*yester ha-tov*), yet not to be displaced by the good inclination nonetheless. See B. Berakhot 5a re Ps. 4:5 and Prov. 4:2, and B. Kiddushin 30b re Gen. 4:7, where "good" is identified with the Torah rather than with any innate human capacity. See, also, Solomon Schechter, *Some Aspects of Rabbinic Theology* (New York: Behrman House, 1936), 264ff.

[23] See B. Baba Kama 85a re Exod. 21:19.

animals depend for our life on earth. Only in that sense is the world created for our use.[24] That means we humans are responsible for what we have done to the world and with it, i.e., whether we have used it to make the world a peaceful human dwelling, or whether we have used it to make the world a hell for ourselves and for all our fellow creatures along with us by taking it to be our own disposable property, when we act like intruders rather than like the guests in the world we are truly meant by God to be.[25] And, finally, subhuman nature, wherever it appears, is to be respected because we learn through scriptural revelation that God respects all he has created by calling it "very good" (Genesis 1:31). That divine respect for all created nature is to be imitated by humans, who because of their unique relationship with God are "God's partners in creation"—junior partners to be sure—as the Talmud puts it.[26] We humans have the unique responsibility for the rest of earthly creation "to work it and to care for it" (Genesis 2:15), because God "formed it [the world] to be a dwelling" (Isaiah 45:18): ours and theirs too along with us. All of this follows from humans recognizing we are made in the image of the active Creator-God and thus made to imitate God who takes responsibility for His creation.[27]

1.2 NATURAL LAW GOVERNS THE INTER-HUMAN REALM

Natural law is about specific interpersonal commands. These commands can only be accepted by rational persons when they believe that the person commanding them to do something or not to do something has a good reason or purpose for addressing the command to them as members of this specific group of persons, who are the subjects of this command. These commands can only be accepted by rational persons when they believe that the command is for the direct

---

[24] See M. Sanhedrin 4.5.

[25] See Lev. 25:23; Ps. 119:19; I Chron. 29:14–15.

[26] See B. Shabbat 10a and 119b. Cf. B. Sanhedrin 38a.

[27] This seems to be something humans can intuit even before it is revealed to them in the Torah. See M. Avot 3.18 (only thereafter quoting Gen. 9:6 about the revelation of this truth). Concerning *imitation Dei*, see, also, B. Sotah 14a and Maimonides, *Guide of the Perplexed*, 3.54 re Jer. 9:22–23.

benefit of the specific group of persons who are the objects of the command. Moreover, these commands can only be accepted by rational persons when they believe that the command also benefits themselves who are its subjects. Finally, the command must be interpreted in the context of the society in which it is an accepted or a rejected social practice. Since natural law commands or precepts are addressed to all humans, i.e., to "humankind," their social context is "humanity" (or what used to be called the "human race"). Natural law is universal insofar as it applies in *any* human society. Unlike revealed law, though, where God is experienced as the source of the law, and where the social context can be found in the world (*metsi'ut* in Hebrew), in natural law both God as the source of the universal law and the universal social or communal context of the law are only inferred as presuppositions of the law. Universality can only be thought; it cannot be directly experienced.

Natural law precepts are essentially different from revealed precepts, which are addressed to a particular human community, and need only benefit that community and its divine Sovereign, though it must not harm anyone else in order to be consistent with the natural law principle "no other is to be harmed" (*alterum non laedere*).[28] When the reason of the command is universal and thus immediately evident to all a priori, the command can be considered a natural law precept. When the reason of the command is not universal and thus not immediately evident to all, the command can only be known through revelation a posteriori. Moreover, it is assumed that God, not being a tyrant, still has his less evident reasons for making these commands, and that the benefit accruing from being both the subjects and the objects of these revealed precepts is also far less evident and might, in fact, be postponed for another world altogether.[29]

Natural law is essentially different from laws of nature: it governs free human action rather than describing and predicting animal behavior (even describing and predicting that type of instinctual behavior embodied human beings necessarily share with all other animals), or describing and predicting the course of plant life or the

---

[28] *Digest*, 1.1.10.1. In the Jewish tradition, even the punishment meted out to criminals is not seen as harm per se, but rather is thought to be for their ultimate (if not immediate) benefit. See M. Sanhedrin 6.2 re Josh. 7:25; B. Sanhedrin 6b re II Sam. 8:15; also, B. Berakhot 10a re Ps. 104:35.

[29] See B. Avodah Zarah 35a.

movements of non-living physical bodies. Freedom, though, is an integral aspect of active human nature. It is the power to act rather than to merely behave: to be *the* cause of one's own actions (and thus responsible for them) rather than only being affected by some impersonal force or other. Only a free person can be the subject of a commandment.[30] That means a fully alive human person has the option to knowingly act one way or another or not to act at all in any particular situation. This free decision will largely be the result of what the active chooser wants his or her relationship to be or not to be with the other person who is the object of the act to be done or not be done. Finally, the free subject of a command is ultimately answerable *to* the source of the command, and responsible *for* the object of the command.

1.3 NATURAL LAW IS THE NORMATIVE MANIFESTATION OF HUMAN NATURE

To speak of *human nature* means that to be adequately human a human person is to be actively and intelligently involved in consistent (i.e., ordered) positive relationships with other human beings. That is what it means to say that humans are "naturally political animals."[31] And, to be adequately human, one is to be concerned with having a consistent (i.e., ordered) actively intelligent relationship with God (humans being created as the unique "image of God").[32] The ubiquity of religion as a concern with God—whether positive or negative—seems to demonstrate that religion, the medium whereby humans are related to God (or abjure if they do not want to be related to God), is something endemic to human nature. That is why totalitarian regimes that are intent on remaking human nature in their own image inevitably—but futilely sooner or later—attempt to suppress religion so fiercely. They know it is their chief opponent, challenging their pretensions at every turn. In the Jewish tradition, the prohibition of idolatry is a natural law precept, incumbent on all human persons, which means it is forbidden to both make a new god or to make a new human being in the image of a new god. Modern

---

[30] See MT: Repentance, 5.1–3.
[31] Aristotle, *Politics*, 1.1/1253a1–5; 3.4/1278b20–25.
[32] See Gen. 1:26–27; 5:1; 9:6.

totalitarian ideologies could well be the modern versions of the new human-made religion Maimonides stressed all humans are forbidden to make.[33] Even though the God–human relationship is endemic to human nature, nonetheless, it is not the immediate concern of natural law. (As we shall see, God is only invoked in the human rights claims formulated as natural law as the indirect source or the One who entitles these claims.) Nevertheless, I cannot go as far as did Hugo Grotius, who famously said of natural law that it could be thought of "even were we to say there is no God" (*etiamsi daremus non esse deum*).[34]

Natural law is most evident in inter-human relationships, since from ordinary experience we learn what humans rightfully require of each other, whereas what God requires of humans for Godself is almost always made known only through the extraordinary experience of revelation. That is why natural law can only govern free, rational beings who live and act beneath their Creator rather than with Him, and who are responsible for their own freely chosen acts. Minimally, that means humans ought to acknowledge that we are, insofar as we are only transient tenants here, in possession of nothing. Nevertheless, we are above all other creatures in the world in terms of our intelligence, our volitional capacity, and our responsibility for them, whereas we cannot reasonably expect these other creatures to be responsible for us. Humans are *in the world*, but not *of the world*. We are in the world that includes human and non-human beings, but we are not parts thereof. (Indeed, most contemporary "environmentalists" who do think humans are parts of the world like all other earthly beings cannot explain *why* one part of the world ought to be responsible for all the other parts, there being no difference in kind between them.) We humans act most naturally when we make legitimate claims upon one another that are consistent with the reasonable needs of both the claimer and the claimant. That is what makes human nature an essentially normative idea.

---

[33] See MT: Kings, 10.9.

[34] *De juri belli ac pacis*, prol. XI. However, for the interpretation of this statement that argues it is not atheistic in the modern sense, but only asserts that one doesn't have to affirm the direct commandments of God in order to formulate natural law, see David Novak, "Law: Religious or Secular?," *In Defense of Religious Liberty* (Wilmington, DE: ISI Books, 2009), 150ff.

Natural law is *law* because it is what God the Creator has *commanded* His human creatures *to actively and authentically be*. Only the Creator God could command His creation with such absolute authority. Natural law is divine law. Nevertheless, unlike divine law that is revealed, natural law is not *immediately received* as God's commandment. Instead, humans learn natural law when we methodically discover (i.e., by the mediation of human reason) what are the authentic requirements of our created nature (i.e., what we naturally need), and by our rational formulation of these requirements into actual norms. Not being directly experienced as God's commandment, though, natural law norms are only referred back to God's commandment of them retrospectively. They are coequal with God's unique creation of humans, but they are only recognized as such during the course of subsequent human experience. God's will here is not a datum; it comes largely from a "hidden God" (Isaiah 45:15). That is why one can be genuinely engaged in the theory and praxis of natural law, but without having to recognize *ab initio* a general divine command of which natural law precepts are its subsequent specifications. In other words, natural law theory need not begin from metaphysical assumptions (especially the assumption "God exits"), though it is not fully adequate to the reality it purports to understand when it represses its metaphysical implications.

1.4 NATURAL LAW IS NOT JEWISH LAW FOR GENTILES

There are those who see Jewish law (*halakhah*) having two domains: one for Jews; the other for gentiles. They see Jewish law as having a particular domain for Jews, and a universal domain for the rest of humankind. So, it seems they are basically saying (irrespective of whether any gentiles actually accept such moral subordination to Judaism for themselves): "We can only recognize a universally valid law when it is done our way, recognizing our authority." Moreover, their arguments are made exegetically rather than rationally, i.e., they cite authoritative Jewish texts and naively assume that gentiles inquiring what is "the" Jewish position on some general normative question are actually interested in being told by Jewish teachers what to do when faced with such a normative question.

The notion of cultural subordination of all people to one particular people's morality comes out when Jewish teachers who are accepted as legal authorities (*posqim* in Hebrew) assume their specific authority is generalizable. This comes out when they speak of "Noahide law" (to be discussed in section 8) as a law gentiles are supposed to turn to Jewish scholars to interpret and actually prescribe to them.[35] But the question these Jewish teachers never seem to deal with, however, is just why any gentile would want to become morally subordinate to them or to any Jew. Why would gentiles want to be, in effect, second-class citizens in a Jewish normative realm when they could easily become first-class citizens in that realm by converting to Judaism?[36]

The problem with this view of Jewish law for gentiles is that it calls into serious question whether those who hold it can argue for the universal rationality of what they represent to be universally obligatory. And how can anyone argue for a moral position in a secular society, which looks to no particular revelation for its moral warrant, by simply citing their authoritative texts rather than engaging in rational persuasion? For if natural law discourse can only be done in a way that recognizes the moral authority of a particular tradition, then how universal can it be? Is natural law only universal in its scope, i.e., is it only meant to govern all humans universally, where this universal scope depends upon the authority of a particular human community, its founding revelation, and its ongoing tradition that teaches this law for all humans?

To be sure, the relation of natural law to any particular revelation is complicated, but to require any particular revelation (as distinct from the overall law of God, all of which need not be revealed supernaturally) to be explicitly taken as the sufficient premise of natural law thinking *ab initio,* undercuts the notion that natural law is equally and immediately available to all rational persons whether they be adherents of my religion, other religions, or even if they have no religion. In other words, even if the acceptance of natural law is taken to be the necessary precondition for the acceptance of revelation (and even if natural law is the constant criterion for saving revealed law from becoming irrational), nonetheless that should not lead one to

---

[35] Along these lines, see J. David Bleich, "Judaism and Natural Law," *Jewish Law Annual* (1988), 7:5ff.; also, Marvin Fox, *Interpreting Maimonides* (Chicago: University of Chicago Press, 1990), 124ff.

[36] See B. Yevamot 22a.

conversely conclude that the acceptance of revelation is the necessary prerequisite for cogent natural law thinking and doing. Nor should one presume that an acceptance of revelation is the necessary consequence of an acceptance of natural law, when natural law becomes a covert form of proselytizing.

Natural law is not an imperialist project. Natural law is not what our Jewish tradition (or any tradition) has represented or should represent to the world as our own innovation *for* the world. It is not what the traditional community has first accepted as God's innovation for us and which we are then allowed or even commanded to share *with* the rest of the world. Accordingly, when the adherents of a religious tradition like Judaism, Christianity, or Islam do advocate natural law precepts in a multicultural secular context, we can only do so by reminding the rest of the world what everyone's implicit acceptance of truly human natural sociality *already* means for the normative public question at hand.

Theologians make a category error when they attempt to actually deduce natural law precepts from revealed teachings rather than more humbly recognizing how revelation itself respects natural law as its necessary and ever-functioning precondition. Theologians commit the category error of confusing natural moral reasoning with supernatural pronouncements or scripturally based inferences. Thus theologians from whatever tradition should only try to reason morally in a way that sees natural law precepts being presupposed by revealed teaching (i.e., *torah* or *sacra doctrina*), or illustrated by revealed teaching (i.e., re-presenting rather than originally presenting them), or alluding to revealed teachings or, at least, not contradicting those revealed teachings. Nevertheless, natural law precepts are not derived *from* those settings; those settings are only their *historical occasion*, not their historical genesis. This suggests why it is better to speak of "natural law" rather than "*the* natural law," which too often becomes one particular tradition's way of claiming universal authority for itself.[37]

---

[37] The first Jewish thinker to actually use the term "natural law" (*dat tiv`it*) was Joseph Albo in the early fifteenth century; and he used it in the sense of *ius naturale* in Roman law. See his *Book of Principles*, 1.7, trans. I. Husik (Philadelphia: Jewish Publication Society of America, 1929), 1:78ff. Nevertheless, though I have used the term to cover more areas of normativity than did Albo, his introduction of the term into Jewish discourse has enabled me to use it, and to defend myself from charges that I am using a term and the concept it names in a fundamentally non-Jewish way. "Natural law," then, is not a subset of Roman Catholic moral theology, even though

1.5 NATURAL LAW IS BEST FORMULATED AT THE JUNCTURE OF THEOLOGY AND PHILOSOPHY

Many theologians and many philosophers have been suspicious of the idea of natural law. For many theologians, natural law seems to be a poor substitute for revealed law. It says too little, and what it does say seems to be of no real use to theology; revelation has already stated that better and more accurately. Conversely, for many philosophers, natural law says too much; and it seems to have barely hidden theological premises. Therefore, it must be shown why a revelation-based theology can affirm natural law and not regard it as an implacable enemy, and why an open-minded philosophy of law ought not to reject natural law as fantastic or a covert totalizing project.

One of the most central doctrines of Judaism—in fact, what could be said to be *the* foundation of Judaism—is that the Torah is the fullest version of the law of God available to human beings.[38] Moreover, this revealed law is taken to be fully sufficient for every question of human praxis and thought, even though discovering the Torah's answer to many questions of praxis and thought often requires much effort.[39] At times, though, no definite answer is actually to be found. When that is the case, it is assumed the Sages have the right, even the duty, to devise answers to questions for which an answer cannot be derived from the text of Scripture.[40] So, if the Torah, whether scriptural or rabbinic, is normatively sufficient, then natural law thinking seems to be basically a form of apologetics. At best, it can be useful for deflecting criticism of the revealed law of God, coming from those who have been attracted to worldly wisdom (i.e., philosophy as content in one form or another) as a possible substitute for the Torah's wisdom.[41] Taken to be a philosophical construct, natural law as philosophically formulated seems to say too little about that which the Torah teaches much more fully and much more compellingly. It only offers silver when gold is readily at hand. As one passage in the Talmud puts it: "Let

---

Roman Catholic thinkers have discussed natural law more often than have thinkers from other traditions.

[38] M. Sanhedrin 10.1.
[39] See M. Avot 5.22; Y. Peah 1.1/15b re Deut. 32:47.
[40] See B. Shabbat 23a re Deut. 17:11; MT: Rebels, 1.1–2.
[41] See M. Avot 2.14.

not our perfect [*shlemah*] Torah be like your empty discourse [*seehah betelah*]!"[42]

What proponents of natural law should say to its theological detractors is that an affirmation of natural law is required in order for the normative claim of revealed law to be intelligible. For the specific intelligibility of revealed law requires that those intelligently subject to it—which means those who have freely and wisely accepted it— have already freely and wisely accepted the necessity of natural law for the world. For Jews, Christians, and Muslims, that means that their intelligent adherents must have a priori awareness of why law is an ever-present necessity for all human life everywhere in the world, and why the assumption of the divine cosmic lawgiver best explains why this ever-present necessity is truly universal. For Jews, that means we were living under the more general Noahide law before we came to live under the more specific and more concrete Mosaic law (as we shall soon see). This is best understood when we look at what might be considered the beginnings of general moral experience in any human culture, employing phenomenology as our method of enquiry. (This might appear to be too long a digression, but I hope its value as a sort of phenomenology of the moral experience that makes law itself intelligible will eventually make sense.) That is why the formulation of natural law by theologians is where theology needs philosophy the most, to supply its "bottom line."

What proponents of natural law should say to its philosophical detractors is that natural law is required if there is to be international, multicultural, global discourse and praxis in the world. Moreover, the fact that most natural law theorists have theological commit- ments should not alarm philosophers. Instead, it should convince them that natural law is not fantastic or a totalizing religious project that attempts to absorb everything outside itself into itself.[43] That is because these religious natural law theorists look elsewhere, i.e., to the revelations upon which their respective traditions are based, for what appears to outsiders to be fantastic and totalizing. Hence a com- mitment to a revelation as the maximal manifestation of God's law limits the range of natural law, making it the minimal manifestation of God's law. In the words of Scripture: "Enlargement and salvation

---

[42] B. Menahot 65b.
[43] See Emmanuel Levinas, *Totality and Infinity*, trans. A. Lingis (Pittsburgh: Duquesne University Press, 1969), 35ff.

[*revah ve-hatsalah*] will arise for the Jews from another place" (Esther 4:14). That is why the formulation of natural law is where philosophy needs theology the most, to supply its "upper limit."

1.6 NATURAL LAW REQUIRES A COSMIC LAWGIVER

The earliest experience of humans as moral beings having free choice is when they respond to a command of somebody having power over them, who is usually a parent. When children also trust the wisdom of these powerful persons, children are more willing to obey their commands, being convinced that their parents (or those acting *in loco parentis*) know what is good for them and intend that it be done by and for all those who live in the familial household the parents have founded. By their willingness to obey these commands, children identify with the overall moral project of their parents for their family, thus desiring to help further it. And that is the case whether or not children fully understand the specific reasons of what they have been commanded to do. (At this level of trust, the command is best experienced as a personal request rather than as a more impersonal order.) These commands are experienced as part of the responsible care these procreating and educating parents are exercising on behalf of their children. And, why would our parents have our benefit in mind if not for the fact that they feel responsible to care for those whom they have helped bring into the world and are to nurture here as a family? So, for example, to tell a child not to hit his little sister, or to help her little brother tie his shoes, is usually justified by a responsible, caring parent saying something like this: "I expect this of you because I care for you just as I care for her or him, and I expect you both to do for each other what I do for you. That is what I want done in our family." Or, sometimes, an act is proscribed by a parent with the words: "But we don't do that in our family!"[44] The command to care for siblings is first expressed by the siblings themselves as their claim upon their more powerful siblings, minimally, not to harm them; maximally, to help them. Yet lying behind this kind of claim is the parents' command to

---

[44] See I Sam. 13:11.

do just that, which is what makes the claim of the weaker siblings a right. In other words, the parent justifies the claim, making it a right rather than a complaint, a right whose violation has a predictable consequence.

Those who do not believe the commands of their parents (and other authority figures) have been motivated by benevolence, often as the result of experience in what we now call a "dysfunctional" family, usually look upon moral law as being an oppressive, malevolent scheme of those who wish to harm them in order to enhance their own selfish tyranny, even their own sadism. When this happens, moral law becomes something to be avoided, manipulated, or destroyed (as in the case of psychopaths).

From this we see that *who* is the source of the command, *what* is the content of the command, and *why* it has been commanded must be seen as functioning in tandem. That is because morality is first learned through the commands or claims those who have power over us make upon us, and only thereafter do we learn how to command or claim others over whom we have power. And, just as those commands are only accepted freely when we are convinced that those making them upon us are doing so because they care for us, so too we can only expect free acceptance of the commands or claims we make upon others when they are convinced we are doing so because we care for them. The objects of our care need to understand *why* we ask them to do what we ask them to do, just as we ourselves had to understand *why* we were commanded to do what we were commanded to do by those who care for us. Our deeds need that understanding of the reasons or purposes for them in order to be intelligent action, i.e., what we do for the reasons or purposes these acts themselves have been so commanded. Without that kind of intelligent and beneficent normativity within one's earliest conscious experience, many psychologists are of the opinion that this normative or moral absence often leads to those who suffer it in their formative childhood experience to grow up to be the type of paranoiacs who are unable to relate to others in a non-threatened way, or sociopaths who are unable to relate to others in a non-threatening way.

However, why do we need to affirm a source of just commands? Why can't we just say that something is *good* per se, irrespective of *who* commanded it?

A command is a moral command, as opposed to a capricious order, when one is commanded to do a *good act*, which *means* that one person is commanded by a second person to benefit a third person in a certain context. Judging the act to be good, though, requires that we know (1) whether the subject of the act (the immediate benefactor) has the capacity to confer the commanded benefit; (2) whether this act will really benefit the object of the act (the beneficiary); (3) whether the beneficiary has a right to receive this benefit; (4) whether the time and place this act is to be done are appropriate for it to be done here and now.[45] That requires acknowledgement of *who originally entitled* the object of the act to deserve such a benefit and thus claim it as their right. (And persons no more confer rights upon themselves than they create themselves.) And that requires acknowledgement of *who authorized* the subject of the act to respond to this rightful claim as their *duty*. Therefore, the commandment to act and the act itself cannot be understood outside the relations in which they are imbedded. The commandment itself is how the source of the commandment is related to the subject of the commandment. The act itself is how the subject of the act is related to the object of the act. But to say that an act is simply to be done for its own sake, which is to say that the act is *good* per se, means that the source of the commanded act, its subject, and its object—all of whom are persons—are acting for the sake of the act itself. In other words, it is as if the act commands itself to be done, rather than the act being for the sake or benefit of its source, of its subjects, and of its objects. In this view, the actor or agent is a cipher for the act itself to be instantiated; and it is the act itself that designates its objects rather than the objects of the act requiring the act be done on their behalf.

To simply advocate that an act be done because it is *good* per se is to ignore the relational context in which designating an act to be "good" can be rationally justified.[46] To judge an act to be essentially good

---

[45] Sometimes, certain acts are proscribed anywhere and anytime. The universality of such proscribed acts inevitably leads to their proscription being formulated in natural law type precepts. See e.g., Gen. 34:7 and Rashi's comment thereon; cf. Gen. 29:26.

[46] Aristotle, though, did regard some acts to be good per se, i.e., to be done for their own sake without any external referent. "The good [*t'agathon*] is that towards which all things aim…sometimes the acts [*energeiai*] are themselves the ends [*tōn telōn*]" (*Nicomachean Ethics*, 1.1/1094a2—my translation; see *Rhetoric*, 1.6/1362a23). He then distinguishes these acts from those acts for which "the end is beyond [*para*] the acts." There, what is beyond the act is some end-product *for which* the act was done, i.e., the act was done in order to make something outside itself. But when the act itself by itself aims towards itself alone, it requires no external object, no "other," neither as its source nor as its object. Moreover, the personal subject of the good act per se is only the means to the act's actualization. That is why, it seems, Aristotle doesn't deem either

requires that one show its essentially personal character, i.e., one must show how the act is a benefit *for someone by someone from someone.* And to judge an act to be essentially good requires that one show its essentially historical character, i.e., one must show how the act is only good when done in a certain place at a certain time. This relational context is also ignored when a good act is seen to be the application of an intelligible entity from beyond the world.[47]

All of this can be seen in the phenomenology of familial morality discussed above. But there is more to human sociality (all morality being social insofar as all morality involves interpersonal relationships) than familial sociality. A true community is more than an extended family, more than a tribe.

The move from the authority of the head (or heads) of one's family to the authority of the head (or heads) of one's community is a move from a more narrow range of authority to a wider range of authority. Yet it is more than a mere extension of a family into a community. So, for example, children can understand why their parents have commanded them to treat their siblings justly and compassionately.

---

inter-human relations or the divine–human relation (when it is normative, i.e., when God is the transcendent source of moral law) to involve action that is good per se, for they both require something external.

[47] Plato, though, did regard an act to be good when it specifically instantiates in time and space a transcendent, eternal, universal Form or "idea" (*eidos*), which functions as an archetype called *the Good itself* (*t'agathon kath'auto*). See *Republic*, 505A-509B, 540A (cf. Aristotle, *Nicomachean Ethics*, 1.6/1096a11ff.). The adjective "good" no longer modifies or qualifies action; instead, the adjective "good" becomes a noun that names a Form; and it is the Form that inspires a philosopher who beholds it to then bring its light (*the Good* being compared to the sun) down from heaven to earth. As such, the adjective "good" no longer modifies an act; instead, *the Good* itself is modified by the act when the actor temporalizes and locates *the Good* by applying it to some situation in the world. Therefore, to use "good" as an adverb when saying an act "has been done *well*" means that the act judged to have been done well has been done properly, according to the standard of its otherworldly archetype (see *Laws*, 716A, 757E). For the problem of why a philosopher would be motivated to descend from the ideal heaven above to a human society below (however optimal) to apply his or her vision of the Good to it, see David Novak, *Suicide and Morality* (New York: Scholars Studies Press, 1975), 21ff. And this action is *imitatio dei*, since Plato's god is the archetypal actor who creates the world by looking to the eternal Forms as the archetype or the ultimate criterion according to which this god transforms chaos into cosmos, i.e., into an intelligible universe (see *Timaeus*, 29Aff.). But how something as impersonal as a Platonic Form could be the inspiration for a morally significant act to be done by one person for another person remains a problem for Platonists. Nevertheless, it is worth noting that Plato's greatest teacher, Socrates, states—according to Plato—that all his intelligent activity in the world is in obedience to the command of a god (which I do not regard as being, in fact, Socratic irony). See *Apology*, 28D, 30B.

Nevertheless, even children need to know that a commandment to treat other members of their community justly and compassionately is beyond the authority of their parents. It can only come from those who have this wider range of authority. Here we have a different range of authority in which one's family participates but neither projects out of itself nor totally subsumes itself into it as a part thereof. (The best example of this is that teachers receive their authority from the community not from the parents of the pupils in their charge, nor are teachers meant to replace the moral authority of parents any more than teachers are to be the agents of the parents of their pupils.[48]) Nevertheless, the head of a community (which can even be a national community) has this parent-like authority, and exercises it best and most effectively, when the commands of that ruler are obeyed because he or she is trusted. (I am reminded of how Canadians during both world wars were asked to risk their lives "for King and country.")

Rulers have the right to ask the citizens of the polity they rule to treat their fellow citizens just as parents can ask their children to treat their siblings, and for the same type of reason: "We are responsible for you both, therefore we want you to help us exercise our political responsibility by living together in justice and in peace." Unlike parents (or at least the parents of little children), though, rulers who are not tyrants, i.e., who rule in some kind of constitutional polity, must be able to argue for the immediate intelligibility of what they are commanding citizens to do.[49] Moreover, the ruler of a community does not procreate his or her constituents like parents procreate their children, hence their authority is not biologically obvious as it is with parents.

Now just as the move from the family to the community is more than a simple extension of the family, so the move from the community to universal humankind is more than a simple extension of the community—or simply adding up nations into some sort of united nations which then encompasses them all. Following this analogy, one could say that just as morality in a family depends on the recognition of the intelligent, beneficent authority of the parental heads of the family, and just as morality in a community depends on the

---

[48] This is illustrated in rabbinic tradition by the notion that teachers are not primarily the agents of parents, but of the community. See B. Baba Batra 21a; MT: Torah Study, 2.1.

[49] Note Y. Horayot 1.1/45b re Deut. 17:11.

recognition of the intelligent, beneficent authority of the heads of the community, so too does the recognition of the universal morality that is natural law depend on the recognition of the Sovereign of the universe who creates the subjects of that law and inspires them to learn that law when they are convinced of God's wisdom and beneficence. Here too, knowledge of *what* the law commands, *why* it has been commanded, and *who* commanded it are all inextricably tied together.[50] And, just as children are in the image of or reflect their parents through imitation of them, and just as a people are in the image of or reflect their rulers through imitation of them, so it might be said that humans are in the image of the God who has created them to imitate His beneficent rule.[51] However, it is important to note, that unlike the situation in the family and the situation in the community, in the context of the whole human world God's sovereignty is not directly experienced (more about this later).

All of the above indicates what philosophy, when done as a phenomenology of moral experience, does for theology, especially for normative theology. It shows us that there is no way to bypass the general normativity of the family, then that of the community, and then that of humankind (or the world) in order to bring oneself under the direct rule of God intelligently (which is what revelation alone initiates). That is, there is no way of assuming that humans can intelligently accept the higher law of God only given in singular revelation without having first (in terms of logical if not chronological priority) already intelligently accepted the more general law of God at work in their natural human condition as familial, communal, and worldly human beings. So, it is most unlikely that somebody without any decent familial experience could become a law-abiding member of a community. And it is most unlikely that somebody without any lawful communal experience (for example, someone who only knew tyranny) could become a truly worldly human being. So too, it is most unlikely that somebody without the experience of being the subject of universal moral law that comes from God through several mediums could accept the law that comes straight from God. Just as children coming from basically dysfunctional families can rarely accept the law of the community in which they live as their own, and just as

---

[50] This seems to be what Thomas Aquinas meant by asserting that natural law needs to be *promulgated* by God who made it. See *Summa theologiae*, I-II, q. 90, a. 4.

[51] See B. Berakhot 58a re I Chron. 29:11.

communities that act in a lawless manner towards other communities can rarely accept a law for all humankind, so too can a human being who has not accepted a law for all humankind ultimately coming from humankind's Creator rarely accept a law coming directly from the God who elects one human community to be singularly in the vanguard of what God finally wants for all humankind. Finally, though, it is only through revealed law that God tells the recipients of that law just *what* God wants for Himself; and since God is unique, what God wants for Himself cannot be formulated in the universal categories of natural law. Sometimes God also reveals or allows us to infer from revelation *why* God wants what He wants for Himself; sometimes, though, that *why* remains mysterious, at least to us.[52]

When it comes to recognition of the relation of God and law, all those who only have familial law only need a household or domestic god. Those who only have the law of their particular community only need a tribal deity. But those who have natural law as universal law truly need the universal God who is the Creator of their human world and the whole created universe as its background. Finally, only those to whom God has directly revealed the law that is meant to constitute God's direct relationship *with* them (what is called a *berit* or "covenant") need the God who not only cares for them, but who desires such an intimate relationship, who desires to be loved by his people. God as Creator (especially as the Creator of universal morality) can be feared and deserves to be feared, but only the God who elects a community and directly reveals his law to them and for them, only this God can be loved and only this God deserves to be loved. This love, unlike fear, is mutual and reciprocal.[53] When God is distant, which is what God is when designated as the law-founding Creator, then God is the object of our fear or awe.[54] Only when God is near enough for us to be His intimate covenantal partners can God be the object of our love. Philosophy can deal with God as awesome; only theology can deal with God as loving and beloved. Only through revelation do we

[52] See e.g., Exod. 20:8–11; Deut. 5:12–15. Cf. Num. 19:1–22 and *Midrash Leqah Tov* thereon, ed. Buber, 119b; B. Yoma 67b re Lev. 18:4.

[53] This mutual and reciprocal love *between* God and Israel is elaborated on in the rabbinic interpretation of Song of Songs, especially in *Midrash Rabbah*: Canticles, passim. This love is *eros* insofar as it involves desire on the part of each of the lovers/beloved.

[54] Thus gentiles, who are not covenanted with God according to Scripture, are only required to fear God. See Gen. 20:11; Exod. 1:17, 21; Job 1:1, 8.

learn that God loves us and how God loves us, and we can only learn from revelation that God is to be loved in return and how we are to be so actively responsive to God. We do not learn that from natural law, even when its divine source is acknowledged.

1.7 NATURAL LAW IS A CULTURAL PROJECTION ONTO THE WORLD

Perhaps the greatest vulnerability of natural law theory, in its ancient, medieval, and modern versions, is its seeming oblivion to and disrespect of cultural diversity, especially when it comes to normative matters. Thus many natural law theorists have represented it as if the "nature" underlying it were some sort of universal datum, something directly experienced and thus easily translatable into actual norms for human praxis. In fact, if one looks at Roman representations of *ius naturale,* which is where the term "natural law" first appears, it seems that *ius naturale* supplies the content of *ius gentium.* Now, originally, *ius gentium* meant the law by which the Romans ruled certain non-Roman citizens who had long been living under Roman governance. Natural law in this historical context was what Roman lawyers assumed is law that should apply to all people and, indeed, is also the substratum of the more highly and elaborately developed law that only applied to Roman citizens called "civil law" (*ius civile*).

Moreover, it is important to note that whereas *ius gentium* in its original meaning could be called "Roman law for *subordinate* nations," its meaning in later Roman jurisprudence denoted laws that seem to actually operate in every human polity, laws that usually but not always seem to be identical or at least consistent with *ius naturale.* One could say here that *ius naturale* is *universal* a priori, but *ius gentium* is only *general* a posteriori.[55]

---

[55] See Justinian, *Institutes,* 1.2ff.; H. F. Jolowicz, *Historical Introduction to Roman Law,* 2nd ed. (Cambridge: Cambridge University Press, 1952), 100ff. But in either version, *ius gentium* is not to be confused with what we now call "international law," which being *inter gentes* avoids the imperialist thrust of *ius gentium,* since it is what is decided or negotiated *by* the nations themselves *among* themselves and *for* themselves rather than being decided by one nation *for* other nations *under* its political control. See R. G. Hingorani, *Modern International Law,* 2nd ed. (Dobbs Ferry, NY: Oceana Publications, 1984), 15ff.

The important thing to remember from this comparison of natural law as a cultural projection to *ius gentium* is that *ius naturale* (as the content of *ius gentium* more or less) was not what the Roman lawyers simply *found* or discovered in the natural world (a world shared with other animals). Instead, it was what they presumed could be taken to be universal, thus providing a rationalization that Roman imperial rule was only administering a law that these people or any people could accept as politically necessary, i.e., if they had the power to rule themselves. Accordingly, *ius naturale* is not what is found in nature, but it is what is being proposed for all humankind.

However, there is a big epistemological problem when presuming one culture can in effect tell all humankind what natural law is.[56] That is because universal thinking by persons of particular and culturally determined identities and attachments seems to be an imaginative attempt to constitute a normative world that *would be the case everywhere if we could overcome being from somewhere.* That is like saying, "we would like to speak and think as if *we* were not part of a singular culture in whose language we actually do speak and think." But does this imagined world truly correspond to anything we have experienced? Any attempt to locate this world as a real datum (which seems to be the mistake that those who speak of "*the* natural law" or "the Noahide Code" are prone to make) is so vague as to be normatively useless. Such attempts to transcend cultural particularity are futile, especially when one realizes that different cultures constitute universality in different ways. What they do hold in common seems more like accidental "overlappings" known a posteriori rather than universal truths known a priori. This seems to be what is meant by the current assertion that the human world today is radically "multicultural" or "pluralistic." As Alasdair MacIntyre has so forcefully argued, everybody speaks from *somewhere* in the world; nobody speaks from either nowhere or everywhere.[57] This "speaking from everywhere" (or *sub*

---

[56] Even Maimonides, who speaks of Jews being obliged to compel gentiles whenever wherever Jews have political power over them to accept universal Noahide law (MT: Kings, 8.9; cf. B. Avodah Zarah 64b; B. Arakhin 29a), clearly means that this is because gentiles are human beings for all of whom God's most basic law is authoritative whenever wherever, and that they already know this. It is not because Jews have any specific authority to actually make law for gentiles or that gentiles have any obligation to live under Jewish rule. In fact, even purchased slaves, who according to rabbinic tradition are quasi-Jews living under Jewish rule, have the right to choose whether or not they want to live under Jewish rule (B. Yevamot 48b; MT: Slaves, 8.12).

[57] See *After Virtue* (Notre Dame, IN: University of Notre Dame Press, 1981), 201ff.

specie aeternitatis) is what Kant tried to do in what he called the "transcendental deduction." Nevertheless, natural law is best formulated by abstracting from its more particular historical settings and projecting them on to a universal horizon.[58] Natural law is not the ground from which a particular kind of law is derived or determined.[59] And it is not an ideal to which even revealed law aspires.[60]

Our imagination can tentatively project itself outside our own culture from time to time, conducting what some might call "thought experiments." Nevertheless, we cannot transcend our own cultural matrix by a meta-culturally conceived Archimedean Fulcrum to radically transform the world. We can no more do that than we could transcend the language we have inherited from our cultural matrix by constructing some sort of meta-language from which we could then deduce our "natural" language, which Wittgenstein warned us against doing.[61] So, instead of an attempt to find some universal phenomenon to ground natural law, or posit some ideal from which to deduce natural law, it seems to be more philosophically astute to see natural law as the projection of a universal horizon by a thinker *in* a particular culture *for* one's own culture. One does that by abstracting certain norms from one's cultural-linguistic matrix, then seeing how they could well apply to all persons and not just to the members of one's own historical community. Because of this, the task of a natural law thinker working in a particular historical tradition like Judaism is to show how the logic involved in his or her constitution of a universal horizon is similar in principle to what is being done by thinkers working in other historical traditions. And in order to do that, one must be in conversation with these other thinkers from other traditions.

This projection of a universal horizon must then be coupled with the comparative work. Moreover, these "overlappings" do admit of

---

[58] This seems to be implied in Aristotle's more circumspect view of natural justice (*dikaion physikon*) in *Nicomachean Ethics*, 5.7/1134b20–35.

[59] While Thomas Aquinas sees human law to be derived from or determined by natural law (*Summa theologiae*, I-II, q. 95, a. 2), nonetheless, he doesn't see divine (i.e., revealed) law to be so derived or determined. Hence, it would seem, natural law can only modify divine law, but not change it or abolish it as it can in regard to human law. In this respect, I find Aquinas' treatment of law to be quite consistent with Jewish theology.

[60] Cf. Hermann Cohen, *Religion of Reason Out of the Sources of Judaism*, trans. S. Kaplan (New York: Frederich Ungar, 1972), 338ff.

[61] See his *Philosophical Investigations*, 1.18, trans. G. E. M. Anscombe (New York: Macmillan, 1958), 8.

actual development, especially in a multicultural society (or even in a multicultural world), and especially when enough people there want their multicultural society to be intercultural as well. (Yet that does not mean an idealistic jump into the creation of some sort of superculture or "monoculture" that swallows up all particular cultural identities like what happened in the story of the Tower of Babel.) And, if this indicates a desire on the part of persons and communities to discover by universal projection criteria for living together in mutual justice and peace, then perhaps this type of natural law theory, which is truly pluralistic both politically and epistemologically, will have some real correspondence with the lives and aspirations of the subjects of natural law. In order for this type of correspondence to be valid, however, the test of its universality and generality will be the extent it is able to be interculturally effective. Perhaps, then, natural law thinking can save multiculturalism from the dead-end of relativism, which denies any moral commonality at all; and perhaps multiculturalism, properly understood, can save natural law thinking from its all too frequent political and epistemological myopia. But multiculturalism needs reasons, not just overlappings that could well be accidental, superficial, and ephemeral. Otherwise, the respective cultures in the "multiculture," paradoxically, have nothing in common but their differences, which means they have nothing in common at all.

1.8 NATURAL LAW IS NOAHIDE LAW

Noahide law is what the ancient rabbinic sages taught is the set of precepts that God demands all humans created in God's image learn and practice.[62] These seven commandments (*sheva mitsvot benei noah*) are: (1) the positive injunction to set up courts of law to apply justice; (2) the prohibition of blasphemy; (3) the prohibition of idolatry; (4) the prohibition of sexual license (specifically, incest, homoeroticism, adultery, and bestiality); (5) the prohibition of homicide (including the prohibition of abortion); (6) the prohibition of robbery; (7) the prohibition of eating a limb torn from a living animal. These

---

[62] The basic rabbinic sources of this doctrine are *Tosefta*: Avodah Zarah 8.4; B. Sanhedrin 56a.

laws are termed "Noahide" because they were reiterated to Noah after surviving the Flood, when he and his family became humankind *redivivus*. However, the first and last of these precepts are different from the other five.

The first precept seems to obligate a society to constitute itself *systematically* through a legal order (what in German is called a *Rechtsordnung*), one that operates most immediately and persistently through its judicial system. The other six precepts obviously obligate individual persons, though to have the status of law, these precepts require a society to interpret them, enforce them, and rectify violations of them. So, perhaps, one can see this first Noahide commandment as being the obligation of individual persons to form a society with a legal order capable of properly enforcing the laws by which these persons are *already* obligated, and rectifying violations of them. This is unlike much of liberal political theory, for which there are no individual obligations *until* society is set up or contracted by individuals to make laws for themselves, most often based on nothing more than agreement for the sake of agreement. In this view, these are the public laws these individuals qua individuals couldn't make for themselves in their pre-political "state of nature" or "original position."[63] In other words, from a natural law perspective, the law makes the state more than the state makes the law.

Along these lines, when the Talmud discusses what was required for one to be a "resident-alien" (*ger toshav*) in the days of the First Jerusalem Temple, when the people of Israel enjoyed complete political independence in the entire land of Israel, the majority opinion is the seven Noahide commandments comprise that requirement.[64] Nevertheless, these commandments are not binding *because* they have been introduced by Jewish authorities; rather, the Jewish authorities make what is originally a universal moral requirement into their own particular political requirement. In other words, they are giving what is morally valid universally a particular political location. But that particular location expresses and applies those universally valid moral norms; those who live there do not presume to have invented them by themselves. That is why Jews can readily see these norms being formulated and applied in many other locations in the world.

---

[63] Cf. John Rawls, *A Theory of Justice* (Cambridge, MA: Harvard University Press, 1971), 17ff.

[64] B. Avodah Zarah 64b.

32   *David Novak*

The most Jews can claim is that we think we have exceptionally illu-
minating political-legal experience in the world, which we should be
happy to share with the rest of the world without making any authoritative demands (which inevitably become authoritarian demands)
upon them.[65] Because of this, Jews can engage in truly normative
relations with members of other societies that affirm these universal norms in one way or another. That is how the fourteenth-century
Provençal theologian, Menahem ha-Meiri, explained the moral
respectability of both Christians and Muslims for Jews (in contrast
to the ancient idolaters): they both are parts of communities living
under divine law (*ha-datot*). [66] Hence Jews who represent (or even
imply) Noahide law to be positive law made by Jews for gentiles are
very much mistaken and misleading to others.

Now the first six precepts are only alluded to in Scripture, i.e., there
are accounts in the book of Genesis that seem to indicate these laws
are already in force and they are accepted by everybody except criminals (who themselves often accept these laws as binding on everybody except themselves). In other words, there does not seem to be
any explicit prescription or proscription of them in Scripture. And, if
one therefore assumes these precepts do not need to be prescribed or
proscribed by specific revelation, then how else could they be known
unless they are evident to universally valid moral or practical reason?
Maimonides says they are known by "rational compulsion," or that
"reason inclines towards them," both terms which could be translated
into the scholastic term *inclinatio rationalis*.[67] But the seventh and
last Noahide commandment, which is the prohibition of eating the
"torn limb" (which presupposes the prohibition of tearing the limb
for food), on the other hand, is derived from a scriptural prohibition,
viz., "Indeed, flesh whose life-blood [*be-nafsho damo*] is still in it,
you shall not eat "(Genesis 9:4). And, although this prohibition could
be interpreted as being an example of a more general prohibition of
abusing nature cruelly (especially, abusing domesticated animals who

[65] See *Tosefta*: Sotah 8.6 and B. Sotah 35b re Deut. 27:8. However, Maimonides
rules that when Jews have political power over non-Jews, they should *enforce* Noahide
law (MT: Kings, 8.10), yet he only requires Jews to enforce what all people should
already enforce among themselves. As such, Jews are only required to be the specific
agents of what is essentially universal law.

[66] See Jacob Katz, *Exclusiveness and Tolerance* (Oxford: Oxford University Press,
1961), 13ff.

[67] MT: Kings, 8.11–9.1.

live with humans in closest proximity), Maimonides separates this prohibition from the other six, which he says were "commanded to the first humans [*nitstaveh adam ha-ri'shon*]." The implication here is that this seventh precept needs a specific scriptural prohibition unlike the other six that do not need one. [68]

Whereas Maimonides seems to think that what was commanded to Noah (then what was commanded to Abraham and finally the whole Torah commanded to Moses) occurred at certain points in human history, the six commandments given the first humans are coequal with creation itself. They are ubiquitous: valid and binding every time everywhere. They would be known even had they not been written down anywhere.[69] The very fact that Maimonides sees six sevenths of the Noahide laws to really be "adamic" or "human" (i.e., human as pertaining to their subjects, not pertaining to their source who is God) indicates his acceptance of basic natural law reasoning. "Adam" is the personification of humankind per se. For Maimonides, then, only the seventh Noahide commandment is truly "Noahide." Thus, for Jews, natural law as Noahide law lies in the background of Judaism, but it does so as a logical and not just a chronological precondition *for* revelation. Accordingly, natural/Noahide law never recedes into the historical past; rather it functions as an ever ready criterion that protects revealed law from appearing or being interpreted in a way by which it seems to be beneath instead of above the general morality of natural/Noahide law.[70] In fact, it has protected Jewish law from the type of fanaticism that willfully denies Judaism any universal dimension.

To be sure, to designate Noahide law as the Jewish version of natural law is highly controversial. It has been disputed in ancient, medieval, and modern Judaism.[71] In fact, one could even say that those Jewish thinkers who have seen the idea of natural law operating within the Jewish tradition, especially the Jewish legal tradition, are a minority—albeit not a minuscule or a marginal minority. Today, especially, most scholars of Jewish law (both those who merely describe it and those who also apply it and judge according to it) are legal positivists, looking at Jewish law as they would look at the constitution of a modern nation-state. (The more modest of these scholars restrain themselves

---

[68] MT: Kings, 9.1.
[69] See *Sifra*: Aharei-Mot, ed. Weiss, 86a; B. Yoma 67b re Lev. 18:4.
[70] See B. Sanhedrin 59a; also, B. Yevamot 22a.
[71] See Novak, *The Image of the Non-Jew in Judaism*, 2nd ed., 231ff.

from telling non-Jews what they should be doing or not doing, since they have no jurisdiction over them *de jure*; and, similarly, they usually restrain themselves from telling Jews who do not accept their authority what they should be doing or not doing, since they have no jurisdiction over them *de facto*.) Nevertheless, there is enough of a tradition of natural law thinking in Judaism for any contemporary Jewish thinker to continue it and even develop it. Critical thinking within a normative tradition like Judaism is itself a normative pursuit.[72] And just as new practical situations require that the tradition be mined for new rulings as to what is to be done here and now, so do new intellectual challenges require that the tradition be mined for new theories as to what is to be thought here and now. This mining of the tradition is not just a process of discovery; it is also a process of imaginative judgment. And such imaginative judgment is always selective, judging which source in the tradition lends itself to development for the situation or case at hand and which does not, whether it be a case calling for a practical conclusion (hence requiring a *modus operandi* to reach it), or a case calling for a theoretical conclusion (hence requiring a *modus cognescendi* to reach it). Finally, the normative Jewish tradition enables interpreters of the tradition for their own time and place to rely on minority opinions if that minority opinion provides the more appropriate answer to the normative question that the situation at hand calls for than does the majority opinion.[73]

1.9 NATURAL LAW IS MOST INTELLIGIBLE AND MOST EFFECTIVE WHEN IT FORMULATES HUMAN RIGHTS

We have already seen a number of times that natural law is discovered through the exercise of human reason. But how does that reason operate? What is the subject matter which that reason reasons about? In dealing with this question, the concept of human rights helps us formulate an answer. In order to do that, though, we need to see how

---

[72] See B. Shabbat 31a re Isa. 33:6; also, Leo Strauss, *Philosophy and Law*, trans. E. Adler (Albany: State University of New York Press, 1995), 60ff.

[73] See e.g., M. Eduyot 1.5; B. Berakhot 9a. Cf. B. Hullin 11a re Exod. 23:2.

human rights lie at the core of the human nature to which natural law teaches us to be true by enabling us to act intelligently in a way that, maximally, enhances human nature; and which, minimally, does not pervert it. Moreover, bringing the concept of human rights into the discussion of natural law enables natural law theory to participate in the overall political conversation in the contemporary world where the issue of rights lies at the core of almost everything being discussed.

Earlier, we saw that our moral experience is first domestic: we begin to act morally in response to the commands of our parents. Our moral experience begins with our experience of being the subject of duty, which is the obedience we owe our parents. A major part of what we are commanded to do is concerned with how we are to treat other family members. Moreover, *mutatis mutandis*, we see the same thing in our communal experience: the head of the community commands us to treat our fellow citizens beneficently. Therefore, those who are to be so treated by other members of the community have been entitled (i.e., given the right) to claim our beneficence when it is not forthcoming. (Usually, this is done when the state redistributes wealth in the form of taxation, or when the state drafts citizens to defend their fellow citizens in time of great foreign danger to the country.) And, here too, that entitlement is usually something we know *already, because* we have received it from the head of the community as our duty. And, when we understand the beneficent reasons for this command having been made, we do our duty voluntarily rather than out of fear of extrinsic consequences from the state's power to punish violators of its commands. In both cases, the domestic and the communal, we benefit from doing our duty when we realize that we are agents bringing more justice and more tranquility into our family and into our community. And we benefit ourselves when we can do good for others and not just have good done for us by others, for doing good is even better than experiencing good done for us inasmuch as our human dignity is more enhanced by our activity than it is by our passivity.

Now the good that our parents have willed for us and commanded us to extend to other family members is because these others are still members of *our* family. But these commands extend no further. And the good communal authorities (which could be a parliament rather than a single ruler) have willed for us and commanded us to extend to other members of the community is because these others are still members of *our* community. These commands, too, extend no further.

However, the subjects of natural law are, as we shall see, the subjects of human rights—what used to be called "natural rights." And that is because they are members of universal humankind. So, what is their community, and who is at the head of it?

There have been natural law thinkers (especially the Stoics) who have seen the family or the domestic community being included in the political community, and then the political community being included in the cosmos or world order. And, just as parents are the authorities of the family, and just as the head(s) of the political community are the authorities there, so too is God the authority or Sovereign of the universe.[74] And, in this view, it could be said that natural law emanates down into the law of human communities, then down into the domestic realm. As such, God is to the head of the political community what the head of the political community is to the head of the family. That is, what is higher transcends what is lower and rules over it. Nevertheless, the higher does not totally absorb the lower into itself. The lower first owes duty to the higher; the higher then entitles the lower with rights.

The problem with this picture of natural law, though, is twofold. One, it assumes that we have actual experience of living within such a cosmic "community," which includes all rational beings (humans being the only such rational beings we can recognize in our world anyway). But, the fact is, we have no such experience of this kind of universal world actually peopled by all human beings. That seems to be some kind of romanticized past or idealized future. Two, this picture of natural law assumes that we have ordinary experience of the cosmic Sovereign, especially enjoying experience of God's giving His command to us and for us. But, the fact is, we have no such ordinary experience. Only communities that claim to be founded on revelation can claim to be directly commanded by God.[75] But even there, one does not expect to regularly experience God's commandment personally. It is usually an accepted tradition.

The way to avoid these two problems raised by much pre-modern natural law theory is not to derive the natural rights codified by natural law from the existence of a cosmic community and of a cosmic Sovereign/Lawgiver as if they were facts known from ordinary experience, which they are not. (But, unlike many modern theorists, we

---

[74] See Cicero, *De Natura Deorum*, 2.2, 11, 29ff.

[75] See Amos 3:1–2; Ps. 147:19–20 and Ibn Ezra's comment thereon.

should not regard human rights to be arbitrary human inventions willy-nilly either; for what humans can invent, they can even more easily destroy.) Instead, we should look directly to the human being making a natural rights claim upon us, the most basic right/claim being: "Do not harm me" (*noli me tangere*)! Now if this claim were made by a sibling, we would already know the answer from the fact that we have already been commanded by our parents not to harm *our* siblings. And that is because our parents care for them as they care for us. The same is true when in a political setting this kind of claim is made by a fellow citizen.

However, in the case of somebody with whom we do not knowingly share a common parent and with whom we are not parts of the same family (or community), we have to begin with the claimants themselves rather than with *who* originally entitled the claimant to make their claim as their right. Nevertheless, that claim does need a justification ultimately, if for no other reason than we need to distinguish a just claim from an unjust claim. And the justification could be something like this: "I am like you and all humankind created in the image of God. Here and now that means I am like you and all humankind specially placed in the world to reflect or imitate God's concern for the world, that justice and peace prevail there among all creation, first and foremost with the human creation who most reflect God's caring for what God has created. Harming anybody created in God's image prevents him or her, you or me, from doing what God has commanded all of us to do in the world." In other words, we infer the source of the claim from the claim itself, which is the claimants' assertion of their human right not to be harmed. Unlike the domestic, political, and covenantal situations, though, we do not derive the right or claim from the authority of the head of the community whom we already know, nor do we assume that we are members of the same real community in the world. In a situation subject to natural law, the universal community that is the context of the law's rule is an abstraction, and the head of this now abstract community can only be assumed *ex hypothesi*.[76] Nevertheless, that hypothesis has tremendous heuristic value.

---

[76] Only at the *eschaton* or "end of days" (*aharit ha-yamim*) will this universal community become a concrete reality, and only at the *eschaton* "will the Lord become King over all the earth" (Zech. 14:9).

Of course, there are other reasons for respecting somebody else's human rights. These reasons should not be dismissed by those who believe that human nature as the image of God is the best reason for respecting the human rights of the bearers of that divine image. For having reasons we consider inferior to our own is still better than having no reasons at all for affirming human rights in practice; and that is still better than basing one's concern with human rights on intuition or feeling or even passion (though any significant human endeavor needs subjective emotional motivation continually). To paraphrase the Talmud: it is better to do something right for an inadequate reason rather than not to do it at all; for one might eventually do what is right for the right reason after all.[77] Furthermore, by not requiring our secular interlocutors, who accept the indispensability of human rights for our political health, to accept our philosophical-theological justification of human rights, we can engage them in ongoing discussion of the theoretical issues involved here in a way that does not threaten them. We need not refute their reasons; we only need to understand why we have better reasons than they have for doing what we both think ought to be done in the world. Indeed, we only need to argue with them when they make arguments against our reasons for doing what we both believe needs to be done in the world. Nevertheless, even when such arguments against our theoretical position are made, we can still work with them for the enhancement and protection of most human rights in the world today.

1.10 NATURAL LAW THINKING PROVIDES THE REASONS FOR SOME OF THE SCRIPTURAL COMMANDMENTS

Natural law type thinking (whether it actually used the term *dat tiv'it* or "natural law" or not) has operated as an important criterion in Judaism for attempts to formulate the "reasons of the commandments" (*ta'amei ha-mitsvot*), both commandments derived from the words of Scripture (*mitsvot de-oraita*) and commandments devised by the rabbinic Sages (*mitsvot de-rabbanan*). And it has been especially

---

[77] See B. Nazir 23b.

fruitful for discovering or projecting reasons of the commandments that govern inter-human relations (*bein adam le-havero*).[78] Natural law thinking in connection with the commandments that pertain in this area, which might be called the "political realm" (in the Aristotelian sense of politics or social ethics), is best pursued when the theologians who engage in it are concerned and familiar with the questions discussed in political philosophy.

Let us look how natural law type thinking operates in the case of scripturally based commandments.

The reasons of scripturally based commandments are discovered a posteriori, i.e., the commandment already there before us, to be done whenever the occasion calls for it to be done.[79] One is expected to keep the commandment irrespective of whether or not one understands the reason why God commanded that this act be done. One can only discover, after the fact as it were, why this is the case. But, why should anyone want to discover why God gave such and such a commandment if the keeping of the commandment does not depend on having that knowledge beforehand? Moreover, isn't there always the chance that one will discover a reason why *not* to keep the commandment?[80] Isn't unquestioning obedience preferable to questioning why the commandment is to be kept, with all the doubt such questioning necessarily involves, doubt that can easily lead to inaction or to our doing something we are commanded not to do? And, what if God has no other reason for commanding us to do something than to test whether or not we will obey out of pure faith in God?[81]

Nevertheless, to assume that God has no reason for commanding us to do x rather than y other than to exercise His powerful authority over us means that we conceive God to be an irrational tyrant, "on a power trip" in today's colloquial parlance.[82] Is it not an insult to God to attribute to God an irrationality that we would abhor in a human ruler?[83] So, first of all we need to assume that all God's commandments have reasons, even though we can never know all of them or

[78] See M. Yoma 8.9.
[79] See B. Shabbat 88a re Exod. 24:7.
[80] See B. Sanhedrin 21b re Deut. 17:17.
[81] See *Midrash Rabbah*: Genesis 44.1 re II Sam. 22:31.
[82] See B. Avodah Zarah 3a.
[83] See Gen. 18:25; Maimonides, *Guide of the Perplexed*, 3.26 re Deut. 32:47 and Isa. 45:19.

even hope to know many of them with certainty.[84] And, whereas we might be unaware of why God has commanded certain command-ments that pertain to the divine–human relationship (*bein adam le-maqom*), we are certainly aware of why God commanded all the commandments that pertain to inter-human relations. Only in the case of the former, which are commandments God commands for His own sake, can we know *what* God wants us to do for Godself; but we only know that when God tells us so through revelation. Sometimes God tells us *why* He wants us to do this or that for Him. And that is sometimes shown to be what God wants to be done for the sake of God's covenantal relationship *with* us, keeping the Sabbath being the best example.[85] Other times God does not tell us why and we can only try to surmise why God wants this or that to be done for Him.[86]

Regarding inter-human commandments, however, the Torah is largely codifying what we already know is good for humans in their life together in the world.[87] This is what makes these commandments universal moral norms. Justice and peace are good for the world. That is why by means of natural law humans are told to pursue these ends and how to do so. Thus, when these natural law precepts are taken up into the revealed law of the Torah, we can assume that the same reasons for them that obtained in natural law also obtain in revealed law. For example when the Torah commands "You shall not mur-der" (Exodus 20:13) it is simply reiterating and recontextualizing the unwritten prohibition of murder that Cain was held responsible for due to his murder of his brother Abel (Genesis 4:8–13).[88] In other words, the fact is that even though we have to keep the command-ments of the Torah with the reasons for them being affirmed only a posteriori, those commandments that have already been manifest as natural law have reasons that can be affirmed a priori. That is, know-ing that a human being is created in the image of God is what enables us to infer from that truth the prohibition on killing the object of God's special concern whenever we are faced with the opportunity of murdering another human being. The fact every human person is

---

[84] See David Novak, *The Election of Israel* (Cambridge: Cambridge University Press, 1995), 251–52.

[85] See Gen. 12:1–3; Exod. 20:8–11 and 31:15–17 and 35:2; also, Y. Rosh Hashanah 1.3/59a-b re Lev. 22:9.

[86] See B. Sanhedrin 21a.

[87] See Israel Lifschuetz, *Tiferet Yisrael* on M. Baba Batra 10.8.

[88] See B. Sanhedrin 56b re Gen. 2:16 and 9:6.

created in the image of God calls for an appropriate response from any other human person encountering that other human person.

Furthermore, understanding the reason of the prohibition of murder gives us the criterion for reinterpreting any other commandment of the Torah that seems to be prescribing murder. Thus when the Torah commands us regarding the Canaanites that "You shall not let any one of them live" (Deuteronomy 20:16), the ancient rabbinic Sages and Maimonides clearly want to avoid the conclusion that the Torah is commanding murder, indeed genocide.[89] So, this commandment is reinterpreted as part of an offer the invading Israelites are seen to have made to the residents of Canaan, viz., they only risk annihilation if they attempt to prevent Israelite settlement in the land of Canaan by waging war with the Israelites. But, this will not be the case if they either emigrate from the land or if they make peace with the Israelites. And, quite significantly, this peace treaty as it were also requires the Canaanites to accept the Noahide law, one of whose main precepts is the prohibition of "shedding innocent blood" (*shefikhut damim*). If they do so, they will be left alone and their cities left intact. In other words, how could the Torah that proscribes murder to gentiles command Jews to engage in it?[90] (And that abhorrence of shedding the blood of *anybody* created in the image of God, even that of a murderer, led some of the ancient rabbinic Sages to advocate qualifying the preconditions for the application of scripturally mandated capital punishment to such an extent so as to make capital punishment virtually impossible to enforce.[91]) Other Torah laws too were reinterpreted so as save the Torah from appearing to be morally inferior to the type of natural law awareness that could be assumed to be prevalent among those who do not have to live under the Torah's rule, but who do have to live under the rule of natural law insofar as it is rationally compelling.[92]

Finally, we need to distinguish here the "reasons of the commandments" from human projects or ideals; for if these reasons are essentially human ideals, there is no need to require the affirmation of a divine lawgiver of the commandments. The commandments could be thus "demythologized" into idealistic ethics. Nevertheless, a theistic

---

[89] Y. Shevi`it 6.1/36c; MT: Kings, 6.4.
[90] See B. Sanhedrin 59b.
[91] See M. Makkot 1.10; B. Makkot 7a.
[92] See B. Baba Kama 113a-b.

ontology prevents that.[93] For God's purposeful creation of the cosmos is not only a datum; it is a task given (*Aufgabe* in German) to humans to imitate and further actively. Indeed, human action gains cosmic significance when it is harmonized with God's own purposes for the world. Thus creation has both origin (*archē*) and end (*telos*). Yet these divine purposes are not ideals we humans could project onto the world, since we humans did not create the world we inhabit (much less the cosmos that is beyond our habitation).[94] We find ourselves already there (*da-sein* in German) in the world. As such, we cannot realistically expect to recreate the world in our own image by our own power. Only God is "the first and the last" (Isaiah 44:6). Both the substance and the form of creation are God's doing alone. The most we humans can do is to willingly and proactively cooperate with God in the ongoing work of creation. This is the most one can do to be like God (*imitatio Dei*) in the world.[95]

1.11 NATURAL LAW PROVIDES THE CRITERIA FOR LEGISLATING HUMAN-MADE JEWISH LAW

Most of those scholars who judge natural law thinking not to be genuinely Jewish forget that the area of Jewish law pertaining to inter-human relations, especially Jewish civil and criminal law, is one where as the Mishnah puts it: "There is little from Scripture, but much more from tradition (*halakhot merubbot*)."[96] Though one can see much of the traditional law that was developed by the rabbinic Sages as having been represented to have been transmitted from ancient sources (even going as far back as Moses), most of the literary evidence suggests otherwise. Thus Maimonides, with considerable (though not unanimous) rabbinic precedent on his side, argues that

---

[93] See David Novak, "The Universality of Jewish Ethics: A Rejoinder to Secularist Critics," *Journal of Religious Ethics* 36 (2008), 198ff.

[94] See Isaiah 45:18; also, Maimonides, *Guide of the Perplexed*, 2.19, for the notion that the Torah teaches that natural ends are not simply in the world eternally (as Aristotle taught), but that God has infused them into the world for the world simultaneous with his creation of the world. Thus the world's creation is for the sake of an end *made for* the world, but which is not inherent in the world per se.

[95] See B. Sotah 14a.

[96] M. Hagigah 1.8.

the only traditional laws not humanly made are those few laws desig-nated as "Mosaic" (*halakhah le-mosheh mi-sinai*; literally, "laws going back to Moses at Sinai").[97] All the rest are clearly devised by human minds. And that is why, at least in principle all of these humanly made laws could be repealed, i.e., if they either fall out of Jewish usage, or if later Sages think the specific reasons for making them are no longer valid; or even if the ends these laws intend are better attained by acts other than those originally commanded for their sake.[98]

However, did the Sages simply exercise their legislative authority arbitrarily as some sort of expression of their own political power? Or did they want to be sure that they were legislating for reasons evi-dent and acceptable to the people they were legislating for?[99] In other words, didn't the justification of their legislation have to be *persuasive*, i.e., didn't there have to be reasons for it, reasons known beforehand a priori? Here the preponderance of evidence from the Talmud and related sources is that rabbinic legislation had to be rationally and politically justified in order to be accepted by a people who even asked God for reasons to accept His law in good faith.[100] In fact, the Talmud notes that there are only three rabbinic laws that seem to have no reason and which are, therefore, like laws that are accepted because of their antiquity alone.[101] Yet even here, later scholars tried to show that these three laws do have reasons, which can be discovered by careful enquiry.[102]

Now the reasoning employed in rabbinic legislation is teleologi-cal: specific laws are made in the interest of more general ends. What Maimonides showed so well, especially in his interpretation of the rabbinic laws pertaining to inter-human relations—aided but not caused by his liking for Aristotelian teleology—is that they are based on what the rabbinic Sages discerned to be universalizable standards of justice and peace.[103] Since there is so little in this area of Jewish

[97] MT: Rebels, 1.3.

[98] B. Avodah Zarah 36a-b; MT: Rebels, 2.6–7.

[99] See B. Avodah Zarah 35a.

[100] See David Weiss Halivni, *Mishnah, Midrash, and Gemara* (Cambridge, MA: Harvard University Press, 1986), passim.

[101] B. Gittin 14a.

[102] See B. Gittin, *Tosafot*, s.v. "ke-hilkhata."

[103] See MT: Sanhedrin, 24.10; Kings, 4.10; also, David Novak, "Can We Be Maimonideans Today?" in *Maimonides and His Heritage*, eds. I. Dobbes-Weinstein, L. E. Goodman, and J. A. Grady (Albany, NY: SUNY Press, 2009), 193ff.

law that is specifically derived from Scripture or the "Written Torah," the reasoning employed here had to be more teleologically conceptual than exegetical. Here is where the philosophically imagined idea of natural law is needed for the coherent explication and development of that type of conceptual reasoning in matters of human experience and practice that can hardly be taken to be uniquely Jewish. The two classical Jewish terms for this type of universalizable reasoned practice are *derekh erets* (literally, "the way of the earth," or less literally, "the worldly road") and *tiqqun ha`olam* (literally, "the mending of the world," or less literally, "constructive public policy").[104] Both of these terms seem to correspond to the philosophical concept of the "common good" (*bonum commune*).[105] When this line of thinking is carefully followed, one can effectively apply natural law criteria as a limit on and corrective of positive law made by humans, even to the point of repeal (more often *de facto*; less often *de jure*).

In conclusion, then, natural law thinking is an authentic Jewish form of thought, influencing how Jews look upon their morally significant relations with the non-Jewish world, and how Jews are to continually interpret and reinterpret morally significant relations among ourselves by the very same criteria. Pursuing this work has given me the task of more than a lifetime. I hope to be able to pursue that task for as long as God gives me the time and the energy to do so.[106]

---

[104] Re *derekh erets*, see *Midrash Rabbah*: Leviticus 3.9 re Gen. 3:24. Re *tiqqun ha`olam*, see M. Gittin 4.5 re Isa. 45:18.

[105] See Aristotle, *Politics*, 1.1/1252a1ff.; John Finnis, *Natural Law and Natural Rights* (Oxford: Clarendon Press, 1980), 156ff.

[106] See M. Avot 2.16.

Response to David Novak's
"Natural Law and Judaism"

Anver M. Emon

David Novak's scholarship on natural law and Judaism spans decades; and from his contribution to this volume, it is obvious that there are many points to which I could address this response. I will focus my response on a narrow range of issues, which I will structure along the lines of Novak's numbered points and considerations. In particular, this response will focus on three points that arise in Novak's essay and which pose important and interesting points of comparison in the spirit of this volume.

I. IS NATURAL LAW ENDEMIC TO ISLAMIC THOUGHT?

Both Novak and I argue for natural law theories within the Jewish and Islamic legal traditions, all the while aware of a critique that rejects such a theoretical possibility. As Novak writes, "[t]here are those who presume coherent natural law thinking presupposes the type of *natural* ontology developed by classical Greek philosophers, especially Plato, Aristotle, and the Stoics."[1] In the case of Islamic natural law theories, the theoretical approaches I have identified in pre-modern Islamic legal philosophy, namely the approaches of Hard and Soft

---

[1] Novak, Sec. 1.

Natural Law, have engendered, among others, the objection that to frame such approaches as "Islamic" natural law theories gives undue priority and authority to a "Christian/Western" tradition that defines the terms of what can count as an "Islamic" approach to natural law. A more philological version of this objection may be to suggest that there can be no "natural law" tradition in Islamic law because the very idea and phrase "natural law" does not occur in Islamic legal history. There are other terms of art that such critics would invoke as more appropriate focus for a study about reason and authority in Islamic law. Those terms might include *maslaha, maqasid, istihsan*. I suspect that similar criticisms can be applied to any other attempt to articulate a natural law approach from traditions other than the Christianized Western one.

In the Islamic studies context, these sorts of critiques draw their significance and strength from the critiques of Orientalist scholarship that sometimes too easily frame the Christian West (and its intellectual tradition) in imperial terms.[2] This is not to suggest that such critiques are unfounded; indeed they are important historiographic contributions to the study of Islam and Islamic law specifically, and the post-colonial world more generally. But to argue from such positions against the possibility of an "Islamic" natural law is arguably to posit as "Islamic" only that which is unadulterated or uncontaminated by ideas that are associated with an Other. By implication, such a position presumes a pure or authentic Islam that, ironically, reifies what Islam is and can be in a fashion akin to what Orientalist scholars of Islam have already done, and for which they have been roundly criticized.[3]

Although these post-colonial forms of critique are important to address and account for, they do not and cannot solely and fully define the scope of what is possible in terms of Islamic legal research. They cannot define and delimit the questions that we can pose of the Islamic tradition. Indeed, to suggest that we can delimit the questions that can be posed of a historical tradition suggests that all we can do is explore

---

[2] Edward Said, *Orientalism* (London: Routledge and Kegan Paul, 1978); Dipesh Chakrabarty, *Provincializing Europe: postcolonial thought and historical difference* (Princeton: Princeton University Press, 2000).

[3] Indeed, this is the critique Mohammad Fadel lays against Wael Hallaq's arguments about Islamization and Islamic reform in the modern nation-state. Mohammad Fadel, "A Tragedy of Politics or an Apolitical Tragedy?" *Journal of the American Oriental Society* 131, no. 1 (Jan-Mar 2011): 109–27.

new answers to old questions. But as the critic of post-colonial theory, David Scott, suggests, critiques such as those posed of my approach to Islamic natural law ignore the pressing imperative of accounting for how changes in our twenty-first century world pose new questions that old answers (or new answers to old questions) cannot satisfy. As Scott writes: "In new historical conditions, old questions may lose their salience, their bite, and so lead the range of old answers that once attached to them to appear lifeless, quaint, not so much wrong as irrelevant."[4] Throughout the Muslim world, we are witnessing how old/new answers to old questions either miss the point of innovative scholarship or actively seek to suppress such scholarship in the name of an Islamic purity. For instance the well-known legal action in Egypt against the late scholar Nasr Hamid Abu Zayd on grounds of apostasy alleged that he had written about the Qur'an in a manner that reflected the heterodox theology of Mu'tazilism—an allegation that was dubious at best,[5] politically motivated at worst.[6]

Drawing upon Scott's critique of post-colonial theory, I suggest that a "natural law" frame of reference provides a valuable starting point for asking new questions of the Islamic tradition. As new questions, though, they disrupt a certain status quo in the historiography of Islamic law. For instance, if Islamic natural law theories posit nature as a mediating concept that makes possible the ontological authority of reason, one can appreciate this as an answer to questions about whether, how, and to what extent jurists understood their ontological authority to develop legal rulings in light of the infinite experience of humanity and the finite sources of authority. So much of the literature on the jurist's legal authority has focused on his epistemic authority (i.e., *ijtihad* and other related methods). Islamic natural law theory, however, shifts the question from epistemology to ontology to explore new approaches to and insights on the issue of authority. Some may

---

[4] David Scott, *Conscripts of Modernity: The Tragedy of Colonial Enlightenment* (Durham: Duke University Press, 2004), 5.

[5] Thomas Hildebrandt, "Between Mu'tazilism and Mysticism: How much of a Mu'tazilite is Nasr Hamid Abu Zayd?" in *A Common Rationality: Mu'tazilism in Islam and Judaism*, eds. Camilla Adang, Sabine Schmidtke, and David Sklare, (Würzburg: Ergon in Kommission, 2007), 495–512.

[6] Nasr Hamid Abu Zayd with Esther R. Nelson, *Voice of an exile: reflections on Islam* (Westport, CT: Praeger, 2004); Baber Johansen, "Apostasy as objective and depersonalized fact: two recent Egyptian court judgments," *Social Research* 70, no. 3 (Fall 2003): 687–710; Susanne Olsson, "Apostasy in Egypt: Contemporary Cases of Hisbah," *The Muslim World* 98 (2008): 95–115.

find this question sufficiently unfamiliar as to be discomfiting. Take for example a fundamental irony about Islamic natural law theories that I discuss in my essay to this volume, namely that despite starting from opposing theological positions, jurists developed distinct natural law theories that are not terribly different from one another. The Islamic natural law approach reveals the theological distinctions between these jurists to be rather insignificant in regard to questions about ontological authority in law. Yet some might prefer focusing on debates about Mu'tazilite and Ash'arite ethics, and in that sense, disregard "natural law" as a useful organizing concept.[7] Clearly uncomfortable with the question posed from a natural law vantage point, David Warren situates his voice squarely in defense of the intellectual status quo. He writes: "Indeed, it is perfectly acceptable to use abstract concepts such as Ash'arite, Mu'tazilite, and so on for hermeneutical or explanatory purposes, whilst noting that they can never capture individual intricacies, and that a particular thinker may display characteristics that are applicable to both, or neither." Indeed, he suggests that such an approach has the merit of focusing on terms and traditions "more firmly rooted in the discipline of Islamic law."[8]

To hold to the status quo is less a critique of a natural law approach, and more an acknowledgment that new questions—such as those posed by a natural law frame of analysis—disturb an intellectual status quo. That does not mean, however, that the natural law approach is invalid or somehow irrelevant to a study of Islamic legal history. Indeed, the approach posits new questions, and thereby opens up new possibilities for research and inquiry. For instance, Rumee Ahmed describes the established categories of Ash'arism and Mu'tazilism as "standard, simplistic" and sees the possibilities posed by the new questions and answers of an Islamic natural law as encouraging "a multifaceted view of legal theory and legal theorists."[9]

What should be evident in this short analysis, therefore, is that whether natural law is a helpful model for understanding pre-modern Islamic jurisprudence depends less on what the pre-modern sources offer, and more on the dispositions of contemporary scholars writing

[7] See for instance, Taneli Kukkonen, "[Review of] *Islamic Natural Law Theories*," *Philosophy in Review* 31, no. 1 (2011): 26–28.

[8] David Warren, "[Review of] *Islamic natural law theories*," *Islam and Christian-Muslim Relations* 22, no. 4 (2011): 495–6, 496.

[9] Rumee Ahmed, "[Review of] *Islamic Natural Law Theories*," *Review of Middle East Studies* 45, no. 1 (Summer 2011): 100–102.

and researching about Islam. In a climate of ongoing debates about what counts as "true," or "pure" or "authentic" Islam, the scholarly defense of old answers and/or old questions all too often reifies what Islamic law was and thereby can be.

II. ISLAMIC NATURAL LAW: TOWARD A PHILOSOPHY OF LAW IN ISLAM

Novak makes an important set of observations when addressing how the universality of natural law is bounded by the circumstances and particularity of the community within which the practical reasoning of natural law takes place. In this regard, he asserts that natural law thinking may aspire to a universal set of values, but always from within a particular tradition or cultural context.[10] Furthermore, he situates the particularity of natural law thinking at the juncture of the disciplinary poles of theology and philosophy.[11] The juxtaposition of these two points offers an important opportunity to reflect upon how the Islamic natural law theories I address in my contribution to this volume are perhaps best appreciated neither as a form of theology (*kalam*) nor as a form of natural philosophy within the tradition of *falsafa*, but rather as a gesture toward a philosophy of law in Islam.

What do I mean by a philosophy of law in Islam? Certainly this is not the place to articulate a robust picture of what philosophy of law in Islam can or should look like. But whatever Islamic legal philosophy is or might be, it cannot be merely elided with the genre of *usul al-fiqh*, or viewed as a set of deductive methods of legal determination (e.g., *qiyas, maqasid* and *maslaha*). To view *usul al-fiqh* as reflecting for the most part a *legal method* betrays the prioritization of epistemological questions over and even against the ontological ones such as authority and its sources. As Rumee Ahmed has shown in his *Narratives of Islamic Legal Theory*, there is more to the *usul al-fiqh* genre than merely debates about method of legal derivation. In the interstices of debates in treatises of *usul al-fiqh*, he shows that there are significant theological and cosmological questions that have

---

[10] Novak, Sec. 7.   [11] Novak, Sec. 7.

implications not just for the epistemology of Islamic legal theory, but also for foundational questions about law, authority, and governance.[12] Additionally, to elide *usul al-fiqh* and Islamic legal philosophy ignores how the detailed *fiqh* debates among jurists and across legal schools can and often do reveal a philosophy of law that might be implicit across a range of issues. Indeed, as I have shown in my treatment of the *dhimmi* rules, there is an implicit relationship between law and the enterprise of governance such that any contemporary approach to Islamic law and pluralism cannot also ignore how the advent of the modern state contributes new conditions of intelligibility for any discussion of what Shari'a can and ought to be.[13]

None of this is to deny that a philosophy of law in Islam would draw upon arguments from *kalam* and *falsafa*. But it cannot be so tied to such arguments as to be over-determined by them. Indeed, as noted above already, a fundamental irony of Islamic natural law theories is that despite starting from opposing theological camps, jurists of competing natural law theories reached roughly similar answers to the question about reason's ontological authority in law. Furthermore, though their philosophy of law was premised upon a certain conception of nature, their approach to nature for purposes of natural law was different and distinct from their consideration of nature for purposes of their natural philosophy (*al-tabi'iyat*). If we examine the conceptual work that "nature" did in the different natural law theories espoused by pre-modern Muslim jurists, we find that it made possible the grant of ontological authority to reason. Whether one agrees or disagrees with any particular theory of Islamic natural law, the conceptual contribution of nature in an Islamic natural law theory does not simply reflect some empirical sense of an objective world, or require one to stake out a position as a hard or soft determinist with respect to causation. Rather, as suggested in my contribution to this volume, "nature" in Islamic natural law theories allows, at the very least, for enough determinacy to make possible the fusion of fact and value, which in turn makes possible the ontological authority of reason.

---

[12] Rumee Ahmed, *Narratives of Islamic Legal Theory* (Oxford: Oxford University Press, 2012).

[13] Anver M. Emon, *Religious Pluralism and Islamic Law:* Dhimmis *and Others in the Empire of Law* (Oxford: Oxford University Press, 2012).

III. ISLAMIC NATURAL LAW,
MAQASID-MASLAHA, AND PRACTICAL
REASONING

For many specialists of Islamic law, *"maqasid"* and *"maslaha"* are important technical terms of art that relate directly to the scope and nature of Islamic legal reasoning. Some specialists might even go so far as to say that any attempt to espouse an Islamic natural law theory is either at worst an imperialist intellectual exercise, or at best inattentive to the resources within the Islamic tradition. No doubt these terms of art are important ones; they have animated Muslim reformist thinking throughout the twentieth century and continue to bolster the hopes of those who look for increased space for inquiry within the rich, deep, and at times constraining tradition of Islamic law. Some might argue that such traditions are so organized against the interests of certain groups (e.g., women) as to preclude a more liberating reading of the tradition. That critique, though, does not preclude the fact that for people of faith, traditions such as Islamic law are repositories of meaning and identity; they are sites of both commitment and contestation. For example, the Muslim women's reform movement Musawah seeks to reform Islamic family law in the Muslim world, in large part by working within the tradition of Islam as opposed to stepping outside of it. While secular feminists might view such an endeavor as quixotic, Musawah's advocates recognize that for many Muslim women around the world, equality *and* belonging to community are both important principles that cannot be, nor necessarily need to be, hierarchized or prioritized in relation to one another.

For reformists, the challenge remains how to argue for a liberating project within the framework of Islamic law. On the one hand, there are inherited doctrines (*fiqh*), which constitute much of the traditional corpus against which reformists argue. Some might argue that these doctrines have a preclusive effect, constituting as they do precedents for issues across a range of topics. On the other hand, the inherited *fiqh* doctrines are themselves embedded as contingent particulars within a normative tradition. Any approach to a liberating model of practical reasoning would need to first recognize how the particularity of these *fiqh* rules limits their normative authority, and thereby limits their preclusive effect on any *de novo* attempt at interpretation within Islamic law. This is not the place to expand upon the authority of *fiqh;* that topic has been addressed elsewhere at length.[14] It suffices here only to summarize basic, but important, findings of existing scholarship on the authority of *fiqh.* As many have shown, despite the all-too-often determinate sounding nature of *fiqh* doctrines, they are embedded in a theoretical structure that limits their scope of authority. As I have shown elsewhere, the *fiqh* are those doctrines that arise from a jurist's interpretive effort (*ijtihad*). Epistemically, these doctrines are premised upon a recognition that the jurist is limited: limited in knowledge, limited in time for research, and limited in his or her ability to know the divine will with any certitude. Indeed, the theoretical structure within which *fiqh* doctrines are embedded generally denies to such doctrines the quality of *certainty* or *certitude.* Rather, as jurists argued, the most a jurist can claim is that his or her legal conclusion is more likely than not to conform to the divine will, or most likely right though perhaps possibly wrong. In Arabic, the technical phrase is *ghalabat al-zann,* with *zann* being the key word that directly conveys the sense of opinion or speculation, and indirectly implies a certain epistemic humility when positing the normative heft of a legal argument.[15] Given this theoretical frame within which *fiqh* doctrines are embedded, it is possible to envision how, despite the existence of these doctrines, a liberating project within the tradition of Islamic law might find a legitimate space to offer critique and espouse a different vision of what should count as *fiqh.*

Once space has been made within the framework of Islamic legal thought, the question remains how to orient such a project. As suggested in my own contribution to this volume, the historical natural law theories in Islam may require certain presumptions or commitments that contemporary thinkers might find unappealing. Some might take issue with the resort to nature, the fusion of fact and value, or a theology of God that espouses particular conceptions of divine justice or grace. Perhaps for these reasons or others, the pre-modern Islamic natural law theories may not find an audience today.

Regardless of the reason for rejecting such pre-modern approaches, there remains a fundamental irony in contemporary recourse to the pre-modern tradition. Reformist thinkers working within Islamic

---

[14] See for example, Ziba Mir-Hosseini. "The Construction of Gender in Islamic Legal Thought and Strategies for Reform." *Hawwa* 1, no. 1 (2003): 1–31.

[15] Anver M. Emon, "To Most Likely Know the Law: Objectivity, Authority and Interpretation in Islamic Law." *Hebraic Political Studies* 4, no. 4 (2009): 415–40.

law often resort to the *maqasid-maslaha* model of reasoning. This model was a pre-modern answer that is used today to respond to the contemporary challenge of clothing a liberating project in the historical language of the Islamic legal tradition. This is in no way to suggest that such projects are illegitimate or inappropriate. The issue of right and wrong, legitimate and illegitimate is less interesting than the irony of how pre-modern answers are made to answer modern questions. I use the term irony only because as suggested in my contribution to this volume, the *maqasid-maslaha* model of reasoning was the Soft Natural Law jurists' attempt to *circumscribe* the scope of natural legal reasoning once they had espoused a theology of grace and a legal philosophy that granted reason ontological authority. The *maqasid-maslaha* model was their way of superimposing an epistemic model that both gave space for reasoned deliberation about the law, and substantially limited it so as to preserve the primacy of source-texts that either had or might otherwise be made to address a given legal controversy. For contemporary reformers to utilize the *maqasid-maslaha* model of reasoning to liberate themselves from the constraining features of *fiqh* is to utilize it for a purpose *against* which it was designed to protect. Here lies the irony.

Does the irony matter? Perhaps not. The historical tradition offers fruits that anyone can pick, if he or she so chooses. There is no police to discipline such usage. In that sense, in the absence of widely accepted institutions of authority, the wide-ranging resort to the *maqasid-maslaha* model, however one aims to use it, reflects a certain democratic spirit in contemporary debates on Islamic law. From a different vantage point, though, the irony does matter. Despite the proliferation of *maqasid* studies and reformist agendas modeled along the line of *maqasid,* there is one thing that links them together—the resort to the same five values articulated by al-Ghazali in the eleventh century: the protection of life (*nafs*), lineage (*nasl*), property (*mal*), mind (*'aql*), and religion (*din*). In some cases, writers will invoke al-Qarafi's reference to dignity (*'ard*) as a substitute for religion or as a sixth value.[16] But all too often, despite the recourse to *maqasid* in a liberatory spirit, the explication of what values count as aims of the law remain tied to and constrained by the historical tradition. So while the *maqasid* values may be broader and more indeterminate

---

[16] Emon, *Islamic Natural Law Theories,* 154–55, 194–99.

than a given *fiqh* rule, the stipulated five (or six) aims in al-Ghazali's *al-Mustasfa* constitute an anchor that keeps the liberatory project clothed with an Islamic attire while limiting how far it can move.

But where do those five values come from? What do they mean? And how do they operate as contemporary guides in a liberatory project toward justice? According to al-Ghazali, these five values are the kinds of values that any legal system would uphold. He then proceeds to illustrate how the Islamic legal tradition upholds these values, namely by reference to Qur'anic injunctions. For example, the Qur'anic injunction against theft protects property. Arguably, his invocation of Qur'anic injunctions does not mean these values are derived from the Qur'an. Rather, his reference to the Qur'an is meant to *corroborate* the five values that al-Ghazali identifies *intuitively*. Corroborating, though, is different from founding or determining or otherwise constituting these values. In other words, the source-texts are not the source of the five values; the values come from somewhere else—they are the values that any society would uphold if it is committed to a social life in which law provides a means of ordering and fulfillment.

But if al-Ghazali posited the five purposes of the law in *al-Mustasfa* intuitively, as if taken for granted, then the question for today's *maqasid* advocate is whether and to what extent al-Ghazali's five purposes prevail as the principle aims of a modern legal system embedded in an international state system that is highly bureaucratized and subject to global pressures of regulation, trade, communication, and so on. If al-Ghazali's five values do not fully capture the scope of values that animate modern legal systems, then what are the purposes of the law that contemporary Islamic legal thinkers should posit? On what basis can they do so, and still claim to be wearing the cloak of an Islamic legal tradition that symbolizes their authority for their respective audiences?

More problematically, though, does positing such purposes of the law, whether old ones or new ones, actually aid in the practice of practical reasoning? For instance, suppose someone posits as new *maqasid* the modern human rights tradition. Such a set of values, though, begs important questions about what that tradition is, how it operates, and to what ends. Indeed, as contemporary scholars of Islamic law, human rights, and the international system have shown, there are serious concerns about how these various traditions, rather than acting in a liberatory fashion, all too often circumscribe certain freedoms and liberties in favor of other interests and values.[17] Suppose a new *maqasid* value is simply *equality*. As much as that might seem straightforward, there is no shortage of debate about what equality means. For instance, does equality refer to formal equality where everyone is treated the same, or substantive equality where we differentiate between peoples who are or are not disadvantaged in term of resource allocation?[18]

The modern recourse to the *maqasid-maslaha* model of reasoning poses notable concerns about whether and to what extent the model promises more than it can deliver given that it was originally designed to limit the scope of reasoned deliberation. It also forces serious questions about what it means to posit broad, abstract ideas as purposes of the law when so much of what legal inquiry concerns are highly contingent and particular issues framed by a broader cultural and linguistic context in which a specific legal issue or conflict arises. For that reason, it is useful to recall Novak's remarks about natural law thinking: "[I]nstead of an attempt to find some universal phenomenon to ground natural law, or posit some ideal from which to deduce natural law, it seems to be more philosophically astute to see natural law as the projection of a universal horizon by a thinker *in* a particular culture *for* one's own culture."[19] Novak is careful to circumscribe the ambit of Jewish natural law thinking so as to forestall any concern that natural law thinking is imperialistic. His remark about the significance of context, though, also serves as a reminder that

---

[17] See for instance, the collection of articles in Anver M. Emon, Mark Ellis, and Benjamin Glahn, eds. *Islamic Law and International Human Rights Law: Searching for Common Ground?* (Oxford: Oxford University Press, 2012). For a critique of the contemporary human rights tradition, see Samuel Moyn, *The Last Utopia: Human Rights in History* (Cambridge: Belknap Press, 2010). On the limits of the international legal system and its perpetuation of the colonial paradigm, see Mark Mazower, *No Enchanted Palace: The End of Empire and the Ideological Origins of the United Nations* (Princeton: Princeton University, 2009); Antony Anghie, *Imperialism, Sovereignty and the Making of International Law* (Cambridge: Cambridge University Press, 2009).

[18] On different approaches to equality in the context of gender, see Anver M. Emon, "The Paradox of Equality and the Politics of Difference: Gender, Equality, Islamic Law and the Modern Muslim State," in *Gender and Equality in Islamic Law: Justice and Ethics in the Islamic Legal Tradition*, eds. Ziba Mir-Hosseini, Kari Vogt, Lena Larson and Christian Moe (London: IB Tauris, 2013), 237–58; Ratna Kapur, "Un-Veiling Equality: Disciplining the 'Other' Woman Through Human Rights Discourse," in *Islamic Law and Human Rights: Searching for Common Ground?*, eds. Anver M. Emon, Mark Ellis and Benjamin Glahn (Oxford: Oxford University Press, 2012).

[19] Novak, section 7.

despite a desire to identify shared, universal values that bring humanity together, the fact remains that legal inquiry remains a sufficiently context-specific endeavor. Recourse to broad, abstract claims about aims or purposes of the law tend to over-determine or over-simplify what ought to remain a context-specific mode of inquiry.

CONCLUSION

There are many other issues that could be addressed in a response to Novak's fine essay. Space prevents me from going further. Nonetheless, the three issues addressed above showcase important points of engagement that can arise by reading and working collaboratively on a project such as this. Each tradition posits questions and ideas, some of which resonate across traditions and others that do not. Dialogue across difference is not meant to undercut or delegitimate the more common and popular pursuit of shared values. But to recognize difference, work through that difference, and appreciate how we are each provoked by that difference increases not only an appreciation for the tradition we each consider "ours," but also enhances our appreciation for the "other" tradition that, through the juxtaposition, helps us see "our" tradition more clearly.

Response to David Novak's "Natural Law and Judaism"

Matthew Levering

The work of David Novak travels down a number of roads worth taking for both Jewish and non-Jewish scholars alike. The eleven propositions sketched in his essay are like maps to these roads, calling the interested observer to deeper engagement with the ways in which Novak fills out these propositions in his books and articles. Since I have elsewhere discussed Novak's earlier works in greater detail, I will limit my response here to certain themes as they are set forth in his eleven propositions.[1] The basic goal of my remarks will be to inquire into the role of God in Novak's natural law doctrine, and to suggest similarities and differences with the way in which, as a Christian student of natural law, I envision the role of God in natural law.

I will begin with Novak's fourth proposition, "Natural law is not Jewish law for gentiles." He also has in mind the converse: natural law is not Christian theology for non-Christians. In addition to its evident "imperialist" problems, such a view would negate the crucial claim that natural law is universal or naturally accessible to rational persons. Novak therefore cautions that "even if the acceptance of natural law is taken to be the necessary precondition for the acceptance of revelation...nonetheless that should not lead one to conversely conclude that

---

[1] See my *Biblical Natural Law: A Theocentric and Teleological Approach* (Oxford: Oxford University Press, 2008), chapter 1; and my *Jewish-Christian Dialogue and the Life of Wisdom: Engagements with the Theology of David Novak* (London: Continuum, 2010).

the acceptance of revelation is the necessary prerequisite for cogent natural law thinking and doing." Were one to suppose that "cogent natural law thinking" required the acceptance of revelation, then one would render natural law essentially useless. Novak puts the problem this way: "Is natural law only universal in its scope, i.e., is it only meant to govern all humans universally, where this universal scope depends upon the authority of a particular human community, its founding revelation, and its ongoing tradition that teaches this law for all humans?"

I fully agree with Novak's cautionary note. To imagine that only Christians (let alone only Catholics listening to the Church's Magisterium) possess natural law would be a terrible mistake. Indeed, Christian thinkers have long seen natural law doctrine in non-Christian sources. But it is worthwhile to probe a bit further into the topic. Christians believe that sin has obscured the human perception of natural law, if not so much in its first principles then in the specific determinations of these principles. Arguably Protestants, more than Catholics, have insisted upon the darkening of human practical reason by sin, but both Catholics and Protestants have affirmed sin's deleterious effects on practical reasoning.[2] Thus Thomas Aquinas held that God revealed to Moses and the people of Israel certain precepts of natural law—such as "Do not steal"—because humans needed the light of revelation to assist their weakened ability to perceive and apply natural law principles by human reason.[3] Aquinas is clear that in its general principles, natural law cannot "be blotted out from men's hearts," even if in particular actions, humans often falter in applying natural law principles.[4] In its "secondary precepts," however, "natural law can be blotted out from the human heart."[5] The effect of sin upon human perception of the secondary precepts of natural law means that there is reason to suppose that revelation will assist human beings in identifying the precepts of natural law.

Yet by insisting on the integrity of philosophical reasoning, and by repeatedly affirming the wisdom of non-Christian and pre-Christian traditions of moral reflection, Christian thinkers have made clear

---

[2] See David VanDrunen, *Natural Law and the Two Kingdoms: A Study in the Development of Reformed Social Thought* (Grand Rapids, MI: Eerdmans, 2009).

[3] See Thomas Aquinas, *Summa theologiae*, I-II, q. 94, a. 6; I-II, q. 99, a. 2, especially ad 2; II-II, q. 2, a. 4.

[4] Aquinas, *Summa theologiae*, I-II, q. 94, a. 6.

[5] *Summa theologiae*, I-II, q. 94, a. 6.

that despite the effects of sin, Christian revelation is not required for the formulation of natural law doctrine. Christian thinkers have also made a crucial distinction between natural law doctrine, on the one hand, and natural law as a reality that exists in all persons, on the other. In particular cultures, including some Western cultures today, it has become difficult to articulate and defend natural law doctrine in a publicly persuasive manner. But this certainly has not eliminated natural law as a reality in the individuals who make up those cultures.

In recent years, some Catholic theologians have challenged the Church's competence to teach about natural law (for instance, with respect to the moral status of abortion).[6] In teaching about the necessary elements of discipleship to Jesus Christ, the Catholic Church affirms that it can teach not only about what God has revealed but also about moral truths accessible without divine revelation. Otherwise, the Magisterium or teaching office of the Church could not instruct believers on the content of discipleship, which includes obedience to natural law precepts that, given the fallen condition of humankind, may not be as evident to believers as these precepts should be. When the Church teaches precepts of natural law, it is teaching Catholics specifically, but there is no reason for a Catholic to suppose that its teaching does not also serve to instruct all humans. But neither is there a reason for a non-Catholic to suppose that the Church has authority to teach non-Catholics. It should be added that the Church does not claim to have articulated the best possible comprehensive natural law doctrine, let alone to have made the natural law reasoning of non-Catholic philosophers superfluous or second-rate.

Novak's comments on the relationship of natural law to God the Creator are particularly attractive and interesting. In proposition three, for instance, Novak says on the one hand that "Even though the God–human relationship is endemic to human nature, nonetheless, it is not the immediate concern of natural law." I can see what he means: most natural law precepts have to do with human-to-human relationships. But I think that human-to-God relationships are also at the core of natural law, since in justice we owe a debt of gratitude to the Creator, which we

---

[6] For a helpful introduction to this discussion, see Avery Dulles, SJ, *Magisterium: Teacher and Guardian of the Faith* (Naples, FL: Sapientia Press, 2007), 78–81; Lawrence J. Welch, "Christ, the Moral Law, and the Teaching Authority of the Magisterium," *Irish Theological Quarterly* 64 (1999): 16–28; Welch, "Faith and Reason: The Unity of the Moral Law in Christ," *Irish Theological Quarterly* 66 (2001): 249–58.

acknowledge in acts of religion. The obligation to worship God belongs to natural law, rather than being discovered first through the light of revelation. This obligation to worship God is further specified by revelation. Novak remarks that "what God requires of humans for Godself is almost always made known only through the extraordinary experience of revelation." Yes, but the truth that God requires worship, of some kind, is not something that humans know only through revelation. This is so even if outside of revelation "God" is often known only intuitively and improperly, due to worship of lesser things (idols).[7]

In the same proposition (three), Novak strongly connects natural law with God. He observes, "Natural law is 'law' because it is what God the Creator has *commanded* his human creatures *to actively and authentically be*. Only the Creator God could command his creation with such absolute authority." Novak goes on to say that natural law, while in this sense a "divine law," is discovered by human practical reason rather than revealed by God as divine commandments. One does not have to recognize the divine command in order to recognize that it is God's commandment, "coequal with God's unique creation of humans." Natural law, Novak states, consists in "the authentic requirements of our created nature." In proposition six, too, Novak emphasizes that "Natural law requires a cosmic lawgiver." Distinguishing natural law from revealed (covenantal) law, he argues that adequately recognizing and living out the universal precepts of natural law depends "on the recognition of the Sovereign of the universe who creates the subjects of that law and inspires them to learn that law when they are convinced of God's wisdom and beneficence." In order to affirm a universally applicable moral law, he suggests, one needs to be able to appeal to the creative work of a universal lawgiver, the "God who is the Creator."

This does not mean that one thereby occupies a position of universal rather than tradition-based moral reasoning.[8] On the contrary,

---

[7] Here I would need to say more about divine revelation and natural theology, as well as about conceptions of gods and "God" in various cultures. See for example David Bentley Hart, *The Experience of God: Being, Consciousness, Bliss* (New Haven, CT: Yale University Press, 2013); Jean Daniélou, SJ, *God and the Ways of Knowing*, trans. Walter Roberts (San Francisco: Ignatius Press, 2003); Luke Timothy Johnson, *Among the Gentiles: Greco-Roman Religion and Christianity* (New Haven, CT: Yale University Press, 2009).

[8] See also Alasdair MacIntyre, *Three Rival Versions of Moral Enquiry: Encyclopaedia, Genealogy, and Tradition* (Notre Dame: University of Notre Dame Press, 1991).

Novak holds that it is "more philosophically astute to see natural law as the projection of a universal horizon by a thinker *in* a particular culture *for* one's own culture." Novak also makes clear that the connection of natural law with the recognition of a Creator-lawgiver should not require us to reject the insights of those who do not accept the existence of a Creator-lawgiver. He warns against "deriv[ing] the natural rights codified by natural law [such as 'do not harm me'] from the existence of a cosmic community and of a cosmic Sovereign/ Lawgiver." He observes that believers should grant that "there are other [non-theistic] reasons for respecting somebody else's human rights. These reasons should not be dismissed by those who believe [as Novak does] that human nature as the image of God is the best reason for respecting the human rights of the bearers of that divine image."

When Novak says that "Natural law is 'law' because it is what God the Creator has *commanded* his human creatures *to actively and authentically be*," I find myself strongly agreeing, even though I would perhaps use slightly different language. So as to combine God's will with his wisdom, and to root natural law ultimately in God's wise plan for the flourishing of his human creatures, I would say that natural law is our participation, as rational animals, in God's eternal law— which is his wise plan for the ordering of all things to himself. We share in this law in a manner that non-rational beings cannot. We are able to know the good and to move ourselves toward it. Novak prefers an emphasis on God's creative command, so as to underscore the fact that creation already involves us in a relationship of obedience to our intelligent and beneficent Creator. Without denying such a relationship, I think that rooting natural law in the divine wisdom—God's wise plan for our flourishing—is perhaps better, so as to avoid any sense of arbitrariness. God's eternal law is his wisdom with regard to creatures; it is his plan from eternity for the ordering of all created things. Since God is not composed of parts (which imply creaturely finitude), God's wisdom or knowledge as regards creatures is none other than God knowing himself and thereby knowing everything to which his power can extend. The freedom of God in respect to creatures is assured by the fact that God does not have to create what he knows. When the eternal God creates, he does so wisely, with the fruition of creation already in view.

Novak's account of God commanding humans regarding how they should "actively and authentically be" corresponds with the authentic life of human flourishing that God, in his wisdom, has in view for us. Even so, Novak has long objected to the language of "eternal law" because, he argues, it claims to know "what God is" rather than simply "that God is." But natural law, as a mode of knowing, participates in God's eternal law not by our knowing *what* God is, but rather as our limited knowledge of God's wise plan for human flourishing (for example, as our knowledge that we should not steal or murder, if we wish to flourish individually and communally). Novak comments in footnote 15: "I do not think natural law stems from God's eternal nature or essence as Thomas Aquinas thought about *lex aeternae* being the ontological foundation of *lex naturalis*.... For, if we cannot know *what* God is but only *that* God is..., how then could what we do not know ground what we do know, viz., natural law?" This seems, however, to misunderstand what Aquinas (and before him Augustine and others) means by thinking of natural law as a participation in eternal law, since Aquinas is claiming only that natural law is a limited, rational sharing in God's wisdom for human flourishing.[9]

In the same footnote, Novak goes on to say that "natural law, which is to govern inter-human relations, is grounded in *what God does*, i.e., what God commands..., which we can know; it is not grounded in *what God is per se*, which is beyond anything we could ever experience in this world and hence beyond anything we could ever know here." If I were to put this in my own words (and thus in a way that Novak might not agree with), I would say that natural law is grounded "in what God does" because it is grounded in God's creative knowledge and will with respect to his human creatures, God's wise plan for the ordering of humans to himself. In this manner, natural law is a rational participation in God's eternal law, but natural law is certainly not a knowledge of "what God is per se," nor is natural law grounded in God's will. Novak's remark that natural law describes "the authentic requirements of our created nature" accords nicely with what I mean by saying that natural law is our rational participation in God's eternal law. These "authentic requirements" are, I take it, the ways of living that foster human flourishing, so that our actions accord with what the Creator intended us to be. When I speak of natural law as teleological, this is what I mean. Teleology, of course, has a very different

---

[9] For discussion see John Rziha, *Perfecting Human Actions: St. Thomas Aquinas on Human Participation in Eternal Law* (Washington, D.C.: Catholic University of America Press, 2009).

meaning in Maimonides, where it conflicts with God's covenantal freedom, and so I can understand why Novak avoids the term.

Novak's view that "Natural law requires a cosmic lawgiver" makes great sense to me. Logically speaking, how could we claim that there is a stable "human nature," open to determinate modes of perfection rather than fluid in an evolutionary or self-determined way, if we denied the existence of a Creator? Even more, how could there be a "natural law" if there were no Creator-lawgiver? Without a lawgiver, the existence of a natural law is much less plausible. One might answer that humans can discover and promulgate a universally applicable law simply by reflecting upon our own moral life, without any appeal to a divine lawgiver.[10] The most brilliant attempt to make this claim, in my view (and I think that Novak would agree), was that of Immanuel Kant with his notion of the categorical imperative. But, as I have argued elsewhere, Kant lacks a way to respond adequately to those who suggest that freedom itself should be its own law.[11] So I am persuaded that natural law requires a Creator God, or at least a divine Reason that governs the universe without being absorbed by it.

Does this mean that natural law doctrine cannot be formulated by those who altogether deny the existence of God, or that practical reasoners outside a theistic orbit cannot know natural law? To the first question, I think that non-theist accounts of natural law have generated valuable insights, but I do not think that they can ultimately be persuasive because the lack of a divine Creator-lawgiver severely undermines the claim that humans possess a determinate "nature" that is governed by a moral "law" to which all humans have access. To the second question, I think that a commitment to natural law doctrine requires one to suppose that everyone, including non-theists, has rational possession of the first principles of natural law. All people who possess the use of reason possess natural law, because God has

---

[10] Leszek Kołakowski accepts that "natural law is present in the world, but it does not logically presuppose a legislating personal God. It does, however, imply a certain metaphysical faith: the faith (which goes back to the Stoics) that there is a Reason which rules the universe, a Reason whose nature we can recognize and which enables us to distinguish truth from falsity as well as good from evil" (Kołakowski, "On Natural Law," in his *Is God Happy? Selected Essays* [New York: Basic Books, 2013], 241–50, at 247). I think it difficult to defend a "Reason which rules the universe" without ultimately invoking a Creator God.

[11] See my *Biblical Natural Law: A Theocentric and Teleological Approach* (Oxford: Oxford University Press, 2008), chapter two.

given us the rational ability to know something of what pertains to our flourishing.

As I noted above, Novak denies that there is an "ordinary experience" of "the existence of a cosmic community and of a cosmic Sovereign/Lawgiver." If Novak means a strong "ordinary experience" of "a cosmic Sovereign/Lawgiver," he may be right, although I think that people do ordinarily know, in a murky and intuitive sense at least, that there is a God. But even supposing that God were generally unknown—that is to say, that our knowledge of God strictly requires tradition-based revelation—we would do well to inquire further into this situation. Why is it that humans so often do not recognize either God or the "cosmic community" of beings? Why is it that human nature is (as Novak says) not "something directly experienced and thus easily translatable into actual norms for human praxis"? Surely it is not inbuilt into creation that we should lack awareness of our Creator, or of what pertains to the flourishing of our nature, or of our unity as human beings.

To take the first instance, God did not create us too dumb to know that he exists. Were God to have done so, then our idolatry would be his fault, not ours. Genesis depicts the first humans as possessed of some knowledge of God, some real communion with him. This communion falters when the first humans rebel against God, by seeking to be God for themselves. Likewise, the first humans—as in the story of Cain and Abel—possessed some knowledge of good and evil (natural law). According to Genesis, however, human sinfulness means that God was quickly forgotten by humans as the generations passed, to the point where "the earth was corrupt in God's sight, and the earth was filled with violence. And God saw the earth, and behold, it was corrupt; for all flesh had corrupted their way upon the earth" (Gen 6:11–12). The story of salvation is intertwined with this story of human corruption. Novak, then, might consider adding a proposition that describes how our knowledge of natural law in its secondary precepts is affected by our moral corruption or sinfulness, and how the light of divine revelation assists us in being awakened to what, if our minds were not weakened, we would be able to know easily by the exercise of practical reason.

I should make clear that I do not mean to suggest that Novak's vision of natural law doctrine lacks a sense of human sinfulness. On the contrary, he is very well aware of it, and this recognition of the terrible things that we humans do to each other—including the unspeakable things that have been done by Christians to the Jewish people—clearly provides an important motivation for Novak's theoretical reflections on natural law. He wishes to contribute, as he says at the end of his essay, to influencing for the good "how Jews look upon their morally significant relations with the non-Jewish world, and how Jews are to continually interpret and reinterpret morally significant relations among ourselves by the very same criteria." The seven Noahide commandments, which in Novak's view express natural law, indicate his sense of the requirements of natural law and the ways in which it is (sinfully) violated: "(1) the positive injunction to set up courts of law to apply justice; (2) the prohibition of blasphemy; (3) the prohibition of idolatry; (4) the prohibition of sexual license (specifically, incest, homosexuality, adultery, and bestiality); (5) the prohibition of homicide (including the prohibition of abortion); (6) the prohibition of robbery; (7) the prohibition of eating a limb torn from a living animal." In his essay, Novak speaks in passing about such problems as uncontrolled libido, abuse of the earthly environment, dysfunctional families, and modern totalitarianisms. But, even so, I think that more direct attention to sin and its effects—including its effects on natural law's practical reasoning—would be of value.

One of the striking elements of Novak's career has been his willingness to engage the work of Christian scholars, and to learn from their insights, while speaking as a Jewish theologian who seeks to build up the covenantal community of the people of Israel. There are many insights about natural law that I have learned from Novak, perhaps especially his insistence that developing a doctrine of universal natural law does not require that we reason from outside the covenantal community. While rightly insisting that natural law doctrine does not depend on revelation, Novak also allows divine revelation, and the Jewish philosophical and theological tradition, to inform his approach to natural law doctrine. In creatively condensing his thought into eleven propositions, Novak displays once again the fruitful intertwining of philosophy, theology, and Scripture that animates his natural law theory. The best Christian approaches through the centuries have followed the same model.

2

Christians and Natural Law

Matthew Levering

Among the sources of Christian reflection on natural law, this essay highlights two in particular: the Apostle Paul's striking remark in his letter to the Romans, "When Gentiles who have not the law do by nature what the law requires, they are a law to themselves, even though they do not have the law. They show that what the law requires is written on their hearts" (Rom 2:14–15); and the commentaries on this passage authored by five influential patristic theologians, namely Origen and John Chrysostom in the East, and Ambrosiaster, Pelagius, and Augustine in the West.[1] These commentaries on Romans 2 are particularly helpful for considering how Christians, from Paul onward, have accounted for universal natural law within the context of a highly particular theology of sin and salvation.[2] By comparison with the extensive development of

[1] Pelagius of course does not count as a "Father" of the Church, since his views on free will and grace were condemned as heretical.

[2] For the later development of Christian natural law doctrine, see my *Biblical Natural Law* (Oxford: Oxford University Press, 2008), which examines Thomas Aquinas's exposition of natural law in the *Summa theologiae* and which also treats the fate of natural law doctrine in mainstream modern philosophy, from René Descartes to Friedrich Nietzsche. In agreement with the theologians of the patristic and medieval periods, I argue that the Bible, while not a foundation for natural law, is supportive of natural law doctrine, largely due to the doctrine of creation. For a different perspective, arguing that Christian natural law doctrine adopts Stoic natural law doctrine, see Ernst Troeltsch, "Christian Natural Law," in Troeltsch, *Religion in History*, trans. James Luther Adams and Walter F. Bense (Minneapolis, MN: Fortress Press, 1991), 159–67. I agree with Troeltsch that "Christian natural law differs very much from modern secular natural law, which has been developed since the times of Hobbes, Locke, Grotius, Pufendorf, Thomasius, Wolf, Rousseau, and Kant...While this secular natural law is genetically related to the natural law of antiquity and of Christianity, it has its own distinct foundations in modern philosophical and social

natural law doctrine by Christians since the medieval period, the Fathers of the Church do not regularly treat the doctrine of natural law. In this sense, Robert Louis Wilken remarks that natural law doctrine "plays but a small role in the church fathers."[3] But in fact, as we will see, the Fathers delve deeply and instructively into natural law doctrine, as Romans 2 makes inevitable.

In the Christian East, Origen holds a central place because his commentary on Romans shaped all further Romans commentaries by the Greek Fathers.[4] Origen argues that the precepts of natural law follow from the Golden Rule: do unto others as you would they do unto you (see Luke 6:31). He holds that non-Christians (and non-Jews) are able to obey natural law and do good works that enable them to be among the saved. Natural law, Origen adds, is not yet the righteousness of God that we see manifested in the humility of Jesus. Indeed, for Origen, the process of trying to follow natural law leads humans to recognize that we all need a merciful Redeemer. Chrysostom builds upon Origen's commentary and adds to it a greater appreciation for

developments and has followed its own course towards liberalism, democracy, and free competition quite independently of the Christian idea" (Troeltsch, 167). See also Troeltsch's "Stoic-Christian Natural Law and Modern Secular Natural Law," in the same volume, 321–42. For the view that Thomas Aquinas's efforts to combine various sources of natural law doctrine failed, see Anna Taitslin, "The Competing Sources of Aquinas' Natural Law: Aristotle, Roman Law and the Early Christian Fathers," in *The Threads of Natural Law: Unravelling a Philosophical Tradition*, ed. F. J. Contreras (New York: Springer, 2013), 47–63. See also my "Knowing What Is 'Natural': Thomas Aquinas and Luke Timothy Johnson on Romans 1–2," *Logos* 12 (2009): 117–42.

[3] Robert Louis Wilken, *The Spirit of Early Christian Thought: Seeking the Face of God* (New Haven, CT: Yale University Press, 2003), 320. At the same time, however, Wilken realizes that "[t]here are passages in the Scriptures in which natural law is assumed, Romans 2, for example," and along these lines Wilken has briefly compared Origen's interpretation of Romans 2 with Augustine's and Aquinas's: see Wilken's "Origen, Augustine, and Thomas: Interpreters of the Letter to the Romans," in *Reading Romans with St. Thomas Aquinas*, ed. Matthew Levering and Michael Dauphinais (Washington, D.C.: Catholic University of America Press, 2012), 288–301, at 295–300.

[4] Origen is the originator of the genre of Christian biblical commentary. Alfons Fürst remarks, "It would obviously be wrong to dub Origen the first Christian exegete. He is not the inventor of Christian exegesis in general. He is rather the inventor of a specific kind of exegesis, namely of a running explanation of the Bible in the form of what came to be called a 'commentary'" (Fürst, "Origen: Exegesis and Philosophy in Early Christian Alexandria," in *Interpreting the Bible and Aristotle in Late Antiquity: The Alexandrian Commentary Tradition between Rome and Baghdad*, ed. Josef Lössl and John W. Watt [Burlington, VT: Ashgate, 2011], 13–32, at 14). Fürst considers that "[i]n methodological approach and exegetical techniques, the ancient Christian commentaries on the Bible correspond to the philosophical commentaries on the writings of Plato and Aristotle" (Fürst, 16).

Paul's theology of sin and grace, as well as for Paul's own context of preaching to communities made up of Jews and Gentiles (a context that is also appreciated by Origen).[5] Chrysostom grants that before Christ's coming there were good Gentiles, and that Gentiles can obey natural law successfully. He argues that Paul seeks to awaken us to the coming divine judgment and to our need for a merciful Redeemer on the day of judgment.

Among Latin theologians, I treat two fourth-century Roman theologians, Ambrosiaster and Pelagius, as well as the greatest Latin theologian, Augustine. Ambrosiaster affirms the existence of natural law in all persons, but he does not really think that natural law doctrine need play any role in Christian thinking about justice, righteousness, and salvation. Pelagius, by contrast, thinks that natural law alone, at least in theory, can suffice for justice, righteousness, and salvation. While accepting natural law, Augustine argues that to fulfill it after original sin requires grace. The issue then becomes how we conceive of grace and whether the drama of sin and grace negates the importance of natural law.

In what follows, my study of these patristic doctrines of natural law is largely expository, but it leads to a set of constructive conclusions. Namely, after sifting and evaluating the Fathers' contributions, I propose seven theses about natural law doctrine. Readers knowledgeable in contemporary Christian theological and philosophical debates about natural law will recognize that my seven theses aim to contribute to these debates.[6] Although the full elaboration of my theses must await the completion of my patristic exposition, let me set them forth succinctly here: (1) Natural law does not obviate the need for the grace of the Holy Spirit and the work of Jesus Christ; (2) In following their conscience and striving to act justly to God and neighbor,

---

[5] See Brian L. Dunkle, SJ, "A Development in Origen's View of the Natural Law," *Pro Ecclesia* 13 (2004): 337–51, at 343.

[6] I have in view primarily Catholic and Protestant discussions, but Orthodox moral theologians have also addressed natural law, as one would expect given the ample patristic witness to natural law. See for example Vigen Guroian, *Incarnate Love: Essays in Orthodox Ethics* (Notre Dame, IN: University of Notre Dame Press, 1987), 21. Guroian cites Basil the Great in favor of the reality of natural law, envisioned not in terms of autonomy but in terms of love. See also the work of Aristotle Papanikolaou, who seems to connect "natural law" with the "nature–grace split" but who nonetheless affirms much of what natural law doctrine affirms: Papanikolaou, *The Mystical as Political: Democracy and Non-Radical Orthodoxy* (Notre Dame: University of Notre Dame Press, 2012), 134 and elsewhere.

humans may be moved by grace that unites them to the salvation won by Christ even though they may not know Christ explicitly; (3) Like all humans, Christians possess natural law and are required to live by its precepts; (4) Natural law doctrine helps to affirm God's universal providence and God's saving power toward all humans; (5) Natural law is our participation in God's eternal law, and it is constituted and promulgated by the Creator God, who imprints it in our mind; (6) Human positive law is properly grounded upon natural law; and (7) Human sinfulness obscures, but does not eliminate, our ability to perceive the precepts of natural law.

2.1 THEOLOGICAL AND PHILOSOPHICAL CONCERNS ABOUT NATURAL LAW DOCTRINE

My seven theses aim to address contemporary theological concerns about the relationship of natural law doctrine to Christian discipleship, on the one hand, and contemporary philosophical concerns about how to articulate natural law doctrine, on the other. During the past century, Christian moral theologians have been especially concerned that natural law doctrine puts in place a universal ethics that relativizes discipleship to Jesus Christ. If natural law doctrine provides a fruitful framework for an ethics that transcends one's own particular religious tradition, then it might seem that we should do without our particular religious traditions, which often divide us and may even foster conflict.[7] Some Christian theologians have also feared that natural law doctrine promotes a notion of human self-sufficiency and that taking natural law seriously as a source of moral reasoning ignores the baleful consequences of original sin upon our moral reasoning.

From a Protestant perspective critical of natural law doctrine, for example, Karl Barth comments, "What is pleasing to God comes into being when all human righteousness is gone, irretrievably gone, when men are uncertain and lost, when they have abandoned all ethical and religious illusions, and when they have renounced every hope in this

---

[7] Along these lines, see Jan Assmann, *The Price of Monotheism*, trans. Robert Savage (Stanford, CA: Stanford University Press, 2010).

world and in this heaven."[8] In Barth's view, when some Gentiles "show that what the law requires is written on their hearts" (Rom 2:15), they show precisely that they no longer cling to any human resource, including "natural law."[9] Stanley Hauerwas similarly warns against the tendency to separate propositions (including natural law precepts) from the broader story on which their true meaning depends, a tendency that in the Enlightenment led to the separation of some "reasonable" doctrines from the seemingly less reasonable story of the salvation won for us by Christ Jesus. Hauerwas considers the problem with natural law doctrine to be that it claims to give us a ground on which to stand before God that is other than the particular story of God, as if our moral actions could be rightly evaluated outside this particular story.[10] From a related angle, quoting Romans 2:14–16, Paul Ramsey complains that "[t]his passage has been made to bear the weight of an elaborate theory of 'natural law.' "[11] Ramsey argues that it matters little whether or not Paul believed in a natural law, since both natural law and the Torah have now been definitively superseded by Christ, who gives us the new covenant that fulfills Jeremiah's prophecy, "I will put

---

[8] Karl Barth, *The Epistle to the Romans*, trans. from the sixth edition by Edwyn C. Hoskyns (Oxford: Oxford University Press, 1933), 68.

[9] For a broadly similar interpretation from a contemporary biblical scholar, see Douglas A. Campbell, *The Deliverance of God: An Apocalyptic Rereading of Justification in Paul* (Grand Rapids, MI: Eerdmans, 2009), 203–05, 550–59; eccentrically, Campbell holds that the views expressed in Romans 2:5–16 are not Paul's.

[10] See Stanley Hauerwas, *The Peaceable Kingdom: A Primer in Christian Ethics* (Notre Dame: University of Notre Dame Press, 1983). Hauerwas also observes that "[e]mphasis on the distinctiveness of Christian ethics does not deny that there are points of contact between Christian ethics and other forms of the moral life. While such points frequently exist, they are not sufficient to provide a basis for a 'universal' ethic grounded in human nature per se" (Hauerwas, 60–61). In addition, he remarks that attempts to deny the story-based, particular character of every morality lead to the temptation to coerce those who do not act in accordance with what they allegedly ought to know by nature. The recent document by the International Theological Commission, "The Search for Universal Ethics: A New Look at Natural Law" (2008), attempts to address such concerns: for discussion see especially J. Budziszewski, "Diplomacy and Theology in the Dialogue on Universal Ethics," *Nova et Vetera* 9 (2011): 707–35; Russell Hittinger, "The Situation of Natural Law in Catholic Theology," *Nova et Vetera* 9 (2011): 657–70. See also Jean Porter, "Does the Natural Law Provide a Universally Valid Morality?" in *Intractable Disputes about the Natural Law: Alasdair MacIntyre and Critics*, ed. Lawrence S. Cunningham (Notre Dame: University of Notre Dame Press, 2009), 53–95.

[11] Paul Ramsey, *Basic Christian Ethics* (Louisville, KY: Westminster/John Knox Press, 1993), 84. This edition of Ramsey's 1950 book contains a Foreword by Stanley Hauerwas and D. Stephen Long.

my law within them, and will write it on their hearts" (Jer 31:33). As
Ramsey puts it, "Whether or not there is actually a natural morality
inscribed in every human heart, this much is certain: this law also
Christian ethics transcends....Regardless of what God did through
Moses in the past, what he has now done in Jesus Christ, and what he
is doing, ought now to become the one and only center of man's existence before God."[12] On this view, even if the Torah and the natural
law were divinely mandated for Jews and Gentiles (respectively), as
soon as Christ comes into the world, "Man's ethical and religious ori-
entation focuses on the Christ, necessarily turning away from the old
Law, away also from the sovereign dictates of natural conscience."[13]
For Ramsey, Christ radically transforms all previous moral codes, so
that "Christian ethics is an ethics of perfection which cuts man to fit
the pattern, not the pattern to fit man."[14]

---

[12] Ramsey, 84. See also Ramsey's response, in his *War and the Christian
Conscience: How Shall Modern War Be Conducted Justly?* (Durham, NC: Duke
University Press, 1961), to the possibility that "the foundation of just-war theory and
practice was a new kind of exercise that was laid in the principles of natural justice
or natural law, and that on this a Christian's participation in political and military
action depended, *alongside* the foundation that was laid by Jesus Christ in the private
lives of men" (Ramsey, *War and the Christian Conscience*, xviii). Against this way of
construing just-war doctrine, Ramsey insists that "the norm of Christian love, and
not natural justice only, was still the main source both of what the Christian could
and should do and of what he could and should never do in military action" (Ramsey,
xviii). Ramsey goes on to argue that Aquinas's appropriation of Augustine's just-war
doctrine included, mistakenly, "an increasing emphasis upon the natural-law concept
of justice in analysis of the cause that justifies participation in war" (Ramsey, 32). See
also, however, Ramsey's extensive and more appreciative engagement with natural law
doctrine in chapters 5, 8, and 9 (on Reinhold Niebuhr, Jacques Maritain, and Edmond
Cahn) of his *Nine Modern Moralists* (Englewood Cliffs, NJ: Prentice-Hall, 1962).

[13] Ramsey, *Basic Christian Ethics*, 85.

[14] Ramsey, 85. Ramsey goes on to argue that Augustine's *On the Spirit and the Letter*,
which I discuss below, accords with Ramsey's viewpoint. As Ramsey states, "Indeed,
by what is Christian ethics to be distinguished from generally valid natural morality, if
some theory of natural law becomes an authentic part and to any degree the *primary*
foundation of Christian morality?...What God has now ordained shifts morality from
foundation in either of these ancient standards for righteousness" (Ramsey, 86–87). In
a manner that recalls Martin Luther's formulations, Ramsey remarks, "Whatever validity Paul assigns the law in his letter to the Romans, it never includes positive instruction
in any aspect of Christian morality. Jesus Christ is the one and only teacher.... While
love frees from the law it binds a man even closer to the needs of others, even as Jesus
Christ was bound; and precisely that which alone frees also binds. The possession of
law—any law, as defined above—'puffs up' the man prepossessed with it.... Love builds
up others, and so doing it also builds up its own unlegislated self-discipline in personal
living" (Ramsey, 87). These formulations strike me as too stark in their oppositions,
especially in their misguided effort to oppose law and love.

By contrast, contemporary Protestant scholars such as Daryl Charles, Craig Boyd, Nigel Biggar, and Carl Braaten have offered positive accounts of natural law broadly similar to the one offered in the present essay.[15] In addition, David VanDrunen has argued that "Calvin's understanding of natural law indeed stood in considerable continuity to the medieval natural law traditions, including the Thomistic," and both VanDrunen and Stephen Grabill have shown that Barth's position on natural law diverges from that of the Reformed tradition within which Barth stands.[16]

Since natural law doctrine is formulated using philosophical resources, my essay also has in view perennial philosophical concerns regarding natural law doctrine, such as how to articulate the basic principles and precepts of natural law, how natural law is a "law," whether natural law is teleological in the sense of being rooted in human natural inclinations that pertain to human flourishing, and whether natural law requires a divine lawgiver. One influential school of Catholic natural law reflection holds that natural law doctrine can and should be fully articulated without any reference to the

---

[15] See J. Daryl Charles, *Retrieving the Natural Law: A Return to Moral First Things* (Grand Rapids, MI: Eerdmans, 2008); Craig A. Boyd, *A Shared Morality: A Narrative Defense of Natural Law Ethics* (Grand Rapids, MI: Brazos Press, 2007); Nigel Biggar, *Behaving in Public: How to Do Christian Ethics* (Grand Rapids, MI: Eerdmans, 2011); Carl E. Braaten, "A Lutheran Affirmation of the Natural Law," in *Natural Law: A Lutheran Reappraisal* (St. Louis, MO: Concordia Publishing House, 2011), 3–16. As Biggar concludes, "To affirm natural law, then, should be to affirm the following: that there is a form of flourishing that is given in and with the nature of human being; that reflection on human nature can achieve an understanding of that flourishing and its component basic goods; that reflection on human experience can produce a grasp of kinds of disposition and action that respect and promote those goods; that all human beings are, despite their sinfulness, *somewhat* capable of an accurate grasp of basic goods and their practical requirements; and that, therefore, there are sometimes areas of ethical agreement between Christians and others. None of this, however, makes the Christian theological salvation-narrative ethically irrelevant. It does not say that sinful humans have the motivation to do sufficiently what they know to be right, apart from the penitence, faith, gratitude, and hope that the story of God's salvific initiative inspires. Nor does it say that they have the power, unaided by biblical tradition, to know completely what is good, what is virtuous, or what is right" (Biggar, *Behaving in Public*, 41–42).

[16] David VanDrunen, *Natural Law and the Two Kingdoms: A Study in the Development of Reformed Social Thought* (Grand Rapids, MI: Eerdmans, 2010), 95; Stephen J. Grabill, *Rediscovering the Natural Law in Reformed Theological Ethics* (Grand Rapids, MI: Eerdmans, 2006). See also VanDrunen's constructive study, *A Biblical Case for Natural Law* (Grand Rapids, MI: Acton Institute, 2006).

Creator God or to theological or scriptural insights.[17] According to this perspective, represented by Germain Grisez, John Finnis, and Robert George, natural law involves the recognition by practical reason of certain basic human goods or values, in no hierarchical order.[18] Another Catholic school of thought on natural law, represented by Russell Hittinger, Stephen Brock, and Steven Long, argues to the contrary that God imprints the natural law upon us, so that we discern in and through our natural inclinations the ordering that God has given us. On this view, with which I agree, a full-scale natural law doctrine requires reference to God and to a hierarchical order of human goods or ends.[19]

What about the effects of original sin upon the knowability of natural law precepts? Russell Hittinger has made this question a central aspect of his lifelong study of natural law.[20] Various other

[17] See Joseph Boyle, "Natural Law and the Ethics of Tradition," in *Natural Law Theory: Contemporary Essays*, ed. Robert P. George (Oxford: Clarendon, 1992), 3–30; for an opposing view see Jean Porter, *Natural and Divine Law: Reclaiming the Tradition for Christian Ethics* (Grand Rapids, MI: Eerdmans, 1999), chapter 3.

[18] See, e.g., Germain Grisez, "The First Principle of Practical Reason: A Commentary on the *Summa theologiae*, 1–2, Question 94, Article 2," *Natural Law Forum* 10 (1965): 168–201; Germain Grisez, "Natural Law and Natural Inclinations: Some Comments and Clarifications," *New Scholasticism* 6 (1987): 307–20; Robert P. George, "Kelsen and Aquinas on the Natural Law Doctrine," in *St. Thomas Aquinas and the Natural Law Tradition*, ed. John Goyette, Mark S. Latkovic, and Richard S. Myers (Washington, D.C.: Catholic University of America Press, 2004), 237–59; Martin Rhonheimer, "The Cognitive Structure of the Natural Law and the Truth of Subjectivity," *The Thomist* 67 (2003): 1–44.

[19] See, e.g., Russell Hittinger, *A Critique of the New Natural Law Theory* (Notre Dame: University of Notre Dame Press, 1987); Steven A. Long, "Natural Law or Autonomous Practical Reason: Problems for the New Natural Law Theory," in *St. Thomas Aquinas and the Natural Law Tradition*, 165–93; Romanus Cessario, O.P., *Introduction to Moral Theology* (Washington, D.C.: Catholic University of America, 2001), 54–99; Stephen L. Brock, "Natural Law, the Understanding of Principles, and Universal Good," *Nova et Vetera* 9 (2011): 671–706; Fulvio Di Blasi, *God and the Natural Law: A Rereading of Thomas Aquinas*, trans. David Thunder (South Bend, IN: St. Augustine's Press, 2006); John M. Rist, *Real Ethics: Rethinking the Foundations of Morality* (Cambridge: Cambridge University Press, 2002).

[20] See, e.g., Russell Hittinger, "Natural Law and Catholic Moral Theology," in Hittinger, *The First Grace: Rediscovering the Natural Law in a Post-Christian World* (Wilmington, DE: ISI Books, 2003), 3–37; Russell Hittinger, "Human Nature and States of Nature in John Paul II's Theological Anthropology," in *Human Nature in Its Wholeness: A Roman Catholic Perspective*, ed. Daniel N. Robinson, Gladys M. Sweeney, and Richard Gill (Washington, D.C.: Catholic University of America Press, 2006), 9–33; Alasdair MacIntyre, "Intractable Moral Disagreements," in *Intractable Disputes about the Natural Law*, ed. Lawrence S. Cunningham, 1–52; Gerald McKenny, "Moral Disagreement and the Limits of Reason: Reflections on MacIntyre and Ratzinger," in *Intractable Disputes about the Natural Law*, ed. Lawrence S. Cunningham, 195–226;

contemporary Catholic philosophers have focused on identifying the theoretical foundations of natural law doctrine, which do not in themselves require an account of the effects of sin or redemption.[21] The philosophical question of how (or whether) natural law has been effectively promulgated comes up especially in discussion of the relationship of natural law doctrine to the positive law of particular human legal systems, a discussion to which Hittinger and Jean Porter have made significant contributions.[22]

2.2 AN OVERVIEW OF ROMANS 1–3

As a brief final step before turning to the five patristic commentaries, let me quickly summarize the main lines of the first three chapters of Romans. Influenced by the Wisdom of Solomon, Paul states that the Gentiles "suppress the truth" about God and have therefore become "futile in their thinking" and prey to "dishonorable passions" (Rom 1:18, 21, 26).[23] Even so, Paul thinks, "what can be known about God is plain to them, because God has shown it to them. Ever since the creation of the world his invisible nature, namely, his eternal power and deity, has been clearly perceived in the things that have been made" (Rom 1:20). As we have seen, he goes on to suggest that some Gentiles actually do what the "law" requires, because "what the law requires

Lawrence Dewan, O.P., "St. Thomas, Natural Law, and Universal Ethics," *Nova et Vetera* 9 (2011): 737–62

[21] See for example Ralph McInerny, *Implicit Moral Knowledge*, ed. Fulvio Di Blasi (Rubbettino: Soveria Mannelli, 2006).

[22] See Russell Hittinger, "Natural Law in the Positive Laws" and "Authority to Render Judgment," in Hittinger, *The First Grace*, 63–91 and 93–112, respectively; Jean Porter, *Ministers of the Law: A Natural Law Theory of Legal Authority* (Grand Rapids, MI: Eerdmans, 2010); Joseph Ratzinger, "That Which Holds the World Together: The Pre-political Moral Foundations of a Free State," in Jürgen Habermas and Joseph Ratzinger, *Dialectics of Secularization: On Reason and Religion*, ed. Florian Schuller, trans. Brian McNeil, C.R.V. (San Francisco: Ignatius Press, 2006), 53–80, at 67–72; Robert Sokolowski, "Discovery and Obligation in Natural Law," in *Natural Moral Law in Contemporary Society*, ed. Holger Zaborowski (Washington, D.C.: Catholic University of America Press, 2010), 24–43.

[23] For discussion of the Wisdom of Solomon, see David Winston, *The Wisdom of Solomon* (New York: Doubleday, 1979); John J. Collins, *Jewish Wisdom in the Hellenistic Age* (Louisville, KY: Westminster John Knox Press, 1997); James Barr, *Biblical Faith and Natural Theology* (Oxford: Oxford University Press, 1993).

is written on their hearts" (Rom 2:15). If Gentiles are "futile in their thinking," how do at least some of them "do by nature what the law requires"? Paul leaves this tension open, and indeed he augments it by affirming not only that God "will render to every man according to his works"—so that God "will give eternal life" to all those who persevere in well-doing (Rom 2:6–7)—but also that "all men, both Jews and Greeks, are under the power of sin" (Rom 3:9), so that without faith in the Redeemer they cannot merit eternal life. Paul concludes, "For there is no distinction; since all have sinned and fall short of the glory of God, they are justified by his grace as a gift, through the redemption which is in Christ Jesus, whom God put forward as an expiation by his blood, to be received by faith" (Rom 3:22–25).

Given the complexity of Paul's teaching here, it is no wonder that the Fathers do not agree fully on what he meant. They differ, for example, on what he means by "law" in his statement that "[w]hen Gentiles who have not the law do by nature what the law requires, they are a law to themselves." They also differ on what "by nature" means. They recognize the problem that if "all have sinned and fall short of the glory of God," it would seem that there could hardly be Gentiles who "do by nature what the law requires." Likewise, they struggle to affirm both that all "are justified by his grace as a gift" and that God "will render to every man according to his works." Within their exegesis of these texts, the Fathers develop their accounts of universal natural law in relation to God's providential care for non-Christians, the value of good actions, the saving righteousness of Christ, the grace of the Holy Spirit, the community of the Church, and judgment and eternal life. So as to get a sense for the development of natural law doctrine within this Christian theological context, let us now turn to these patristic interpretations, beginning with the Christian East.

2.3 ROMANS 2:14–15 IN THE CHRISTIAN EAST: ORIGEN AND JOHN CHRYSOSTOM

2.3.1 Origen of Alexandria (185–254)

Origen's *Commentary on the Epistle to the Romans*, written around 246, comes to us in an abridged form. As with most of Origen's works, the original Greek text is no longer extant: apart from some Greek

fragments; what remains is Rufinus's Latin translation, which significantly condenses the Greek text.[24] The views that we find in the commentary, however, fit with the views that Origen expresses elsewhere,
and so we can safely assume them to be Origen's own.[25] Brian Dunkle
has argued that Origen's *Commentary on the Epistle to the Romans*
marks a turning-point in his natural law doctrine. According to
Dunkle, prior to writing his commentary on Romans, Origen "tends
to see the natural law either as the physical regularity governing the
cosmos or as the law of reason that guides human thought. In the
Commentary on Romans, by contrast, Origen discusses the natural
law primarily in moral terms and argues that many of Paul's references to 'law' apply to a set of universal ethical norms binding all
rational agents."[26]

[24] In translating the work around the year 406, Rufinus obeyed the request of
the monk Heraclius that he abridge Origen's commentary by half, even though the
work is still quite long. While defending the general reliability of Rufinus's translation, Thomas Scheck accepts that "Rufinus has left out large blocks of text," and notes
the likelihood that Rufinus "reformulated (or updated) heterodox-sounding passages,
particularly those pertaining to the Trinity, since his translations assume that heretics
had falsified some passages in Origen's works." See Thomas P. Scheck, "Introduction"
to Origen, *Commentary on the Epistle to the Romans, Books 1–5*, trans. Thomas P.
Scheck (Washington, D.C.: Catholic University of America Press, 2001), 1–48, at 19.
The issues that Origen discusses here would have been of significant interest in 406
due to the emerging Pelagian controversy. See also the background to the commentary provided in Theresia Heither, *Origenes. Commentarii in epistulam ad Romanos/
Römerbriefkommentar* (Freiburg im Breisgau: Herder, 1990). Rufinus appears to have
accentuated (but not distorted) Origen's discussions of natural law: this is Caroline
Hammond Bammel's conclusion in her comparison of Greek fragments of the commentary on Romans with Rufinus's Latin translation. See Bammel, "Philocalia IX,
Jerome, Epistle 121, and Origen's Exposition of Romans VII," *Journal of Theological
Studies* 32 (1981): 51–81.
[25] For Origen on Romans and for the later reception of his commentary, see
especially Thomas P. Scheck, *Origen and the History of Justification: The Legacy of
Origen's Commentary on Romans* (Notre Dame: University of Notre Dame Press,
2008); Mark Reasoner, *Romans in Full Circle: A History of Interpretation* (Louisville,
KY: Westminster John Knox Press, 2005).
[26] See Dunkle, "A Development in Origen's View of the Natural Law," 338. See also
William Banner, "Origen and the Tradition of Natural Law Concepts," *Dumbarton
Oaks Papers* 12 (1958): 49–82; Riemer Roukema, *The Diversity of Laws in Origen's
Commentary on Romans* (Amsterdam: Free University Press, 1988); Henry Chadwick,
"Origen, Celsus, and the Stoa," *Journal of Theological Studies* 48 (1947): 34–49. For
further background see Richard A. Horsley, "The Law of Nature in Philo and Cicero,"
Harvard Theological Review 71 (1978): 35–59; Helmut Koester, "νόμος φύσεως: The
Concept of Natural Law in Greek Thought," in *Religions in Antiquity: Essays in Memory
of E. R. Goodenough*, ed. J. Neusner (Leiden: Brill, 1968); Fernando Llano Alonso,
"Cosmopolitanism and Natural Law in Cicero," in *The Threads of Natural Law*, ed. F.
J. Contreras, 27–36; John W. Martens, *One God, One Law: Philo of Alexandria on the*

Let me begin with Romans 2:5-6, "But by your hard and impenitent heart you are storing up wrath for yourself on the day of wrath when God's righteous judgment will be revealed. For he will render to every man according to his works." Hardness of heart, Origen says, occurs when we know what is good but refuse to do it. "Storing up wrath" contrasts with storing up "treasure in heaven" (Mt 6:20). If we are hard of heart, we store up evil works. Those who are not evil but who pay no attention to spiritual things foolishly store up earthly treasures and have no spiritual reward. By contrast, the spiritual person "is wise and rich in relation to God and who, though he lives on earth, has his citizenship in heaven."[27] The "day of wrath" is the day of the Lord prophesied by Amos, Joel, Zephaniah, and Isaiah. This is the day of judgment, when nothing will be hidden any longer. Our inner hearts, our thoughts and motivations, will be revealed. On that day, says Origen, those who have fallen into many sins "shall be in need of remedies of fire," while the saints will immediately receive "the riches of God's goodness."[28] The day of judgment will occur at the end of the world because the judgment needs to include not only the deeds of each person, but also the impact that the person's deeds had upon other people across the centuries.

On the day of judgment, God will judge us according to what we have done. God "will render to every man according to his works." Indeed, Origen says that even though they were unable to have faith in Christ, "the Gentiles will in nowise seem to be excluded when they

Mosaic and Greco-Roman Law (Leiden: Brill, 2003). Dunkle notes, "Hellenistic philosophers applied the language of natural law to the intellectual, physical, and moral norms that govern the various spheres of the universe. The Stoics developed all of these strains, often against the Epicureans, who saw disorder underlying the physical realm and personal preference providing the only guidance for ethical inquiry. The Stoics took the proper human end as living 'according to man's nature which is reason.' Chrysippus, whom Origen appears to have read, asserts that justice is a universal value that does not vary with local codes: 'That which is just is so by nature and not by imposition [*thesis*], so that it is both the law [*nomos*] and right reason [*orthos logos*].' During the period dominated by Middle Stoicism and Middle Platonism in the first and second centuries after Christ, when both schools appear to have been influenced by the other's thought, theories of natural law and natural justice became an increasingly common response to Epicureans and Skeptics. Alexandria was especially alive with these Hellenistic debates. Philo, who has been called, with some exaggeration, the progenitor of *all* natural law language, takes the natural law to conform, in general, to the ancient Hebrew law" (Dunkle, "A Development in Origen's View of the Natural Law," 339).

[27] Origen, *Commentary on the Epistle to the Romans, Books 1-5*, 107.
[28] Origen, 110.

themselves do good and behave correctly."[29] Origen is troubled, however, by Ezekiel's prophetic statement that if a good person becomes
bad, the good works that the person has done will not be remem-
bered by God in his favor (Ez 18:24). It would seem then that God
will not do what Paul says God will do, namely "render to every man
according to his works." In response, Origen explains that Ezekiel
means that a good person's works will be forgotten by God only if
a good person falls away so far as to commit *all* the sins of a bad
person.

This eschatological focus only increases when Origen arrives at the
next portion of Romans 2,

> To those who by patience in well-doing seek for glory and honor and
> immortality, he will give eternal life; but for those who are factious and
> do not obey the truth, but obey wickedness, there will be wrath and fury.
> There will be tribulation and distress for every human being who does
> evil, the Jew first and also the Greek, but glory and honor and peace
> for every one who does good, the Jew first and also the Greek. For God
> shows no partiality (Rom 2:7–11).

Origen wants to insist that Gentiles—the pagans who lived before
Christ—were able to do good and to receive eternal life. Because
"God is not only the God of the Jews but also of the Gentiles,"[30] God
will give eternal life to those Gentiles (and Jews) "who by patience in
well-doing seek for glory and honor and immortality," that is to say to
those persons who care for spiritual things rather than merely living
as though this world were all there is. Here Origen emphasizes Paul's
commendation of "patience in well-doing." Those who do good works
will have to struggle and persevere. One cannot just say good things,
one must do them, often at significant cost.

Those who "seek glory and honor and immortality" are those who
understand material things spiritually, so as patiently to seek God and
to participate in his glory. Persons who persevere in good works will
receive the "honor" that properly belongs to humans as spiritual creatures, the "honor" of communing with God as did Adam and Eve
before the Fall. Good works also will lead the person to the immortality of the resurrection. By contrast, the unjust deprive themselves of
God's gifts, and this deprivation causes suffering. Unlike the reward
of the just, which God causes, God does not cause the suffering of

---

[29] Origen, 112.   [30] Origen, 113.

the unjust; rather the unjust cause it themselves by their actions, just as people cause their own sickness by eating bad food against their physician's orders. Origen explains that souls that do evil become crimped and anguished, whereas souls that do good and share in spiritual truth are enlarged and filled.

Gentiles, says Origen, could know God from creation (Rom 1:20), but they could not know God's will; God revealed his will to the Jews alone. What then does Paul mean when he refers to Jews and Greeks in Romans 2:9–10? Origen suggests that "Jews" here means those who know God's will—and therefore ultimately means Christians—and that "Greeks" means pagans who do not know God's will because they have not yet believed. On this interpretation of the meaning of "Jews" and "Greeks," however, a problem arises: "How then does Paul here make the Gentiles sharers of the glory and honor and peace in the second place after the Jews?"[31]

Origen answers that perhaps Paul in fact envisions a threefold distinction. First, there are Christians, that is, Jews and Greeks who believe in Christ. They will receive eternal life because they "seek for glory and honor and immortality" (Rom 2:7) as spiritually minded persons. Second, there are unbelieving Jews and unbelieving Greeks, and they will "have tribulation and distress" (Rom 2:9). Third, however, these same unbelieving Jews and unbelieving Greeks will be repaid for their good works, as Paul says in Romans 2:10: "But glory and honor and peace for every one who does good, the Jew first and also the Greek." Origen's concern is to ensure that no good work goes without its reward. He is persuaded that many Gentiles, lacking either the Mosaic law or faith in Christ, nonetheless perform good works. Such Gentiles must be rewarded by the God who "will render to every man according to his works" (Rom 2:6).

This brings us to the topic of natural law. Without yet turning to Romans 2:14–15, Origen states that there are clearly many Gentiles who believe neither Moses nor Christ, yet who nonetheless exercise their "natural reason" sufficiently well so as to "hold fast to justice or observe chastity or maintain wisdom, moderation, and modesty."[32] The virtues of justice, temperance, and prudence are not unknown among the Gentiles. Such a Gentile is indeed "a law to himself, showing the work of the law in his heart" (cf. Rom 2:14).[33] It would seem,

---

[31] Origen, 123. [32] Origen, 125. [33] Origen, 125.

as Origen says, that a Gentile of this kind could not receive eternal life, since eternal life comes through faith and baptism. According to Romans 2:10, however, God does indeed intend to give "glory and honor and peace for every one who does good, the Jew first and also the Greek." Recall Origen's supposition that the "Greek" of Romans 2:10 is the same Greek of Romans 2:9. In the first passage this person is condemned, but in the second passage this person is rewarded. Origen states, "I do not think it can be doubted that the one who had merited condemnation on account of his evil works will be considered worthy of remuneration for his good works, if he indeed had performed good works."[34]

How can the same person both be condemned and rewarded? Before resolving this problem, Origen makes clear that his central aim is to address the fact that there are non-Christians who do good works, and that God must reward them in rendering "to every man according to his works" (Rom 2:6). He recalls Peter's statement that because God is impartial, "in every nation any one who fears him and does what is right is acceptable to him" (Acts 10:35). The flip side of the good Gentile is the wicked Christian, and Origen also observes that there are Christians whose evil works will receive condemnation. All evil works will receive condemnation, just as all good works will receive reward. Origen presses the point that "the unbeliever shall not lose the remuneration for the good works he has done, his unbelief notwithstanding."[35]

In Romans 2:12–13, Paul states that Gentiles sin "without the law" and Jewish people sin "under the law"; both will be punished. The eschatological difference consists in whether people are "doers of the law." Are there people, then, who are not only "without the law" but beyond all law, so that they cannot be "doers of the law" in any sense? Origen denies that this can be the case. He appeals to Romans 2:14–15, "When Gentiles who have not the law do by nature what the law requires, they are a law to themselves, even though they do not have the law. They show that what the law requires is written on their hearts" (Rom 2:14–15). They do not have the Mosaic law, and yet "what the law requires is written on their hearts." According to Origen, this "natural law...dwells in all men generally."[36]

---

[34] Origen, 126.   [35] Origen, 127.   [36] Origen, 128.

It could be, however, that natural law, which is distinct from the law of Moses, is what Paul has in mind when he says that "[a]ll who have sinned without the law will also perish without the law" (Rom 2:12). Does Paul mean that Gentiles will utterly perish "without the law" because they have sinned against natural law? Origen argues that to be "without the law" in the severest sense means to reject even natural law, so as to "comply neither with written laws nor with their conscience and their own thoughts, which rebuke and convict them [cf. Rom 2:15]."[37] He considers the prodigal son to be an exemplar of just such a person who has rejected even natural law. But far from perishing utterly, the prodigal son calls forth the Father's love. The same attitude of God is revealed in Ezekiel 34:16, where God, after rebuking Israel's shepherds, promises to seek and heal those sheep who have strayed and are perishing. Such passages show that God never destroys anyone. Origen thinks that "practically no one" lacks natural law, even though in some persons natural law "seems to be obliterated and nullified" because of hardness of heart. Such persons are the ones whom Paul says will "perish without the law" (Rom 2:12), but as Origen has shown, such persons are also the ones that God promises to seek and heal.

To make clear the different meanings of "law" in Romans 2, Origen points out that when Paul speaks of "the Gentiles who have not the law" doing "by nature what the law requires" (Rom 2:14), Paul could not mean that these Gentiles are naturally observing circumcision, the Sabbath, new moons, and sacrifices, let alone such laws as "You shall not wear a mingled stuff, wool and linen together" (Deut 22:11). These precepts of the Mosaic law cannot be what Paul means by "what the law requires." What then does Paul mean? Origen answers, "The reference is instead to what they are able to perceive by nature, for instance, that they should not commit murder or adultery, they ought not steal, they should not speak falsely, they should honor father and mother, and the like."[38] In other words, Origen has the second table of the Decalogue in view as descriptive of natural law. Does natural law also include knowledge of God? Origen thinks that the answer may be yes. Although he is not sure, it may be "written in the hearts of the Gentiles that God is one and the Creator of all things."[39] But

---

[37] Origen, 128.   [38] Origen, 131.   [39] Origen, 131.

he holds that what Paul primarily means are the precepts of "natural justice," those things that can be known by application of the Golden Rule: "And as you wish that men would do to you, do so to them" (Lk 6:31).

Origen goes further: he also considers that the Decalogue and the Golden Rule provide the lens by which to understand spiritually the other Mosaic precepts. The laws about such things as wool and linen, along with the laws about sacrifices, are fulfilled according to the Holy Spirit when people understand them spiritually as teaching justice and righteousness.[40] Understood in this way, they can be fulfilled even by the Gentiles who do not know their letter, as Paul states. The Gentiles possess natural law through "the soul's rational power," which is what Paul means by saying that "what the law requires is written on their hearts" (Rom 2:15).[41]

If this is so, what is the distinction between the rational power of the soul and "conscience," to which Paul refers in Romans 2:15? Origen reviews other biblical passages that speak of "conscience," especially 2 Corinthians 1:12, "For our boast is this, the testimony of our conscience that we have behaved in the world, and still more toward you, with holiness and godly sincerity, not by earthly wisdom but by the grace of God." Origen concludes that "conscience" rejoices over good works and condemns evil works, but does not itself commit deeds. It stands in judgment over the works of the soul. He reasons that when Paul refers to "spirit" and "soul," the former is the conscience. The conscience serves as a "pedagogue to the soul, a guide and companion, as it were."[42] A wicked soul, after death, is separated from its spirit/conscience.

Origen has Marcion on his mind throughout much of this discussion. Near the outset of the section we have examined, Origen states, "Now we need to ask about the righteous judgment of God in which he will pay back to each one according to his own works. In the first place let the heretics who claim that the natures of human souls are either good or evil be shut out."[43] Marcion held that we are either good or evil by nature, rather than by freely chosen works. Commenting on

---

[40] For discussion see Peter W. Martens, *Origen and Scripture: The Contours of the Exegetical Life* (Oxford: Oxford University Press, 2011), 133–60.

[41] Origen, *Commentary on the Epistle to the Romans, Books 1–5*, 132.

[42] Origen, 133.

[43] Origen, 111.

Paul's reference to "that day when, according to my gospel, God judges the secrets of men by Christ Jesus" (Rom 2:16), Origen observes: "As for Marcion and all who, by different kinds of fictional constructions, introduce the concept of different kinds of natures of souls, they are confuted in a most clear way in this passage."[44] Marcion's anthropology and eschatology cannot account for the fact that, as Romans 2:15–16 makes clear, "each person must be judged not by the privilege of possessing a certain nature, but by his own thoughts, accused or defended by the testimony of his own conscience."[45] Similarly, by means of his emphasis on the spiritual reading of the Old Testament, Origen seeks against Marcion to "defend the God of the law and of the prophets as being not only just but also good."[46]

Origen is particularly skillful at highlighting the connection between Paul's eschatological concerns and Paul's construal of the law that is written on the heart. As we have seen, Origen emphasizes Paul's statement that God "will render to every man according to his works" (Rom 2:6), and Origen does not for a moment doubt that there have been and are many Gentiles "who by patience in well-doing seek for glory and honor and immortality" and thereby receive "eternal life" (Rom 2:7). By contrast to Marcion, Origen insists with Paul that Israel's God is the God of the Gentiles, and thus cares for the Gentiles as the father cares for the prodigal son. Similarly, by contrast to Marcion's supposition that some people are evil by nature, Origen argues that God's gift of rationality and conscience ensures that all people possess knowledge of right and wrong, as inscribed in the Decalogue and the Golden Rule. Although Origen does not think that God will permanently condemn anyone, he does think that all our evil works will be condemned and that we will suffer for them. The eschatological fulfillment will be supreme goodness, rather than the everlasting polarity that Marcion teaches.

Origen wants to show that both Gentiles and Jews, Christians and non-Christians, can do good works and will be among the

---

[44] Origen, 135.
[45] Origen, 135.
[46] Origen, 113. For Origen's polemic against Marcion, see Martens, *Origen and Scripture*, 108–31. On Marcion, see the classic (and enthusiastic) work of Adolf von Harnack, *Marcion: The Gospel of the Alien God*, trans. John E. Steely and Lyle D. Bierma (Eugene, OR: Wipf & Stock, 2007); see also the succinct presentation of Marcionite dualism in Yuri Stoyanov, *The Other God: Dualist Religions from Antiquity to the Cathar Heresy* (New Haven, CT: Yale University Press, 2000), 90–91.

saved. Has Origen thereby done away with the significance of Jewish and Christian revelation, by suggesting that Jesus Christ is not the Redeemer of all human beings, as though some could receive eternal life simply by doing what the law requires without the work of Christ and the Holy Spirit?

To answer this question it is necessary to probe a bit further into Origen's commentary, specifically his discussion of Romans 3:21–6,

> But now the righteousness of God has been manifested apart from law, although the law and the prophets bear witness to it, the righteousness of God through faith in Jesus Christ for all who believe. For there is no distinction; since all have sinned and fall short of the glory of God, they are justified by his grace as a gift, through the redemption which is in Christ Jesus, whom God put forward as an expiation by his blood, to be received by faith. This was to show God's righteousness, because in his divine forbearance he had passed over former sins; it was to prove at the present time that he himself is righteous and that he justifies him who has faith in Jesus.

Origen begins with the point that Paul uses "law" in different senses. In general, according to Origen, when Paul wishes to refer to the Mosaic law, he uses the article "the" before "law"; when Paul wishes to refer to natural law, he does not use the article. When Paul says that "the righteousness of God has been manifested apart from law," he does not use the article before "law." The righteousness of God, then, has been manifested apart from *natural law*, whereas the Mosaic law and the prophets "bear witness to" the righteousness of God. Origen explains that natural law does not reveal God's righteousness, but instead sets forth only a human knowledge and righteousness. The righteousness of God is none other than Christ Jesus. The fact that Christ is the Son of God cannot be perceived "from nature alone."[47]

In this vein, Origen emphasizes that "the righteousness of God surpasses and rises above whatever the human mind can scrutinize by natural senses alone. For the mind does not suffice, not so much for every kind of human righteousness, but for grasping the righteousness of God and the judgments which descend from it."[48] God's humility and generosity are simply beyond the power of natural reason; the virtues of Christ go beyond what natural reason could

[47] Origen, *Commentary on the Epistle to the Romans, Books 1–5*, 214.
[48] Origen, 210–11.

envision. Origen observes that natural law can teach us not to do to others what we would not want done to ourselves (Lk 6:31), but natural law cannot teach us the humility that Jesus teaches when he says, "when you give alms, do not let your left hand know what your right hand is doing" (Mt 6:3). Only Jesus' teachings, as prepared for by Moses and the prophets, can reveal God's righteousness to us. As Origen concludes, "Wherefore the law of nature will be of no help whatsoever for knowing God's righteousness, though it appears to understand something about human righteousness."[49]

Against Marcion, Origen makes clear that the "faith in Jesus Christ" to which Paul refers in Romans 3:22 is not a faith that can do without the Mosaic law and the prophets. The whole Scripture is necessary for apprehending the disclosure of God's righteousness. Origen knows that "since all have sinned and fall short of the glory of God" (Rom 3:23), no one can receive or merit glory on his or her own. Sinners cannot stand before the glory of God; God is too holy and powerful. A Redeemer from sin is needed, because both Jews and Gentiles have become "[c]aptives conquered by sin, as if by war."[50] The Redeemer, Christ Jesus, spilled his blood for us as the "price" of our redemption, and in this way made fully manifest the merciful righteousness of God.[51] God worked through "the mediation of a propitiator so that those who were not able to be justified through their own works might be justified through faith in him."[52] This propitiation was symbolized by the mercy seat that God commanded Moses to build for the ark of the covenant in Exodus 25. The mercy seat signifies the pure soul of Jesus, and the ark signifies Jesus' holy flesh. Jesus is both priest and sacrificial offering, which he accomplishes "by the shedding of his own blood for the forgiveness of past sins. And this propitiation comes to every believer by way of faith."[53]

Natural law, then, is not enough for sharing in God's righteousness and glory. We need a Redeemer to forgive our sins by the shedding of his blood, and this Redeemer must be perfectly holy. Jesus Christ, who cannot be understood outside the Mosaic law and the prophets, accomplishes this redemption and, in his humility, reveals to us the righteousness of God. Now that the deficiency intrinsic to natural law has been made apparent, however, does this overthrow

---

[49] Origen, 211.   [50] Origen, 215.   [51] Origen, 216.
[52] Origen, 217.   [53] Origen, 223.

Origen's earlier concern for the salvation of those Gentiles who "show that what the law requires is written on their hearts" (Rom 2:15)? By no means. Origen cites 1 John 2:2, which teaches that Jesus Christ "is the expiation for our sins, and not for ours only but also for the sins of the whole world." Putting this into his own words, he states that "Jesus is the propitiator not only of believers and the faithful but also of the whole world; yet not first of the world and then of us, but first of us and only then of the whole world."[54] The fact that only Christians, and not yet the whole world, have embraced the Savior does not tell against the salvation of the whole world. Ultimately, those who "do by nature what the law requires" (Rom 2:14) and "by patience in well-doing seek for glory and honor and immortality" (Rom 2:7) will find that this glory is inaccessible without a Redeemer; but we can equally be assured that there will be "glory and honor and peace for every one who does good, the Jew first and also the Greek" (Rom 2:10).

2.3.2 John Chrysostom (c.347–407)

While serving as a priest at Antioch in the late fourth century, John Chrysostom preached a series of homilies on Romans.[55] How does he address our passage? Chrysostom emphasizes that it is the human sinner, not God, who stores up the "wrath" (Rom 2:5) that the sinner will receive at the day of judgment. God created us with the power to discern between good and evil, and God patiently calls us to repentance. God's "wrath" is not a passion but rather describes his "righteous judgment" (Rom 2:5), according to which each human receives what he or she deserves in justice. According to Chrysostom, then, Paul's warning about judgment in Romans 2:5 is mainly about God's goodness, love, and justice and our ability to choose the good.

Since Paul seeks to awaken us to judgment but not to frighten us away from God, in Romans 2:6–7 Paul proclaims that God, in rendering to us what our works deserve, "will give eternal life" to "those who

---

[54] Origen, 224. On Origen's eschatology, see Panayiotis Tzamalikos, *Origen: Philosophy of History and Eschatology* (Leiden: Brill, 2007).

[55] For Chrysostom's portrait of Paul, see Margaret M. Mitchell, *The Heavenly Trumpet: John Chrysostom and the Art of Pauline Interpretation* (Louisville, KY: Westminster John Knox Press, 2002). See also the background provided by J. N. D. Kelly, *Golden Mouth: The Story of John Chrysostom—Ascetic, Preacher, Bishop* (Ithaca, NY: Cornell University Press, 1998). For brief discussion of Chrysostom on natural law, see Charles, *Retrieving the Natural Law*, 86–87.

by patience in well-doing seek for glory and honor and immortality." Paul thereby reminds us that faith is not sufficient without works. The glory and honor that God will give the blessed are far greater than the earthly glory and honor for which many people strive. God will give an immortal and incorruptible glory and honor rather than the fleeting honor that can be attained in earthly life. Paul also mentions "glory and honor" in addition to "immortality" because not all will rise to glory and honor; some will rise to everlasting punishment. When Paul turns in Romans 2:8 to describe the punishment of "those who are factious and do not obey the truth, but obey wickedness," Chrysostom comments that Paul speaks of obedience to wickedness so as to make clear our free choice in evildoing.

Thus far Chrysostom's commentary has stressed that our evildoing arises from free choice, because God created us with the ability to know good and evil and to choose between them. God therefore will judge us on our works, and our works will either condemn or excuse us. When in verse 9 Paul warns that "[t]here will be tribulation and distress for every human being who does evil, the Jew first and also the Greek," Chrysostom interprets this as showing that no matter how great the person, he or she will not escape judgment. Indeed, Paul's statement "the Jew first" means that those who possess the most advantages in this life will receive greater punishment for sins, since the Jewish people had the great advantage of having received God's law. Chrysostom then faces the problem of what Jews and Gentiles Paul has in mind when Paul says, "but glory and honor and peace for every one who does good, the Jew first and also the Greek" (Rom 2:10). Can Jews and Gentiles who reject Christ gain "glory and honor and peace," as if faith in Christ were of no value?

Chrysostom reasons that Paul must be speaking of Jews and Gentiles "before Christ's coming."[56] In Chrysostom's view, Paul's earlier words about God rendering "to every man according to his works" and God giving eternal life "to those who by patience in well-doing seek for glory and honor and immortality" (Rom 2:6–7) also have in view the era before Christ's coming. Paul's purpose is to make clear that before Christ, God cared for both Jews and Gentiles and ensured

---

[56] John Chrysostom, *Homilies on the Epistle to the Romans*, trans. J. B. Morris and W. H. Simcox, revised by George B. Stevens, in *Chrysostom: Homilies on the Acts of the Apostles and the Epistle to the Romans*, ed. George B. Stevens, Nicene and Post-Nicene Fathers, First Series, vol. 11 (Peabody, MA: Hendrickson, 1995 [1889]), Homily V, 362.

that they could do good and receive salvation. The Jews were God's chosen people, but this did not give them a large advantage over the Gentiles. Chrysostom adds that Paul is referring to the good Gentiles rather than the idol-worshipping Gentiles. The good Gentiles, such as Melchizedek, Job, Cornelius and others, worshipped the one God, "obeyed the law of nature," and "strictly kept all things, save the Jewish observances, which contribute to piety."[57] During this time, of course, there were many wicked Gentiles too, just as the Jewish people was comprised both of idolaters and faithful worshippers of God. Paul's point, says Chrysostom, is that (prior to Christ's coming) the good Jew had no advantage over the good Gentile in terms of salvation, "[f]or it is upon works that both punishment and reward depend, not upon circumcision and uncircumcision."[58]

Chrysostom thinks that Paul is challenging the reasons why Jews, after Christ's coming, might stand aloof from Gentiles. Certainly the idolatrous Gentiles will be punished, because "what can be known about God is plain to them, because God has shown it to them" through creation, with the result that "they are without excuse" (Rom 1:19–20). But since many Jews too have committed idolatry and failed to observe the Mosaic law, the Jews are hardly in a better position than the Gentiles; rather, having been given more, the Jews are more culpable for their failings. Both the good Jews and the good Gentiles will be rewarded with "glory and honor and peace" (Rom 2:10). Between the Jews and the Gentiles, then, "God shows no partiality" (Rom 2:11). Chrysostom recognizes that this is a rather startling claim, because it would seem that God has certainly shown partiality toward the Jewish people by giving them the Mosaic law and the prophets. He explains that Paul is speaking not of this kind of partiality, but of partiality between "every one who does good, the Jew first and also the Greek" (Rom 2:10). Not the status of being a Jew or Gentile, but the actions of particular Jews and Gentiles determine whether God will reward or punish them. This is the point, too, of Romans 2:12, "All who have sinned without the law will also perish without the law, and all who have sinned under the law will be judged by the law." Gentile and Jewish evildoers will both receive punishment, and indeed the violation of the Mosaic law might make

---

[57] Chrysostom, 363.   [58] Chrysostom, 363.

the punishment greater for Jewish evildoers than for Gentile ones. Paul is showing, says Chrysostom, that Jews need the grace of Christ just as much as Gentiles do.

Among the greatest privileges of the Jewish people is having been "hearers of the law" (Rom 2:13), because the Mosaic law was given to the Jewish people. According to Chrysostom, then, Paul finds himself needing to critique those who would rest in this privilege. Paul does this by insisting that it is not the "hearers of the law" but the "doers of the law who will be justified" (Rom 2:13). Could Gentiles, who did not know or observe the Mosaic law, have been "doers of the law"? In Chrysostom's view, this is precisely what Paul means to say. Many "hearers of the law" were not doers, and many doers never heard the law. The possession of the Mosaic law per se cannot be relied upon for salvation. What then is the meaning of Romans 2:14, "When Gentiles who have not the law do by nature what the law requires, they are a law to themselves, even though they do not have the law"? Chrystostom explains that Paul is both affirming the goodness of the Mosaic law, and arguing that "by the reasonings of nature" the Gentiles can perform the works of the Mosaic law.[59] Paul is insisting that the Jewish people, despite the privilege of receiving God's law, did not have an exclusive access to God's law, and Paul commends Gentiles who performed the works of the Mosaic law despite not having the privilege that the Jewish people had. The purpose of this praise of the Gentiles is both to urge the Jewish people not to hold themselves aloof from the Gentiles, and to show that "conscience and reason" suffice to enable people to obey God's law.[60]

Chrysostom particularly has in mind Paul's statement in Romans 2:15, "They show that what the law requires is written on their hearts, while their conscience also bears witness and their conflicting thoughts accuse or perhaps excuse them." In creation, God gave humans rationality and conscience. These created powers of human nature ensure that humans are "able to choose virtue and to avoid vice," something that could only be possible if humans possessed the ability to know God's law (that is, to know what is good and what is evil).[61] God has given humans this ability in creation. In giving a law to Moses, God enables the Jewish people to apprehend more

---

[59] Chrysostom, 364.   [60] Chrysostom, 365.   [61] Chrysostom, 365.

clearly what is good and what evil, but this privilege does not leave the Gentiles bereft. Rather, God has always cared for the Gentiles. Were it otherwise, then it would seem that Christ should have come much earlier. For Chrysostom, then, Paul is responding to those who might say, "Why ever is it, that Christ came but now? And where in times before was this mighty scheme of Providence?"[62] By explaining that there were Gentiles who were able to "do by nature what the law requires," Paul shows that "even in former times, and before the Law was given, human nature fully enjoyed the care of Providence."[63] Humans would have been bereft indeed had they been left without an ability to know God and to know good and evil, but Paul makes clear (especially in Romans 1:19–20 and Romans 2:14–15) that this was never the case. Chrysostom also supposes that Romans 2:15 can just as well apply to Jews, who know God's law both through the written law and through reason and conscience.

Yet it seems that Paul ends Romans 2:15 in an awkward way. Paul has been talking about Gentiles (and Jews) who by natural reason do "what the law requires." Why then does he finish his sentence by commenting that "their conflicting thoughts accuse or perhaps excuse them"? After all, if they are doing what the law requires, then their thoughts will not accuse them. Chrysostom explains that Paul has here shifted his discussion to include not only those who do the law, but all humans. Those humans who have done evil will be accused not by God extrinsically, but by their own reason and conscience intrinsically. Furthermore, not only our publicly known acts but also our hidden acts and our inward acts will come under judgment. In verse 16, therefore, Paul points us toward "that day when, according to my gospel, God judges the secrets of men by Christ Jesus."

It is the thought of that judgment day that should persuade all people, Jews and Gentiles, about their need not simply for the law but for a merciful Redeemer. Chrysostom urges, "Now let each man enter into his own conscience, and reckoning up his transgressions, let him call himself to a strict account, that we be not then condemned with the world."[64] He pictures how embarrassed each of us would be if our worst sins were publicly manifested before the

---

[62] Chrysostom, 365.   [63] Chrysostom, 365.   [64] Chrysostom, 366.

whole congregation, and he reminds us that on the day of judgment everything will be apparent to everyone. In this context, he confesses that each of us have turned away from God; indeed, "now we are so wretchedly disposed, that, were there no fear of hell, we should not even choose readily to do any good thing."[65] Through this analysis of our condition, Chrysostom shows his awareness of how conflicted each of us is. He then compares our lack of love with God's great love. God has blessed humans in every way. Despite our turning away from him, God has run toward us, not only by sending prophets but even by sending his own Son. Christ redeems us from sin and promises us eternal union with God in love. Yet Christians continue to fail miserably: "We need much that is His [God's], and nonetheless we cleave not unto His love, but money we value above Him, and man's friendship, and ease of body, and power, and fame, before Him who values nothing more than us."[66] Chrysostom's message to us is that despite our continued failings, Christ's mercy is still available to us. If we avail ourselves of the mercy of Christ, we can even now learn to glorify God the Father, Son, and Holy Spirit by works of love.

In short, Chrysostom is often quite close to Origen, as should be expected. He assumes that Paul is speaking about Jews and Gentiles prior to Christ. In Chrysostom's view, Paul is arguing that the Jewish people, while privileged to receive the written law, should not therefore hold themselves aloof from the Gentiles. The Gentiles were not bereft of natural reason and conscience, and so they too could know God's law and do it. Many Gentiles were idolaters, but so were many Jews; there were holy Gentiles (such as Job) just as there were holy Jews. Thanks to our natural gifts, we humans can direct ourselves toward the good and know when we are doing evil. At the same time, Chrysostom also never loses touch with the significance of Jesus. His argument about the Jews and Gentiles, and about natural law, is intended to show that Paul aims to bring Jews and Gentiles together in the knowledge that we all need a merciful Redeemer and that this Redeemer is Jesus Christ.

---

[65] Chrysostom, 366.
[66] Chrysostom, 367; translation slightly modified.

2.4 ROMANS 2:5–16 IN THE CHRISTIAN
WEST: AMBROSIASTER, PELAGIUS, AUGUSTINE

2.4.1 Ambrosiaster (fourth century)

The identity of Ambrosiaster is not known with certainty, nor is the exact date of the composition of his commentary on Romans. Scholars have dated it to the mid to late fourth century, a little more than a century after Origen's commentary and two or three decades before Chrysostom's.[67] Not least because Ambrosiaster commented on all the Pauline letters (except Hebrews), his succinct commentary remained influential in the Christian West through the medieval period. Sophie Lunn-Rockliffe observes that Ambrosiaster "showed a keen interest in law in its broadest, most cosmic sense: in natural law, God's law written in creation."[68] This keen interest is less apparent in his comments on Romans 2:5–16, which makes his comments in certain ways all the more interesting for our purposes.

---

[67] See Gerald L. Bray, "Translator's Introduction" to Ambrosiaster, *Commentaries on Romans and 1–2 Corinthians*, trans. and ed. Gerald L. Bray (Downers Grove, IL: InterVarsity Press, 2009), xv–xxiii, at xvi. Augustine knew the commentaries of "Ambrosiaster" and attributed them to a certain "Hilary." Bray considers that Augustine may have had in view either Decimus Hilarianus Hilarius, a Roman Christian layman of the late fourth century, or Hilary of Poitiers. In the medieval period the commentaries were attributed to Ambrose. Seventeenth-century editors coined the term "Ambrosiaster." For further discussion of Ambrosiaster's Pauline commentaries, focusing on his commentary on 2 Thessalonians, see Kevin L. Hughes, *Constructing Antichrist: Paul, Biblical Commentary, and the Development of Doctrine in the Early Middle Ages* (Washington, D.C.: Catholic University of America Press, 2005), 38–50.

[68] Sophie Lunn-Rockliffe, *Ambrosiaster's Political Theology* (Oxford: Oxford University Press, 2007), 50–51. On pages 51 and 139, she quotes an important passage on natural law from his *Quaestiones Veteris et Novi Testamenti*, ed. A. Souter, CSEL 50 (Vienna: 1908). In Q. 4.1, Ambrosiaster writes, "Originally law did not have to be given formed in letters, because it was somehow sown in nature itself, and knowledge of the creator did not lie hidden from the generations of men. For who does not know what is appropriate to the good life, or who is ignorant of the fact that what he does not want done to himself, should not be done to another? But when the natural law faded away, oppressed by habitual sin, then it had to be made manifest, so that among the Jews, all might hear; not because it had vanished without trace; but they laced the great authority of the [natural] law; they applied themselves to idolatry; there was no fear of God on earth; they devoted themselves to fornication…. And so the law was given, so that what was known should have authority, and that which had started to be concealed might be made manifest." For background to the *Quaestiones Veteris et Novi Testamenti* see Marie-Pierre Bussières, "Ambrosiaster's Method of Interpretation in the Questions on the Old and New Testament," in *Interpreting the Bible and Aristotle in Late Antiquity*, 49–65.

Commenting on Romans 2:5, "By your hard and impenitent heart you are storing up wrath for yourself on the day of wrath when God's righteous judgment will be revealed," Ambrosiaster says that such a person "hopes he can get away with his sins" rather than ever having to undergo God's punishment.[69] Such a person will therefore be punished even more severely when God renders "to every man according to his works" (Rom 2:6). God is delaying this "day of wrath" in part to deliver greater punishment to the impenitent. But as regards "those who by patience in well-doing seek for glory and honor and immortality" (Rom 2:7), God will soon give them eternal life with a glory and honor that endures, by contrast to the fleeting glory and honor possible in this life.

Unlike Origen and Chrysostom, then, Ambrosiaster here does not have in view the question of what happens to good Gentiles who know neither Moses nor Christ. Rather, Ambrosiaster interprets Paul to be speaking about good Christians, who are contrasted with impenitent sinners. Good Christians "are not merely those who believe correctly, but those who live correctly as well."[70] Those who do not believe will experience "wrath and fury" and "tribulation and distress" (Rom 2:8–9). Since God does not have passions, God's wrath signifies the eschatological punishment endured by the unbeliever. Ambrosiaster underscores that "[e]vil is not just a matter of deeds but of unbelief as well."[71] He explains that Paul promises punishment or reward to "the Jew first and also the Greek" (Rom 2:9–10) because Jewish people, as the descendents of Abraham, will receive extra punishment if they do not believe in Christ and extra honor if they do believe in Christ. Only believers do "good" and receive "glory and honor and peace" (Rom 2:10). Since all are justified by faith, God "shows no partiality" (Rom 2:11) to those of Jewish ancestry.

Ambrosiaster notes affirmatively that "Paul says that everyone is subject to the law of nature."[72] This prompts a question: how can anyone sin "without the law" (Rom 2:12)? He answers that in Romans 2:12 Paul means the Mosaic law. Gentiles who do not possess the law of Moses or the law of Christ will certainly "perish" (Rom 2:12). The way to avoid perishing is to have faith, which enables people to obey

---

[69] Ambrosiaster, *Commentary on Romans*, 16.
[70] Ambrosiaster, 17.
[71] Ambrosiaster, 17.
[72] Ambrosiaster, 17.

"the law without knowing it" and to be justified.[73] By faith, people not only avoid evil but also believe in God. Furthermore, even if we avoid sinning against our fellow humans—a temporal righteousness—we still are not in right relationship to God. Without faith, the Gentiles cannot know the true God and thus they cannot receive eternal righteousness.[74] The Jewish people know the true God through the law of Moses, a law in which Christ is promised. Jews who do not believe in Jesus will therefore "be judged by the law" (Rom 2:12) and punished by the loss of what the law of Moses promised. Ambrosiaster considers that the Jews who do not believe in Christ are the "hearers of the law" (Rom 2:13) who do not keep the law. Since the Mosaic law promises Christ, the only way to be "doers of the law" (Rom 2:13) is to believe in Christ. By believing in Christ, the Gentile thereby keeps the whole Mosaic law, and also natural law, without knowing it.

How then does Ambrosiaster interpret Romans 2:14–15, which Origen understood in terms of natural law possessed by all people? Recall Paul's words: "When Gentiles who have not the law do by nature what the law requires, they are a law to themselves, even though they do not have the law. They show that what the law requires is written on their hearts, while their conscience also bears witness and their conflicting thoughts accuse or perhaps excuse them" (Rom 2:14–15). Intriguingly, Ambrosiaster argues that the "Gentiles" here are in fact Gentile Christians. Natural reason is most itself when it acknowledges its Creator. Gentile Christians certainly do not practice circumcision, celebrate Jewish festivals, or follow the food laws of Israel. But Gentile Christians do "acknowledge the God of the law."[75] They do so by believing in God and in Jesus Christ (the Father and the Son). In so doing, they display their wise exercise of reason. Using "natural judgment," humans must go "beyond what the law commands" and believe in Jesus Christ.[76] Conscience, bearing witness within our minds, shows us that it is right to believe in God and Christ. "What the law requires" is that we have faith in our Creator and Lord. This

---

[73] Ambrosiaster, 18.

[74] As Lunn-Rockliffe observes, for Ambrosiaster the "unwritten, natural law and instinctive justice was not strong enough by itself to prevent man, endowed by God with free will and 'fragile', from sinning" (Lunn-Rockliffe, *Ambrosiaster's Political Theology*, 52). Ambrosiaster considered the ten commandments to be the revelation of precepts of natural law.

[75] Ambrosiaster, *Commentary on Romans*, 18.

[76] Ambrosiaster, 19.

is a reasonable thing to do, and its necessity is "revealed in the Word of God."[77]

The last phrase of verse 15—"their conflicting thoughts accuse or perhaps excuse them"—leads Ambrosiaster to suggest that in verse 15, Paul takes up those Gentiles who reject belief in Christ. Gentiles who do not believe in Jesus will be accused by their own conscience and thoughts, whereas Gentiles who believe will be excused by their conscience and thoughts. Gentiles who do not believe are thinking unreasonably, because they deny Christ despite the fact that evidence sufficient to sway human reason has been presented. Alternatively, Ambrosiaster supposes that one could also read verse 15 as being strictly about Christian Gentiles. In this case, the meaning is that orthodox Christians will be excused by their conscience and thoughts, while heretical and schismatic Christians will be accused by their conscience and thoughts.

In Ambrosiaster, the difficulties that Origen raises regarding good Gentiles who know neither Moses nor Christ are absent. As we noted, Ambrosiaster considers Paul to be speaking about belief or unbelief in Jesus Christ. Ambrosiaster differentiates between a natural use of reason and a distorted, perverse use of reason. Gentile Christians "do by nature what the law requires" (Rom 2:14) because they use their reason in accord with its natural inclination toward truth. Since the Mosaic law promises the coming of Christ, to do "what the law requires" is to believe in Christ when he comes. Refusing to believe in Christ despite the powerful evidence in his favor is irrational. Natural law comes into Ambrosiaster's commentary insofar as he argues that even if Gentiles keep natural law by not sinning against humans, Gentiles will perish unless they also believe in God and Christ. Ambrosiaster is adamant that natural law is not a path of salvation.

By interpreting Romans 2:14–15 to be about consciously Christian Gentiles, Ambrosiaster runs into difficulties that do not trouble Origen's interpretation. Above all, it would seem clear that Paul in fact is speaking about Jews and Gentiles in Romans 2, not about Gentile Christians. Perhaps because of Paul's own later affirmation that "all have sinned and fall short of the glory of God" (Rom 3:23),

---

[77] Ambrosiaster, 19. Lunn-Rockliffe points out that for Ambrosiaster, "The new law was less onerous than the Mosaic law and entailed a return to the simplicity of natural law coupled with the ancient, Abrahamic trait of faith" (Lunn-Rockliffe, *Ambrosiaster*, 53).

Ambrosiaster does not take seriously Paul's claims that Gentiles have
the law "written on their hearts" and that some Gentiles "do by nature
what the law requires." But there are other exegetical difficulties as
well. For example, in supposing that doing "by nature what the law
requires" means having faith, he stresses that faith is the exercise of
natural reason responding to the sufficient evidence that has been
provided for God and Christ. If so, then how is faith a gift of grace, as
Paul repeatedly affirms?

2.4.2 Pelagius (c.350–c.430)

Pelagius was a Roman layman who wrote his commentary on the letter to the Romans sometime around 405–410. He does not seem to
have read Chrysostom, but he was familiar with the commentaries of
Origen and Ambrosiaster.[78] He was also writing in response to various works by Augustine, including Augustine's *Propositions from the
Epistle to the Romans* (which Pelagius admired) and *To Simplician*.[79]

In his short treatment of Romans 2:5–16, Pelagius begins with those
who are "storing up wrath" for themselves because of their impeni-
tence. Such persons spurn God's merciful love in Christ, and thereby
"use the very remedy to sustain greater wounds."[80] God has appointed
a day of judgment, which will take place at the end of history. In this
life, good works are often not rewarded, but the day of judgment will
manifest their eternal reward. Pelagius depicts the "glory and honor
and immortality" (Rom 2:7) that the blessed will receive. To attain

---

[78] See Theodore De Bruyn, "Introduction" to *Pelagius's Commentary on St Paul's
Epistle to the Romans*, trans. Theodore De Bruyn (Oxford: Oxford University
Press, 1993), 1–53. De Bruyn translates the critical edition produced by Alexander
Souter: *Pelagius's Expositions of Thirteen Epistles of St Paul* (Cambridge: Cambridge
University Press, 1922–1931). Souter's task was rendered difficult by the fact that
Pelagius's text was revised and augmented twice, first by a Pelagian between 412 and
432, and second by Cassiodorus.

[79] In *To Simplician*, Augustine explains why he changed his views on the relationship between God's grace and human good works/free will, so as now to emphasize
the radical priority of God's grace. For a highly sympathetic treatment of Pelagius's
theology, see Gerald Bonner, *Freedom and Necessity: St. Augustine's Teaching on Divine
Power and Human Freedom* (Washington, D.C.: Catholic University of America
Press, 2007). For further background see also Robert F. Evans, *Pelagius: Inquiries and
Reappraisals* (New York: Seabury Press, 1968); Carol Harrison, *Rethinking Augustine's
Early Theology: An Argument for Continuity* (Oxford: Oxford University Press, 2006).

[80] Pelagius, *Commentary on St Paul's Epistle to the Romans*, 70.

this blessedness, we must seek for it by "patience in well-doing" (Rom 2:7), which God will reward with eternal life. We must strive to be holy by doing works of love, and we should worry if we are frequently falling into strife with our neighbor, especially if such strife is caused by our defending things that are against our conscience.

According to Pelagius, those who "do not obey the truth" (Rom 2:8) are those who reject the gospel of Jesus Christ. Such people serve the creature rather than the Creator, and will experience punishment— God's "wrath and fury" (Rom 2:8)—at the judgment. At the judgment, their repentance will be too late, and they will have "tribulation and distress" (Rom 2:9). Those who do good will receive the promised "glory and honor and peace" (Rom 2:10). Paul's phrase "the Jew first and also the Greek" (Rom 2:9–10) does not mean that the Jewish people are favored by God at the judgment; they are "first in time, not in honour."[81] At the judgment, they will not be able to depend on their privilege of having received the law of Moses and the covenantal sign of circumcision. Nor do the Gentiles, despite their claim to knowledge, possess anything that will give them an advantage at the judgment.

Pelagius interprets Romans 2:12, "All who have sinned without the law will also perish without the law," to refer to the Gentiles, who did not have the written law but instead had only "the law of nature."[82] To "perish" means to be judged a sinner by God on the day of judgment. Paul's contrast between "hearers of the law" and "doers of the law" (Rom 2:13) brings the Jews to the same level as the Gentiles. If all we had to do was to hear the law, then the Jewish people would have a great advantage thanks to the written law of Moses. Since righteousness depends upon doing the law, however, Jews and Gentiles occupy the same ground before God. Pelagius adds that Jews need to have faith in Christ in order to avoid perishing; indeed, as Pelagius later makes clear, to be a doer of the law includes believing in Christ, because "it is also part of the law to believe in him."[83] In this sense, keeping the commandments of the law could, for the Jews prior to Christ, merit eternal life. Christians must be careful to be "doers of the law" rather than merely hearers.

Commenting on Romans 2:14, where Paul says that Gentiles "have not the law," Pelagius points out that if they had no law, there would be

---

[81] Pelagius, 72.   [82] Pelagius, 48.   [83] Pelagius, 122.

no standard by which Gentiles could be judged. In fact, the Gentiles lack the Mosaic law but "they do not lack a law."[84] The Gentiles have a law because "[n]ature produces a law in [their] heart through the testimony of the conscience."[85] We experience this when we sin; our conscience causes us to feel guilty and, when we overcome sin, our conscience rejoices. Pelagius interprets Paul's mention of "conflicting thoughts" that accuse or excuse us (Rom 2:15), as being a reference to the process of free choice. Through Jesus Christ, God will judge us on whether we have chosen properly.

Pelagius also inquires about who are the Gentiles whom Paul is describing. Are they righteous Gentiles who lived before the Mosaic law, such as Melchizedek? Or are they Gentiles "who even now do some good"?[86] Pelagius allows for either interpretation, thereby granting the possibility that even after Christ's coming, there exist righteous non-Christian Gentiles. All humans know good and evil, and all can do good and gain reward from God.

Pelagius's commentary is quite spare, and we might sum it up by noting three points that are especially significant. First, Pelagius finds in Paul's words a strong incentive to constant striving, "by patience in well-doing" (Rom 2:7), for eternal life. Second, he considers that to be a "doer of the law" means to believe in Christ, because Christ is prefigured and prophesied by the law. This is significant because it is "the doers of the law who will be justified" (Rom 2:13). Third, he holds that God judges us through Jesus Christ on the basis of our decision-making, guided by our conscience. We possess a conscience as part of human nature, and our conscience apprehends what is good and what is evil (natural law). All of us, including Gentiles today who do not know Moses or Christ, have the ability to follow conscience and make good moral decisions. If we succeed in making good moral decisions, our conscience will excuse us on the day of judgment, and God will give us eternal life in accord with our good works (cf. Rom 2:6–7).

Like Origen and Chrysostom, then, Pelagius thinks that Romans 2:5–16 has to do largely with the situation of Jews and especially Gentiles prior to Christ, and he also includes Gentiles after Christ. Despite lacking a revelation, the Gentiles never lack a law, and they access this natural law through reason and conscience. Yet he also

---

[84] Pelagius, 73.   [85] Pelagius, 73.   [86] Pelagius, 73.

holds that being a "doer of the law"—with regard to Jews—should mean believing in Christ, since Christ is the fulfillment of the law. By contrast, the Gentiles do not seem to need Christ in order to accomplish the law, so long as they follow their conscience and thus follow the dictates of natural law.

2.4.3 Augustine (354–430)

After a lengthy religious exploration, detailed in his *Confessions*, Augustine received baptism in 387 and devoted most of the remainder of his life to serving as bishop of Hippo in North Africa. His voluminous writings do not include a full commentary on Romans. Nonetheless, given the importance of his insights for later natural law doctrine, it is worth examining here his remarks on Romans 2:14–15 in his *On the Spirit and the Letter*, written around 412 with the goal of refuting a Pelagian view of grace and free will.[87]

Before turning to this text, we should briefly note the central aspects of his teaching elsewhere on natural law. In his *On Free Will*, written around 395, Augustine describes a "law which is called supreme reason, which must always be obeyed, by which the evil deserve an unhappy life and the good a blessed life, [and] by which the law we have agreed to call temporal is rightly laid down and rightly changed."[88] Drawing on Cicero and others, Augustine terms this law or supreme reason "eternal law." It is the divine order of all

---

[87] See also Augustine's very brief discussion of Romans 2:15—in which he uses the phrase "lex naturalis"—in his *De sermone Domini in monte* II.32. In *Confessions* II.4 and in his commentary on Psalm 58, he uses the phrase "lex scripta in cordis hominum." For these references, I am indebted to Taylor Marshall. For further references see Richard J. Dougherty, "Natural Law," in *Augustine through the Ages: An Encyclopedia*, ed. Allan D. Fitzgerald, O.S.A. (Grand Rapids, MI: Eerdmans, 1999), 582–4. Augustine's treatment of Romans 2:13–16 in his various works has been analyzed by Simon J. Gathercole, "A Conversion of Augustine: From Natural Law to Restored Nature in Romans 2:13–16," in *Engaging Augustine on Romans: Self, Context, and Theology in Interpretation*, ed. Daniel Patte and Eugene TeSelle (Harrisburg, PA: Trinity Press International, 2002), 147–70. Gathercole shows that "the shift between *On the Spirit and the Letter* and *Against Julian* lies in Augustine's greater reluctance to admit the validity of the 'non-Christian' reading of 2:13–16, and his greater emphasis on the exclusion of reference to *veras virtutes*" (167–68). Even so, Augustine's interpretations of Romans 2:13–16 in *On the Spirit and the Letter* and *Against Julian* are basically the same, and so I do not treat *Against Julian* here. Gathercole's work is also helpful for introducing contemporary biblical scholarship on these verses.

[88] Augustine, *On Free Will*, in Augustine, *Earlier Writings*, ed. and trans. J. H. S. Burleigh (Louisville, KY: Westminster John Knox Press, 2006), 113–217, at 120–21.

things to their proper ends. So as to obey eternal law and to make temporal laws in light of it, we must participate in eternal law. This participation of human reason in "supreme reason" is what is meant by natural law.[89] Similarly, in *Answer to Faustus, a Manichean*, probably written around 408, Augustine affirms that sin is "contrary to the eternal law."[90] He defines eternal law as "the divine reason or the will of God, which commands that the natural order be preserved and forbids that it be disturbed."[91] The "natural order" here is the God-given order regarding the teleological flourishing of created things. In human beings, this order requires that we love God above created things, for example. Again, we know this order through our rational participation in God's eternal law (i.e., through natural law). In *City of God*, too, Augustine observes in a crucial passage that "peace between mortal man and God is an ordered obedience, in faith, in subjection to an everlasting law" and that "the peace of the whole universe is the tranquillity of order," which will be fully achieved eschatologically.[92]

Given this background, let me turn to Augustine's discussion of Romans 2:14–15 in his *On the Spirit and the Letter*. In this work, Augustine wishes to show that "to lead a holy life is the gift of God," not only as regards God's gift of free will or God's gift of the Mosaic law, but also as regards the necessity for fallen humans of the grace of the Holy Spirit.[93] His opponents hold that "without God's help the

---

[89] Following Augustine, Thomas Aquinas states that "the rational creature is subject to divine providence in the most excellent way, in so far as it partakes of a share of providence, by being provident both for itself and for others. Wherefore it has a share of the eternal reason, whereby it has a natural inclination to its proper act and end: and this participation of the eternal law in the rational creature is called the natural law." See Thomas Aquinas, *Summa theologiae*, I-II, q. 91, a. 2, trans. the Fathers of the English Dominican Province (Westminster, MD: Christian Classics, 1981 [1920]).

[90] Augustine, *Answer to Faustus, a Manichean*, trans. Roland J. Teske, SJ (Hyde Park, NY: New City Press, 2007), XXII.27, 317.

[91] Augustine, *Answer to Faustus, a Manichean*, 317.

[92] Augustine, *City of God*, trans. Henry Bettenson (New York: Penguin, 1984), XIX.13, 870. For discussion see Peter Slater, "Goodness as Order and Harmony in Augustine," in *Augustine: From Rhetor to Theologian*, ed. Joanne McWilliam (Waterloo, Ontario: Wilfrid Laurier University Press, 1992), 151–59; Oliver O'Donovan, "The Political Thought of *City of God* 19," in Oliver O'Donovan and Joan Lockwood O'Donovan, *Bonds of Imperfection: Christian Politics, Past and Present* (Grand Rapids, MI: Eerdmans, 2004), 48–72.

[93] Augustine, *On the Spirit and the Letter*, in Augustine, *Anti-Pelagian Works*, trans. Peter Holmes and Robert Ernest Wallis, revised by Benjamin B. Warfield, Nicene and Post-Nicene Fathers, First Series, vol. 5 (Peabody, MA: Hendrickson, 1995 [1887]), 83–114, at 85.

mere power of the human will in itself can either perfect righteousness, or advance steadily towards it," so that by God's instruction about what to desire and what to avoid, and by free will, a person can persevere in a righteous life and can merit "to attain to the blessedness of eternal life."[94] Augustine argues on the contrary that "even man's righteousness must be attributed to the operation of God, although not taking place without man's will."[95]

In making this case, Augustine treats numerous biblical passages, but I will focus on his interpretation of Romans 2:14–15. How can Paul say that the Gentiles "show that what the law requires is written on their hearts" (Rom 2:15), given that God promised that in the new covenant, "I [God] will put my law within them, and I will write it upon their hearts" (Jer 31:33)? In other words, does God promise through Jeremiah to do for Israel what he has *already* done for the Gentiles? Augustine recognizes that this would be absurd. It would mean not only that Israel was worse off than the Gentiles, but also that the new covenant itself merely advances the followers of Christ to the level of the Gentiles, which most Christians were already.

Augustine therefore proposes a possible solution: perhaps the Gentiles to which Paul refers already possess the grace of the Holy Spirit. Augustine holds that people could and did—through faith—receive the grace of the Holy Spirit prior to Christ's coming, even in times and places where no explicit knowledge of Christ was available. In Romans 1, Paul has been speaking about the power of the gospel and of faith: the gospel "is the power of God for salvation to every one who has faith, to the Jew first and also to the Greek. For in it the righteousness of God is revealed through faith for faith; as it is written, 'He who through faith is righteous shall live'" (Rom 1:16–17). The remainder of Romans 1 condemns the Gentiles for unrighteousness: they knew God through the creation, but they turned away from God and worshipped creatures, with the result that "God gave them up to a base mind and to improper conduct" (Rom 1:28). The beginning of Romans 2 then warns all humans against judging each other, because all humans are sinners and under the just judgment of God. Augustine quotes Romans 2:9–13, which, as we have seen, promises punishment for those who do evil and reward for those who do good, that is, for Jewish and Gentile "doers of the law" (Rom 2:13).

---

[94] Augustine, 84.   [95] Augustine, 85.

As Augustine notes, Paul interchangeably uses "Gentile" and "Greek." The Gentile of Romans 2:10 is the same "Greek" for whom the gospel "is the power of God for salvation to every one who has faith" (Rom 1:16). He concludes that this same "Greek" is the Gentile of Romans 2:14, and so the Gentile of Romans 2:14 has faith. Indeed, without "the grace of the gospel," no Gentile could be promised "glory and honor and peace" (Rom 2:10) for his or her good works.[96] If Gentiles (or Jews) could "be justified" without faith, Paul's quotation of Habakkuk 2:4, "He who through faith is righteous shall live" (Rom 1:17), would be emptied of real meaning. If Gentiles could be justified without faith, then Paul could not say that "since all have sinned and fall short of the glory of God, they are justified by his grace as a gift, through the redemption which is in Christ Jesus" (Rom 3:23–24). If Romans 2:14–15 and Romans 2:10 mean that the Gentiles justify themselves by their good works, Paul would be contradicting his insistence that God "justifies him who has faith in Jesus" and that all persons, Jews and Gentiles, are "justified by faith apart from works of the law" (Rom 3:26, 28). As Paul goes on to say, "But if it is by grace, it is no longer on the basis of works; otherwise grace would no longer be grace" (Rom 11:6). The "doers of the law" certainly "will be justified," but this is because as doers of the law, they are already just persons (or, at least, are already accounted just by God). God's grace has caused them to be the kind of people who do the law. If so, then these Gentiles belong to the Israel of the new covenant, the Israel that God prophesied through Jeremiah.

What about Paul's statement that "by nature" some Gentiles do "what the law requires" (Rom 2:14)? If it is by nature, how can we say that it is by grace, without contradicting Paul? Something that is done by nature typically indicates a natural ability that does not require the added gift of the grace of the Holy Spirit. Augustine answers that something that is done by nature can in fact also be done by grace, when the Holy Spirit restores "in us the image of God, in which we were naturally created."[97] Given human nature's fallen condition, there are some things that we were created to do by nature, for which we now need the aid of grace healing and restoring our nature. If one considers human nature per se, then one can rightly say that "it is by nature that men do the things which are contained in the law."[98] All sin is contrary to human nature, which naturally inclines toward

---

[96] Augustine, 101.   [97] Augustine, 103.   [98] Augustine, 103.

the good of human flourishing. To do what is natural, fallen human nature now needs to be healed by grace. Augustine goes so far as to suggest that God's law has been erased in fallen humans; grace must restore fallen human nature by writing the law afresh in the heart. As he remarks, "By this grace there is written on the renewed inner man that righteousness which sin had blotted out; and this mercy comes upon the human race through our Lord Jesus Christ."[99]

Augustine adds that some think that when Paul refers to Gentiles who "do by nature what the law requires," Paul has in mind people who have not received Christ's grace but who nonetheless quite evidently do many good and praiseworthy deeds, even if their motive is not rooted in charity. On this view, there are many people who can do good deeds despite their fallen condition, because the image of God in them has been obscured but not erased by sin; "what was impressed on their hearts when they were created in the image of God has not been wholly blotted out."[100] In response, Augustine grants that God's law in the human heart cannot be "wholly blotted out" by sin. Sin does not destroy our rational powers, which include some ability to know what is good and what evil. Without grace, both Jews and Gentiles certainly possess "that power of nature, which enables the rational soul both to perceive and do what is lawful."[101] But without grace, they are unable to be holy, and so they remain turned away from God. Their actions are a mixture of good and evil, so that "their conflicting thoughts accuse or perhaps excuse them" (Rom 2:15). Yet "on that day when…God judges the secrets of men by Christ Jesus" (Rom 2:16), they will still lack the righteousness needed to be united to God. As Augustine says, "there are some good works which are of no avail to an ungodly man towards the attainment of everlasting life."[102]

In Augustine's view, then, two solutions are possible: it may be that Paul has in view Gentiles who have been justified by faith, even if they lived in times and places where explicit knowledge of Christ was unavailable; or it may be that Paul is thinking of Gentiles who do some good (thanks to the fact that the image of God is not destroyed by sin) and whose good works are valued by God when they come to have faith. Either way, the main point is that without grace humans cannot be "doers of the law who will be justified" (Rom 2:13). The best

---

[99] Augustine, 103.
[100] Augustine, 103.
[101] Augustine, 103.
[102] Augustine, 104.

anyone can do without grace is to do some good works that demonstrate that the knowledge of good and evil, while obscured, cannot be obliterated in the image of God.

Augustine emphasizes that through the mercy of Christ, we receive the Holy Spirit in our hearts and are filled with the love of God, a love that leads us into everlasting communion with God. Even though we cannot avoid venial sins in this life, nonetheless by faith in the merciful Redeemer we can be forgiven and the image of God in us can be renewed and elevated. The indwelling Holy Spirit enables us to do works of love that merit the gift of eternal life. Grace is necessary for justification and for deification; only by Christ's grace can fallen humans receive the promised "glory and honor and peace for every one who does good, the Jew first and also the Greek."[103] Although grace is here inextricably linked with faith in Christ, it is worth repeating that for Augustine, such faith is possible even for those who do not know Christ explicitly.

2.5 CONCLUSION

With regard to how natural law should be conceived and to the relationship of universal natural law to Christian discipleship, what might we learn from these early Christian theologians? Origen insists that Israel's God is the good Creator of all humans, and that natural law is one way that God cares for the Gentiles. For Origen, the precepts of natural law can be identified simply by reflecting on the limits imposed by the Golden Rule, "Whatever you wish that men would do to you, do so to them; for this is the law and the prophets" (Mt 7:12). These limits can be found preeminently in the precepts of the Decalogue. Origen argues that natural law does not include the mode by which we observe the law, for example humility and charity. By embodying and commanding this mode, Jesus teaches a morality that goes beyond natural law. Lastly, Origen notes that we all need a merciful Redeemer because otherwise our sins would not be expiated and we could not share in God's righteousness. John Chrysostom likewise highlights God's providence for the Gentiles, including Melchizedek and Job. Natural law is a means by which the Gentiles participate in God's providential plan for

---

[103] Augustine, 104.

human fulfillment, although everyone needs the merciful Redeemer so as to be able to stand before God at the final judgment.

Arguing that faith in Jesus Christ is rational, Ambrosiaster wards off the supposition that natural law pertains to universal reason whereas faith is opposed to such reason. Lest it appear that God leads non-Christians by way of natural law and Christians by way of Christ, Ambrosiaster shows that Christians too must follow and obey the precepts of natural law, and he makes clear that natural law alone is not a salvific path. For his part, Pelagius insists that the Gentiles have a law—natural law—and that even after Christ's coming, there can be righteous Gentiles. Augustine shows that the image of God in us needs to be renewed by grace so that we can better understand and obey the precepts of natural law. Crucially, he affirms that humans can be united to the salvation won by Christ, even when such persons do not have explicit knowledge of Christ. But he notes that without grace, humans cannot sufficiently obey natural law so as to be righteous; Paul does not intend for what he says about the law written on the heart to be placed in opposition to the universal need to be "justified by [God's] grace as a gift, through the redemption which is in Christ Jesus" (Rom 3:24). Augustine's discussion of "eternal law" clarifies that natural law is human reason's participation in God's wisdom regarding the actions that conduce to human flourishing.

These early Christian theologians, then, understand Paul to be speaking about natural law in Romans 2:5–16, although they differ with regard to its value for eternal reward and to the status of the Jews and Gentiles envisioned by Paul. Like Paul, they embed the topic of natural law within a host of other theological and philosophical issues, including the value of free choice, degrees of righteousness, the need of all people for a Redeemer, grace, the reasonableness of faith, implicit faith, the coming judgment, and eternal life. For this reason, I think that their efforts to reflect upon natural law as a universal possession of human nature, in light of the particularity of divine revelation and salvation in Jesus Christ, can benefit contemporary natural law discussions, perhaps especially within an interreligious framework.[104] Specifically, I suggest that we might broadly derive from these early Christian thinkers the following seven theses as a constructive conclusion to this study.

---

[104] This is true even if some of their views require emendation, as can be seen, for example, by comparing their views on the Jewish people with the teaching of the Second Vatican Council's *Nostra Aetate* (in *Vatican Council II*, vol. 1: *The Conciliar and*

The first four theses pertain to the relationship of natural law to Christian discipleship, which as we have seen was an issue of particular importance to the Fathers. As noted above, this relationship remains a controversial one today in Christian moral theology, and it is pressing as well for questions regarding the status of non-Christians in God's plan of salvation, an important topic for the Second Vatican Council.[105] My four theses seek to integrate elements that we found in various Fathers and in Paul, while avoiding the theological and inter-religious pitfalls that some of the Fathers fell into.

Postconciliar Documents, new revised edition, ed. Austin Flannery, O.P. [Northport, NY: Costello Publishing Company, 1996], 738–42). See also Paula Fredriksen, *Augustine and the Jews: A Christian Defense of Jews and Judaism* (New York: Doubleday, 2008); Robert Louis Wilken, *John Chrysostom and the Jews: Rhetoric and Reality in the 4th Century* (Eugene, OR: Wipf & Stock, 2004).

[105] See the Second Vatican Council's Dogmatic Constitution on the Church, *Lumen Gentium*, no. 16: "Finally, those who have not yet received the Gospel are related to the People of God in various ways. There is, first, that people to which the covenants and promises were made, and from which Christ was born according to the flesh (cf. Rom. 9:4–5): in view of the divine choice, they are a people most dear for the sake of the fathers, for the gifts of God are without repentance (cf. Rom. 11:28–29). But the plan of salvation also includes those who acknowledge the Creator, in the first place amongst whom are the Muslims: these profess to hold the faith of Abraham, and together with us they adore the one, merciful God, mankind's judge on the last day. Nor is God remote from those who in shadows and images seek the unknown God, since he gives to all men life and breath and all things (cf. Acts 17:25–28), and since the Saviour wills all men to be saved (cf. 1 Tim. 2:4). Those who, through no fault of their own, do not know the Gospel of Christ or his Church, but who nevertheless seek God with a sincere heart, and, moved by grace, try in their actions to do his will as they know it through the dictates of their conscience—those too may achieve eternal salvation. Nor shall divine providence deny the assistance necessary for salvation to those who, without any fault of theirs, have no yet arrived at an explicit knowledge of God, and who, not without grace, strive to lead a good life" (*Vatican Council II*, 367–68). For discussion of this point in relation to the Congregation for the Doctrine of the Faith's *Dominus Iesus* (2000) and to the perspectives of Joseph Ratzinger and Jacques Dupuis, SJ, see Edward T. Oakes, SJ, *Infinity Dwindled to Infancy: A Catholic and Evangelical Christology* (Grand Rapids, MI: Eerdmans, 2011), 408–17, 429–30. For further discussion see Avery Dulles, SJ, "Who Can Be Saved?," in Dulles, *Church and Society: The Laurence J. McGinley Lectures, 1988–2007* (New York: Fordham University Press, 2008), 522–34. It remains the case, however, that as Ralph Martin observes (in light of Paul's letter to the Romans and paragraphs 16 and 17 of *Lumen Gentium*), "vast numbers of people within and without the Church do not appear to be seeking God and trying to do his will, following the light of their consciences, but are rather exchanging the truth of God for a lie, suppressing the truth, and living in rebellion and immorality, needing desperately to be invited to faith and repentance in order to be saved" (Martin, *Will Many Be Saved? What Vatican II Actually Teaches and Its Implications for the New Evangelization* [Grand Rapids, MI: Eerdmans, 2012], 202).

(1) Natural law does not obviate the need for the grace of the Holy Spirit and the work of Jesus Christ. The knowledge of the precepts of natural law does not mean that we will observe them, or that our outward observance of them will be matched by our interior attitude. For example, natural law teaches us to honor our parents, but we can sometimes honor them outwardly without loving them interiorly. The exterior action signals our interior righteousness only if the spirit with which we honor our parents is one of love. Furthermore, our sinfulness obscures the precepts of natural law and makes it impossible for us to know them adequately, let alone to observe them rightly. We need to be renewed and transformed by the grace of the Holy Spirit; we need a Redeemer by whom our sins are forgiven, so that we might be reconciled to God and be the righteous people that God created us to be.[106]

(2) In following conscience and striving to act justly to God and neighbor, humans may be moved by grace that unites them to the salvation won by Christ, even without knowing Christ explicitly. This explains the presence in the Bible of righteous Gentiles such as Melchizedek and Job. Grace is not limited to the time after Christ. God cares for all humans, and not just for the people of God. Those who are not members of the visible people of God (Israel/Church) are cared for by God in various ways, including natural law that enables them to distinguish right from wrong.

(3) Like all humans, Christians possess natural law and are required to live by its precepts. Imitating Christ would not suffice, indeed would not be possible, if Christians lacked natural law. Put another way, the cruciform moral path of Christians should not be set at odds with the natural law precepts that one finds in the Golden Rule and the Decalogue, as Jesus himself affirmed. Part of the task of Christian natural law doctrine, then, is to remind Christians of what Christians should be doing, rather than solely to call upon others to value the dignity of all human persons.

---

[106] See Russell Hittinger, "Human Nature and States of Nature in John Paul II's Theological Anthropology," in *Human Nature in Its Wholeness: A Roman Catholic Perspective*, ed. Daniel N. Robinson, Gladys M. Sweeney, and Richard Gill (Washington, D.C.: Catholic University of America Press, 2006), 9–33.

(4) Natural law doctrine helps to affirm God's universal providence and God's desire to save all humans (see 1 Tm 2:4). Natural law doctrine affirms the worth of each human being. It shows that there are certain things that no human being or institution can rightly do to other humans.[107] It upholds the moral value of free choice, so that oppressors in every society are distinguishable from those whom they oppress. Since God "will render to every man according to his works" (Rom 2:6), natural law doctrine supports the obvious point that moral knowledge and praiseworthy works are by no means limited to Christians.

The final three theses have to do with philosophical issues regarding natural law doctrine. Theological reflection has to balance natural law and discipleship, reason and Scripture, sin and salvation. Philosophical reflection, by contrast, asks what kind of "law" natural law is, where it comes from, how we discern it, and other such questions. It seems to me that Paul and the early Christian theologians, all of whom exhibit the influence of Hellenistic philosophy, can give us some guidance on these matters.

(5) Natural law is our participation in God's eternal law, and it is constituted and promulgated by the Creator God, who imprints it on our hearts. Although people can know natural law precepts without recognizing God, therefore, natural law doctrine requires the recognition of a divine lawgiver.[108] As a rational sharing in God's providence, natural law is ordered toward human fulfillment or human flourishing, which involves hierarchically ordered ends or goals.[109] The teleological character of natural law, its rootedness in human inclinations (shaped by human rationality), follows from the fact that God creates

---

[107] See Matthew Levering, *Jewish-Christian Dialogue and the Life of Wisdom: Engagements with the Theology of David Novak* (London: Continuum, 2010), chapters 3 and 4.

[108] See J. Budziszewski, *The Line through the Heart: Natural Law as Fact, Theory, and Sign of Contradiction* (Wilmington, DE: ISI Books, 2009), 23–40; Fulvio Di Blasi, *God and the Natural Law: A Rereading of Thomas Aquinas*, trans. David Thunder (South Bend, IN: St. Augustine's Press, 2006); Levering, *Biblical Natural Law*, especially chapter 2.

[109] For Thomas Aquinas, the general principles of natural law have their root in our pursuit of good and avoidance of evil; thus at a basic level "whatever is a means of preserving human life, and warding off its obstacles, belongs to natural law" (*Summa theologiae*, I-II, q. 94, a. 2).

humans in his image and for the goal of communion with God and with fellow humans.[110]

(6) Human positive law is properly grounded upon natural law. Murder would still be wrong even if the positive law of a particular society approved murder.[111] People know by natural law, for example, that the preservation of human life is good and thus that murder is evil. Law is not solely a historical and cultural construct, according to which certain actions are right or wrong depending upon the time and place. Some actions are simply wrong, because they violate God's law which we know, however imperfectly, by natural law.

(7) Human sinfulness obscures, but does not eliminate, our ability to perceive the precepts of natural law.[112] One of the common rebuttals to natural law doctrine is that human beings have not been able to agree on its content. With the exception of certain basic precepts, such as the prohibition against murder, people often disagree about what natural law entails. Even with regard to murder, people differ as to when the killing of another human being is actually "murder" and therefore falls under the prohibition. People have different conceptions of what human flourishing involves. The fact that sin obscures but does not obliterate the perception of natural law makes sense of what

---

[110] For further discussion see Servais Pinckaers, O.P., *The Sources of Christian Ethics*, trans. Mary Thomas Noble, O.P. (Washington, D.C.: Catholic University of America Press, 1995), 400–56; Stephen L. Brock, "National Inclination and the Intelligibility of the Good in Thomistic Natural Law," *Vera Lex* 6 (2005): 57–78; Steven A. Long, "Teleology, Divine Governance, and the Common Good—Reflections on the ITC's *The Search for Universal Ethics: A New Look at Natural Law*," *Nova et Vetera* 9 (2011): 775–89, at 776–80; Jean Porter, *Nature as Reason: A Thomistic Theory of the Natural Law* (Grand Rapids, MI: Eerdmans, 2005), chapter 2; Jean De Groot, "Teleology and Evidence: Reasoning about Human Nature," in *Natural Moral Law in Contemporary Society*, ed. Holger Zaborowski, 141–69. See also Alasdair MacIntyre, *Dependent Rational Animals: Why Human Beings Need the Virtues* (Chicago: Open Court, 1999); David Oderberg, "The Metaphysical Foundations of Natural Law," in *Natural Moral Law in Contemporary Society*, ed. Holger Zaborowski, 44–75.

[111] See especially Hadley Arkes, *Constitutional Illusions and Anchoring Truths: The Touchstone of the Natural Law* (Cambridge: Cambridge University Press, 2010).

[112] Aquinas considers that with respect to practical reasoning, sin can obscure even the general principles of natural law—and sin more easily obscures the precepts that should follow from these principles. This happens "either by evil persuasions...or by vicious customs and corrupt habits, as among some men, theft, and even unnatural vices, as the Apostle states (Rom. i), were not esteemed sinful" (*Summa theologiae*, I-II, q. 94, a. 6).

would otherwise be a strange paradox, namely that both the Torah and Jesus Christ reveal precepts that belong to natural law. The obscuring of natural law also helps to explain the historical variance with respect to what has counted as the content of natural law. Over the course of history, and for all sorts of historical reasons, different individuals and societies will perceive the precepts of natural law more or less clearly.

The Fathers that I have examined in this essay, along with Paul, focus on how natural law fits with salvation through Jesus Christ and the grace of the Holy Spirit. In this essay, therefore, I have hardly cleared up all questions; indeed, the variety of patristic approaches and the difficulty of Pauline exegesis make for an array of challenges. But the example of the Pauline and patristic approaches to natural law doctrine will be especially instructive to religious thinkers who wish to appreciate the character and significance of natural law without relegating revelation to a secondary role in the moral life.

Response to Matthew Levering's "Christians and Natural Law"

Anver M. Emon

Matthew Levering's learned article on natural law doctrines in the patristic period reveals a diversity of approaches to fundamental questions of *Christian* natural law. I emphasize the adjective *Christian* to bring to the fore a fundamental issue that casts a shadow on most natural law debates, and certainly the contributions in this book. That skulking issue is *difference*. It casts shadows in the sense that it is a principal antagonist for natural law theorists, at least as long as natural law is associated with universal value claims knowable by human reason, a faculty all people share regardless of their various forms of bounded identities. While some might argue, and quite correctly, that this is a far too simplistic or reductive notion of natural law, this notion nonetheless captures a core idea in natural law debates that certainly finds expression in the pages of this collection. To bring to the forefront the concern about difference, and juxtapose it with natural law might seem to admit defeat for those committed to universal claims of value that all can experience firsthand, given a shared human capacity to reason. Yet, Levering (and Novak as well) shows how a recognition of difference need not preclude natural legal reasoning. Rather, as this response to Levering will suggest, religious natural law traditions, such as those delineated in this book, not only espouse theologies and philosophies of natural legal reasoning, but in doing so, also reveal how natural legal reasoning does not occur *ex nihilo*. Natural law arguments come from somewhere; and to be intelligible as a particular "somewhere" implies the need to think about boundaries—boundaries of inclusion and exclusion that help constitute the very enterprise of natural law thinking.

This response consists of three parts. Part I will return to Levering's analysis of the patristic theologians using the lens of difference. Difference as a lens will illustrate that Levering is doing more than asking "what is natural law?" or even "what is Christian natural law?" The theological dimension of his analysis poses a perplexing question that challenged each theologian he addresses, namely, how inclusive can a natural law theory be before it undermines the boundaries that help define a faith community. The question of inclusion and its corollary of exclusion are implicit (though often explicit) throughout Levering's analysis. Returning to the patristic arguments for natural law in light of Romans 2—but with attention to the dynamic of difference, inclusion, and exclusion—raises further questions about whether and to what degree a natural law theory can (or even ought to) transcend boundaries of inclusion and exclusion. Part II will juxtapose Levering's analysis of patristic theories of natural law with Islamic natural law theories to illustrate how the doctrines across both traditions situate their natural law doctrines. For Levering's patristic theologians, natural law is situated in relationship to faith in Christ Jesus as the Redeemer. There is a fascinating comparison to be made between the arguments among the patristic theologians about the salvation of those who do not know Jesus or Moses (i.e., before the coming of Christ Jesus) and the arguments by Muslim jurists about the authority of reason as a matter of law "before revelation" (*min qablu wurud al-shar*'). In both cases, the debates in each tradition are framed in terms of time (e.g., before Jesus' coming, before revelation). As will be suggested, though, time functions as a place-holder for a type of absence or void into which natural law theories are fit. The problem for patristic and Muslim natural law exponents is what remains of natural law when there is no such void, or in other words, after Jesus has come or after revelation came to Muhammad. Part III is designed to contrast the Islamic example with the patristic accounts Levering shares by returning to the lens of inclusion and exclusion. As will be shown in Part I, Levering's essay suggests that the Church Fathers developed their natural law doctrines in part by addressing the salvation of the religious Other—the Jew and non-Christian Gentile—who might nonetheless participate in natural reasoning. In the Islamic legal context, the religious Other appears elsewhere, as part of a different but equally compelling debate about obligation (*taklif*). Muslim jurists debated whether and to what extent non-Muslim permanent residents in Islamic lands (i.e., *dhimmis*) could be obligated to abide by Islamic law, which they argued is based on a scriptural source (i.e., the Qur'an) in which non-Muslims do not believe. For some jurists, the *dhimmis* were obligated to abide by the Shari'a-based doctrines on account of their shared human capacity to reason to the same conclusions of Shari'a-doctrines. Others disagreed that a universal, shared reason was sufficient to establish the *dhimmis'* obligation to Shari'a. Instead they argued that the basis and scope of the *dhimmis'* obligation to Shari'a are founded upon the contract of protection (*'aqd al-dhimma*), which *dhimmis* are presumed to accede to and by which they abide. By focusing on obligation and the religious Other, Part III highlights how claims about universal and shared reason— whether in debates on natural law or obligation—cannot escape the specter of difference that certainly animated the Church Fathers and pre-modern Muslim jurists.

I NATURAL LAW, RELIGION, AND RELIGION'S OTHER

A reading of Levering's essay shows that he is not simply trying to answer in the abstract "what is natural law?," or even "what is Christian natural law?" from some purely philosophical perspective argued or posited from nowhere in particular. Rather he asks "what is natural law" from a specifically Christian perspective, and thus inserts into what might be a philosophical question a different dimension, namely the theological one. The theological dimension does not merely pose a question about God, but more fundamentally asks whether and to what extent a robust account of natural law might have the side-effect of performing an end-run around central tenets of Christian faith, such as belief in Jesus Christ as the Redeemer. Indeed, Levering's analysis of each patristic theologian, from Origen to Augustine, reveals how each theologian grappled with this possible consequence of a natural law doctrine.

According to Levering, Origen recognized that Gentiles who believed in neither Moses nor Jesus nonetheless did good works, which they knew were good by virtue of natural reason. The good works of these Gentiles, Origen argued, would not go unrewarded. Indeed, that was Origen's understanding of Romans 2:6, according to Levering ("[God,] who will render to every man according to his deeds"). But as Levering notes, reward for doing good works is different from being saved; the latter requires faith and baptism. As much as Origen argued that good works would allow one to be saved—whether Gentile, Jew, Christian, or non-Christian—he could not avoid addressing whether being saved by good works provides a natural law end-run around the centrality in Christianity of faith in Jesus Christ as redeemer. As Levering shows, Origen made clear that since all people were sinners, there was no real possibility of redemption before the glory of God without a redeemer whose purity and holiness provides a bridge of mercy that permits the sinner to pass into the eternal life. As Levering writes, "Natural law, then, is not enough for sharing in God's righteousness and glory. We need a Redeemer to forgive our sins by the shedding of his blood, and this Redeemer must be perfectly holy."[1] In other words, as much as Gentile non-Christians could engage in natural law thinking, that alone could not ensure their salvation. Does that mean that without faith in Christ as Redeemer, these Gentile non-Christian natural reasoners will necessarily perish in eternity? According to Origen, that is not the case since Jesus was a redeemer not only for Christians but also the whole world. Quoting Origen, Levering writes: "Jesus is the propitiator not only of believers and the faithful but also of the whole world; yet not first the world and then of us, but first of us and only then of the whole world."[2] Jesus as Redeemer has come to redeem all who inhabit the world. In fact, Origen makes clear that even those without faith and baptism, but who "do by nature what the law requires" (Rom 2:14) can still enjoy salvation. Levering's analysis of Origen showcases a fascinating example of an early Christian theologian thinking about his faith and the possibility of salvation in the most capacious manner possible. Nonetheless, difference remains an important point for Origen. Reading Levering's analysis of Origen with an attentiveness to difference, one cannot escape noticing how Origen's global salvific aspirations remain beset by the imperative of difference. As much as Christ is a redeemer for the whole world, he is first for "us" and only thereafter for the rest.

---

[1] Levering, section 2.3.1.
[2] Levering, section 2.3.1.

Levering's account of Ambrosiaster so emphasizes difference that those hoping for a universalist account of natural law will surely be disappointed. In his commentary on Romans 2, Ambrosiaster was not concerned with good non-Christian Gentiles as Origen was. Rather, Ambrosiaster held that Gentiles could obey the natural law but still perish. According to Levering's reading of Ambrosiaster, "even if we avoid sinning against our fellow humans—a temporal righteousness—we are still not in a right relationship with God. Without faith, the Gentiles cannot know the true God and thus they cannot receive eternal righteousness."[3] Consequently, when Paul wrote in Romans 2 about the Gentiles who did not have the law, but did by nature what the law demanded, Ambrosiaster presumed the Gentiles in question to be Christian Gentiles, namely those without the law of Moses (i.e., the Jews), but with faith in Christ. [4] Consequently Ambrosiaster's view of natural law was couched within a paradigm of faith and disbelief. Those who believe in Christ will exercise a natural reason, while those who do not believe will exercise perverted reason. Nonetheless, it is noteworthy that the frame of faith and disbelief allowed Ambrosiaster to espouse a natural law doctrine without running the risk of transcending the very boundary that for him made possible a Christian identity.

John Chrysostom also worried about natural law as an end-run around faith in Christ as the path to salvation. He located this concern in Romans, where Paul wrote: "but glory and honor and peace for every one who does good, the Jew first and then the Greek" (Rom 2:10). According to Levering, Chrysostom argued that Paul was here referring to Jews and Greeks who lived *before* Christ's coming.[5] As Levering notes: "in Chrysostom's view, Paul's earlier words about God rendering 'to every man according to his works' and God giving eternal life 'to those who by patience in well-doing seek for glory and honor and immortality' (Rom 2:6–7) also have in view the era *before* Christ's coming."[6] According to Levering, Chrysostom's aim was to ensure that prior to Christ's coming, the Jew did not have an advantage over the Gentile, given the former's commitment to the law of Moses. Consequently, after the coming of Christ, Chrysostom believed that

---

[3] Levering, section 2.4.1.
[4] Levering, section 2.4.1.
[5] Levering, section 2.3.2.
[6] Levering, section 2.3.2 (emphasis added).

Jews should not look askance at or stand back from Gentiles. Indeed, both were equally capable of salvation prior to Christ's coming, the Jew in terms of the law of Moses and the Gentile in terms of the natural law. As Levering writes, Chrysostom's view of Romans 2:14 is that "Paul is insisting that the Jewish people, despite the privilege of receiving God's law, did not have an exclusive access to God's law."[7]

Importantly, after Christ's coming, Chrysostom argued that the very enterprise of natural reasoning changed. As Levering shows, Chrysostom viewed the coming of Christ as re-calibrating the natural reason that once paved the way to salvation. Christ as Redeemer provides the bridge to salvation for a world of sinners. Though natural legal reasoning may have led people to salvation *before* the coming of Christ, natural reason *after* Christ's will point us all toward belief in Christ as the merciful redeemer who will help us face our sins, transcend our fears, and find eternal life when we are confronted with our deeds on Judgment Day. Consequently, for Chrysostom's theory of natural law, the differences that matter are faith and disbelief on the one hand, and living before or after Christ's coming on the other hand. Prior to Christ's coming, the difference between Jew and Gentile did not preclude either from salvation through natural law. After Christ's coming, both were still able to engage in natural law thinking. But the historical discontinuity posed by Christ's presence in history so altered the world that natural reasoning itself transformed. After Jesus' coming, natural reasoning for Chrysostom was not geared toward pursuing good deeds that would lead to salvation. After Jesus' coming, natural reasoning leads one toward faith in Jesus Christ as redeemer, which thereby becomes an important, constitutive element of any route to salvation.

As much as we might find Origen and Chrysostom striving for a capacious theology to make salvation possible for the unbeliever who nonetheless reasons to the natural law, Pelagius seemed to go slightly further in the case of Gentile non-Christians living after the coming of Christ. On Levering's account, Pelagius made clear that to be a "do-er" of the law requires believing in Christ. Prior to Christ's coming, Jews who abided by the Mosaic law were do-ers and thereby merited eternal life. Likewise Gentles before the coming of Christ had the natural law imprinted on their hearts; they too were not without a law. In this sense,

---

[7] Levering, section 2.3.2.

much like Chrysostom, Pelagius relied on the difference of time to provide a capacious account of natural law that allowed non-Christians (prior to Christ's coming) to be saved. But what about the Jews and Gentiles *after* Christ's coming? On the Jews, Pelagius argued that one feature of the Mosaic law was that it prefigured and prophesied Jesus as Redeemer and a bridge to salvation. Consequently, Pelagius argued that to be a do-er of the Jewish law required having faith in Jesus as the Redeemer through which we can find our route to eternal life. On Gentiles, Pelagius granted "the possibility that even after Christ's coming, there exist righteous non-Christian Gentiles."[8] In Pelagius' case, therefore, the capacity of natural law to make an end-run around faith in Christ seems to exist, but only in the case of non-Christian Gentiles after the coming of Christ. These Gentiles, though without faith in Christ as Redeemer, are nonetheless capable of making good and moral choices, and thereby merit eternal life on the Day of Judgment.

Whether or not Pelagius considered his argument about non-Christian Gentiles an end-run around faith in Christ, his position certainly raises a fascinating counter-example to the other theologians addressed above who recognized difference as both inclusive and exclusive, and thereby as constitutive of what makes being "Christian" intelligible. Indeed, Pelagius' expansion of salvation to righteous Gentiles living after Christ was not without its detractors, such as Augustine, who premised salvation through the natural law upon the transformative power of divine grace to set the natural law thinker on the right path toward the good. As Levering notes, Augustine "emphasizes that without grace, humans cannot sufficiently obey the natural law so as to be righteous."[9] For Augustine, divine grace is a gift in the form of the Redeemer Christ Jesus, which gives teleological content to our capacity for natural reasoning.[10]

The above discussion of Levering's account of Origen, Ambrosiaster, Chrysostom, Pelagius, and Augustine is meant to illustrate that alongside the inquiry into natural law lay the specter of difference that limits the salvation possible for those who reason to the good, but without having faith in Jesus as Redeemer. That the specter of difference co-exists alongside natural law accounts should not be evidence of the failure of natural law; attentiveness to difference hardly suggests

---

[8] Levering, section 2.4.2.
[9] Levering, section 2.4.3.
[10] Levering, section 2.4.3.

that natural law is illusory. Nothing about difference precludes jurists, theologians, or Rabbis from reflecting on the capacity of human reason to know the good, and the normative authority of such rationally determined good for purposes of human behavior. This volume indeed showcases how each tradition creates space for reason as a source of normative authority. To recall Novak's remarks in his seventh principle: "[I]nstead of an attempt to find some universal phenomenon to ground natural law, or posit some ideal from which to deduce natural law, it seems to be more philosophically astute to see natural law as the projection of a universal horizon by a thinker *in* a particular culture *for* one's own culture."[11] Each tradition conditions the scope of reasoned deliberation, and in that fashion thereby limits both the space within which reasoning can occur and the subjects that it can address. Without such limits, the very coherence of a tradition is put at stake. Consequently, any pursuit of the good from within a tradition of natural law (Islamic, Christian, Jewish, or otherwise) will follow a course that may also limit the scope of reason's sway.

Importantly, this limitation on the universal claim of reason and certain core human values is not only a feature of religious traditions. Rather, attentiveness to religious natural law theories sheds light on how other modes by which we claim the universality of certain values anticipate certain limits. For instance, as much as advocates of human rights seek to proclaim the universality of such rights (e.g., the Universal Declaration of Human Rights), such rights are in fact highly contingent. At a formal level, proclamations of rights and freedoms are quickly subjected to limiting clauses. For instance, Article 9 of the European Convention of Human Rights proclaims a right to religious freedom. But in Article 9(2), the scope of that freedom is limited in the interest of the needs of a democratic society; public order, health, or morals; or the protection of the rights of others.[12] At a more substantive and applied level, recent studies[13] and cases in

---

[11] Novak, section 1.7.

[12] For the text of the Convention, see http://www.echr.coe.int/NR/rdonlyres/ D5CC24A7-DC13-4318-B457-5C9014916D7A/0/CONVENTION_ENG_WEB.pdf (accessed August 30, 2012).

[13] See for instance, Roger Normand and Sarah Zaidi, *Human Rights at the UN*, United Nations Intellectual History Project Series (Indianapolis: Indiana University Press, 2008); Samuel Moyn, *The Last Utopia: Human Rights in History* (Cambridge: Belknap Press, 2010); Anver M. Emon, Mark Ellis, and Benjamin Glahn, eds., *Islamic Law and International Human Rights Law: Searching for Common Ground?* (Oxford: Oxford University Press, 2012).

human rights tribunals[14] have showcased the contingent and particular nature of human rights. Far from fulfilling the claim of shared human values, their formation, articulation, and application reflect highly particularized contexts and politicized interests that cannot simply be distinguished or disregarded as irrelevant or separable from their more lauded aspirations. Consequently, to view natural law from the vantage point of difference is not meant to undercut the authority of reason as a source of value and authority within different traditions. Rather it reveals the fundamental conceit of those who discount how notions like "the right," "the good," and "the bad" are themselves deeply embedded within communities of tradition or value.

II TIME AS ABSENCE: POSITIONING NATURAL LAW DOCTRINES IN RELIGIOUS TRADITIONS

One fascinating feature of Levering's essay has to do with time and its implications for the authority of natural law as a path to salvation. Time certainly featured in Chrysostom's account of natural law. According to Levering, Chrysostom allowed for natural reasoning about the good and good deeds to offer a path to salvation *before* the coming of Christ. *After* Christ's coming, though, natural reasoning was fundamentally transformed to point Jew and Gentile to Christ as the redeemer and conduit to eternal life. In other words, the notion of time signals an important difference, a difference between a world without Christ and a world with Christ. That difference mattered not only for Chrysostom, but also for the various theologians Levering addresses. For Ambrosiaster, that difference limited the scope of who could participate in natural legal reasoning. For Pelagius, the difference of *before* and *after* worked to the disadvantage of Jews who did not believe in Jesus. In all of these cases, time is meant to signal an absence or void into which natural law is deposited, or a presence and

---

[14] The religious freedom case law from the European Court of Human Rights has come under intense scrutiny, given its views on head scarves and crosses in the classroom. See for instance, Urfan Khaliq, "Freedom of Religion and Belief in International Law: A Comparative Analysis," in *Islamic Law and International Human Rights Law: Searching for Common Ground?* eds. Anver M. Emon, Mark Ellis, and Benjamin Glahn, 183–225 (Oxford: Oxford University Press, 2012).

affirmative content against which the authority of natural reasoning must be balanced.

Whether natural law is viewed as opposing faith, conducive to faith, or an instrument of fulfilling the promises of faith will vary across the theologians Levering reviews. For the patristic theologians Levering analyzes, the time after Jesus' coming positions natural law in relation to faith in Christ. For Origen, natural law reasoning after Jesus' coming is separate and distinct from the role Jesus plays as Redeemer. The natural legal reasoner cannot, without the intervention of Jesus, achieve salvation. Origen's promise, though, is that Jesus is a mercy for everyone, Christians first and then the rest. For Pelagius, before Jesus' coming, the Jews had the Mosaic law and the Gentiles had the natural law, both of which could lead them to salvation. But after Jesus' coming, Pelagius argued, Jews could no longer achieve salvation through the Mosaic law alone without faith in Jesus. On Pelagius' account, the Jewish law anticipates the coming of Christ; consequently, failure to believe in Jesus as a mercy and redeemer violates the law. But Gentile non-Christians could still hope for salvation by pursuing the natural law. Time stands for something important in all these theologians' doctrines of natural law: it stands for a discontinuity not only in history, but also in the nature of natural reasoning in relation to faith. Indeed, the discontinuity in time posits the initial foundations for and boundaries of a tradition that these theologians use to situate the claims of natural reasoning.

In comparison, Muslim jurists also used the idea of time to reflect on the authority of natural legal reasoning. Though in their case, time denoted a different kind of absence and presence, namely the absence or presence of revealed scripture. Hence, it is not surprising that they discussed natural law theories by reference to the phrase *min qablu wurud al-shar'*. This phrase has been translated as "before revelation," which is certainly a literal translation of the phrase.[15] But it is important to recognize that Muslim jurists writing about the nature of legal decision making "before revelation" were doing so as a counterfactual. By the time they were theorizing about natural law, there was no doubt that revelation had occurred and was a constituent feature of the Islamic legal landscape. Viewing the phrase, therefore, as a

[15] Kevin Reinhart, *Before Revelation: The Boundaries of Muslim Moral Thought* (Albany: SUNY Press, 1995)

counterfactual suggests that they were perhaps not addressing what constituted normative authority *before* there was revelation, just as it is doubtful that the main thrust of Chrysostom's natural law doctrine (at least going forward) is whether or not Jews and Gentiles before Christ's coming were capable of achieving salvation. Rather, the Islamic counterfactual of *min qablu wurud al-shar'* calls forth the specter of difference that so often plagues natural law theories. That difference is constituted by the discontinuity in history (i.e., the revelation of the Qur'an and the prophecy of Muhammad) and its implication on the authority of reason as a source of normative authority.

This brief comparison about the use of time in Islamic natural law accounts and the patristic ones that Levering recounts signals the strategies used within religious natural law theories to situate the authority of reason in light of the inherited traditions or articles of faith that define and demarcate the boundaries of religious identity. These boundaries are important; they define a religious tradition as a tradition, and give some coherence to the adjectives *Christian* and *Islamic*. But at the same time, these boundaries do not preclude serious reflection on the relationship between reason and tradition, and the ways each helps constitute the scope and breadth of the other.

III OBLIGATION, REASON, AND DIFFERENCE IN ISLAMIC LAW: THE OTHER UNDER THE LAW

In the context of Levering's analysis, we see how being attentive to difference can help us understand what was at stake for each Church Father as he developed a natural law doctrine. On Levering's account, the patristic period illustrates not only that natural law was a point of considerable interest to the Church Fathers, but also that their natural law doctrines had to account for the scope to which non-Christians could participate in natural law, to what end, and in what relationship to the arrival of Jesus Christ. In the Islamic context, this dynamic of difference did not play out in Islamic natural law theories, but rather in theories of obligation to the law, called *taklif* in Arabic. The question for Muslim jurists was whether, why, and to what extent non-Muslims were subjected to the laws of Islam. Part of the answer depended on the relationship of the non-Muslim to the lands held and governed by

Muslims. In some cases the non-Muslim entered and exited Muslim lands quickly, as in the case of traders seeking to sell their wares and return home (e.g., the *musta'min*). In other cases, non-Muslims lived outside of Muslim lands, thereby rendering them outside the law. But in other cases, and most significantly for this analysis, some non-Muslims were permanent residents in Islamic lands. These non-Muslim permanent residents were called *dhimmis* and Muslim jurists developed complex legal doctrines governing the scope of their freedom and liberty.[16] What is noteworthy is how for Muslim jurists, the issue of obligation under Islamic law had to do with the capacity to reason that is shared among all humans. Consequently, though the Islamic debates on obligation (*taklif*) and natural law (i.e., *min qablu wurud al-shar'*) were considerably different, the two shared a common theoretical query, namely the capacity of human reason to know the law. The difference though was that in the case of obligation, Muslim jurists were not asking about the authority of rationally based law in the absence of scripture. Instead they were addressing the scope of the legal subject's obligation under a taken-for-granted legal order in the absence of shared faith commitments.

A fundamental question for Muslim jurists was whether *dhimmis* could be held liable to Islamic law. This was not an easy question for jurists. In some cases, Islamic legal doctrines were directly taken from the Qur'an—a text that Muslims believed was revealed by God, but in which non-Muslims did not believe. How can laws based on the Qur'an (either directly or indirectly) be applied to *dhimmis* given that they did not believe in the Qur'an as a sacred, let alone authoritative, text in the first place? At the same time, jurists recognized that so many of the Islamic legal doctrines both benefited and burdened all who lived under the Muslim imperium. Legal doctrines could range from contract formation, to tort liability, to the legal obligations to one's neighbor. All of these rules regulated different forms of inter-personal interaction in which *dhimmis* participated. Since *dhimmis* benefited from these rules, why should they be excluded from any corresponding liability to these rules? Or perhaps they should be exempted from

---

[16] For a more extensive analysis of this legal regime in Islamic legal history and its relationship to governance, see Anver M. Emon, *Religious Pluralism and Islamic Law: Dhimmis and Others in the Empire of Law* (Oxford: Oxford University Press, 2012).

some rules and not others? If *dhimmis* were to be obligated to abide by at least some Islamic legal doctrines but not all, how to distinguish between them, and more to the point, what was the basis for their obligation at all?[17]

The jurist Sayf al-Din al-Amidi (d. 631/1233) wrote that before one can be obligated under the law, he must have rational capacity (*'aqil*) and understand what it means to be obligated (*fahim li'l-taklif*).[18] These conditions, he held, were necessary in order for one to know and appreciate the nature of God, the obligations stemming from the divine discourse (*khitab*), and the requirement to obey the divine will. In short, one must have the ability to know God and to know the requirement to obey the divine will before being legitimately subjected to the Shari'a.[19] For al-Amidi, the requirement to obey the divine will, though, will differ depending on one's relationship to God and the divine message. Consequently, he held that the basis for and scope of obligation to Shari'a for a Muslim was different than for a non-Muslim since the two relate to God differently. Others argued, to the contrary, that all human beings have the same capacity to know what obligation means and to morally reason to the good and the bad (*husn, qubh*). For the latter group, no distinction should be made between Muslims and non-Muslims for the purpose of determining whether someone is obligated to abide by the Shari'a. Rather, the universality of reason justified subjecting the *dhimmi* to Shari'a-based norms to the same degree and extent as Muslims.[20] On either of these two theories of obligation, humans, whether Muslim or not, have the capacity to reason to Shari'a-based norms. But the theories differed over whether or not the difference in faith required different bases for obligation to abide by Shari'a.

---

[17] The discussion that follows is drawn from chapter 2 of my book *Religious Pluralism and Islamic Law*.

[18] Sayf al-Din al-Amidi, *al-Ihkam fi Usul al-Ahkam* (Beirut: Dar al-Fikr, 1997), 1:106–07.

[19] Al-Amidi, *al-Ihkam*, 1:107.

[20] On the debates about *husn* and *qubh*, see Reinhart, *Before Revelation*; Anver M, Emon, "Natural Law and Natural Rights in Islamic Law," *Journal of Law and Religion* 20, no. 2 (2004–2005): 351–95; Emon, *Islamic Natural Law Theories* (Oxford: Oxford University Press, 2010). Others opposing this view on *husn/qubh* and the determination of the law where there is no scripture (*min qabla wurud al-shar'*), also believed it implicated the nature and definition of obligation (*taklif*). See 'Ali b. 'Abd al-Kafi al-Subki and Taj al-Din al-Subki, *al-Ibhaj fi Sharh al-Minhaj* (Beirut: Dar al-Kutub al-'Ilmiyya, n.d.), 1:155.

Notably, despite the different perspectives on the basis for obligation, jurists of both theoretical persuasions acknowledged that *dhimmis* have historically enjoyed certain immunities from Shariʿa-based obligations—immunities that have been transmitted over generations and constitute authoritative precedent. This historical fact posed a problem for jurists espousing the sufficiency of universal reason as a justificatory basis for imposing Shariʿa-based norms on the *dhimmi*. If reason is universal, what explains these precedential limits on the *dhimmi*'s scope of obligation? The difficulty of harmonizing a commitment to universal reason with inherited precedent—which circumscribed the scope of the *dhimmi*'s obligations—suggested to pre-modern jurists that something more than mere reason was required to establish and define the *dhimmis*' obligation to abide by Shariʿa-based norms. That something more was a form of acquiescence.

For Muslim jurists, there were at least two forms of acquiescence for the *dhimmi*. The first was conversion to Islam. In this case, the *dhimmi* no longer remained a *dhimmi* and instead shifted his status once he became Muslim. In the absence of conversion, though, the other model was based on contract, which was in fact the dominant model jurists relied upon to determine the scope of the *dhimmis*' obligation to Shariʿa-based norms. The contract of protection (*ʿaqd al-dhimma*) was the political and legal site of deliberation about the scope, extent, and limits of the *dhimmis*' obligations. *Dhimmis* were rendered liable to some Shariʿa-based obligations because both Muslims and non-Muslims mutually benefitted from them. These rules, the *muʿamalat*, pertained to matters of general, day-to-day concern (*maʿna dunyawi*), and thereby worked to the benefit of both Muslims and *dhimmis*.[21] Of course, determining what constituted a general concern and a desired benefit was something that jurists fiercely debated when considering which rules did or did not apply to the *dhimmi*. Once having determined that distinction, the *dhimmi* was theoretically obligated to abide by the relevant category of rules, all of which were legally deemed to be implicit in the contract of protection. The contract of protection delineated the scope of the *dhimmi*'s liability, and thereby the *dhimmi*'s inclusion in the Muslim polity. But by delimiting the scope of the *dhimmis*' obligation to Shariʿa

---

[21] Abu Bakr al-Sarakhsi, *al-Muharrar fi Usul al-Fiqh,* ed. Abu ʿAbd al-Rahman ʿAwida (Beirut: Dar al-Kutub al- Ilmiyya, 1996), 1:52.

doctrines, the contract was also a reminder of how the *dhimmi* was not an insider to the Muslim community, not one of "us."

CONCLUSION

This response has relied upon the theme of difference to address not only the possibilities for a religiously defined natural law, but also the salience of exclusion as a constitutive feature of the traditions within which Christian theologians and Muslim jurists thought and reflected. Difference as a theme reminds us of how borders and boundaries both include and exclude. To address natural law alongside difference and exclusion might, for some, seem counter-intuitive if not self-defeating. But it is only self-defeating if we presume to give to reason such hegemony as to ignore the ways in which its operation is always and at all times embedded, whether in a tradition, in a historical context, in a discipline, or in a community. The exclusion that can arise from difference does not preclude an ontology of reason for purposes of legal authority, for instance. Indeed, a focus on difference and exclusion is a reminder that an unchecked commitment to a universalist ethos may instead operate hegemonically upon those who might express their reasoned deliberation using a different set of terms entirely.

Response to Matthew Levering's "Christians and Natural Law"

David Novak

I. BEYOND MERE COMPARISONS

I am grateful for this opportunity to respond to Matthew Levering's essay, "Christians and Natural Law," because of the insightful and sympathetic way he has treated my own natural law theory in two earlier books of his, plus his response to my essay in this book.[1] In this response of mine to the essay he has written for this book, I hope to emulate the insight and sympathy he has shown in his treatment of my past work (and the work of other thinkers who have influenced him). Yet there is more than gratitude for past favors motivating this response to Levering's essay here. This response is meant to be an ongoing engagement with his thought, especially with his own constructive natural law theory. Indeed, I detect the same project in his ongoing engagement with my own constructive natural theory.

This response to Levering's essay is meant to be more than the type of comparative study that has become popular recently, i.e., one that takes interest in "other voices." Levering and I (and Anver Emon as well) are more than academics. We are deeply committed members of our respective faith communities (as is Emon as well). Our concern for each other's work, then, might be considered to be existential

---

[1] The two earlier books are *Biblical Natural Law* (Oxford: Oxford University Press, 2008), and *Jewish-Christian Dialogue and the Life of Wisdom: Engagements with the Theology of David Novak* (New York: Continuum, 2010).

inasmuch as it is concern for what we share in common at the deepest level possible, even if we are not and ought not consider ourselves to be members of the same faith community in this world.[2] There are three reasons for this existential concern with Levering's work on my part. None of these reasons, though, would have to be stated were this a merely academic comparative exercise, whose only reason for being conducted would be because it is "interesting."

(1) Both Levering and I are quite insistent that Christian or Jewish natural law thinkers must explicitly talk about natural law essentially being God's law. When the question of divine law is either ignored or even sidelined by a Jewish or Christian (or Muslim) natural law thinker, one rightly wonders how Christian or how Jewish (of how Muslim) this kind of "atheological" natural law thought really is, irrespective of whatever the personal piety of such a Christian or Jewish (or Muslim) natural law thinker might happen to be.

(2) The God we both affirm to be the source of natural law is the same God. This is easier for Levering to do than it is for me to do, because he can readily rely on the Church's rejection of Marcion's teaching that the God of Israel, who is the God who speaks in the Old Testament, is not the same God as the God of Christians, who speaks in the New Testament. In fact, this was the first heresy the Church declared, already in the 2nd century.

In my own case, truth be told however, there is a considerable body of Jewish opinion that argues that Christians affirm a different god than the Lord God of Israel. According to this opinion, Christianity is "strange worship" (*avodah zarah*), i.e., idolatry (even when it is not iconic), which everybody in the normative Jewish tradition holds to be universally proscribed for all humankind. Nevertheless, there is also a body of opinion that holds that Christianity like Islam (which hardly anybody in the Jewish tradition took to be idolatry per se) is only "strange worship" when Jews embrace it.[3] Thus a Jewish thinker has ample precedent in

---

[2] See Maimonides, *Mishneh Torah* [hereafter "MT"]: Kings, 8.11.

[3] See David Novak, *Jewish–Christian Dialogue* (New York: Oxford University Press, 1989), passim; Novak, *Les Juifs et les chrétiens révèrent-ils le même Dieu?* in *Le christianisme au miroir du judaïsme*, ed. Shmuel Trigano (Paris: In Press, 2003), 95ff.

the Jewish tradition for asserting that Jews and Christians do affirm the same God, especially the same Creator/Lawgiver, even though there are other aspects of God's relation to the world about which Jews and Christians differ significantly. (The difference is greatest in the area of the aspects of God's relation to the world that are named in our respective liturgies, but that area has little or no relevance for natural law theory.)

(3) Since the Enlightenment, liberal proponents of democracy, have proposed natural law as "natural rights." More recently, they have proposed that natural law is about "human rights."[4] Moreover, until recently, Jews and Christians living in democratic societies have used this modern notion of natural law in polemics against each other (polemics in which Muslims have been too new a presence in the West to be involved, yet). Many Christians have long argued that Jews, because they regard themselves to be a separate people, are not universal enough in their historical outlook to be truly committed to liberal democracy. For liberal democracy, in principle anyway, is supposed to be made up of citizens who are taken to be human beings per se. Many Jews have argued (almost as long) for the notion that modern democracy, which is "non-sectarian" in principle, disestablishes any particular religious tradition from being its foundation, i.e., the metaphysical source from which the society gains its moral legitimacy. But, as many Jews (and non-Jews, who are usually former Christians) have argued, haven't orthodox Christians, since Constantine, regarded the Church to be the only legitimating source for any society worthy of anybody's moral allegiance?

However, more recently, perceptive (and more traditionally oriented) Jews and Christians (and most recently, joined by some perceptive Muslims in the West) are awakening to the sad fact that militantly secularist proponents of democracy regard both Judaism and Christianity (and now Islam) to be enemies of their version of natural law as human rights. At the deepest level, their objection is to the inherent inequality affirmed by traditions that posit a divine Lawgiver who is superior in every way to His human subjects. Moreover, they see this as

---

[4] For an important scholarly monograph that argues for continuity between mediaeval notions of natural law and modern notions of natural rights, see Brian Tierney, *The Idea of Natural Rights* (Atlanta, GA: Scholars Press, 1997), 43ff., 316ff.

the metaphysical undergirding of the inherent inequality that manifests itself as "patriarchy" and "heterosexism." For that reason, Jews and Christians (and now Muslims too) need to think out natural law positions together with each other in and for the secular world. Indeed, we have to provide better reasons for those aspects of human rights where egalitarianism is appropriate, and for those aspects of human rights where egalitarianism is inappropriate. And at the deepest level, that means showing why inter-human equality is best grounded in divine–human inequality. In fact, this is what the Canadian Charter of Rights and Freedoms calls "the supremacy of God and the rule of law," which can be taken as phrases in apposition: God's supremacy is manifest in God's law being the foundation of all authentic law.

Let us now turn to the conclusions Levering draws from his study of the Church Fathers, i.e., his normative conclusions for the present. Unfortunately, due to limitations of space, I can only deal with the first three of Levering's seven conclusions. Each subsection of the section below will begin with a quote from the specific normative conclusion Levering draws from his thorough and profound study of some of the most important Church Fathers who have talked about natural law. I shall try to show analogues in the Jewish tradition, analogues that seem to have the same normative significance as do Levering's conclusions.

II. RESPONDING TO LEVERING'S FIRST THREE CONCLUSIONS

1. "The knowledge of the precepts of natural law does not mean...that our outward observance of them will be matched by our interior attitude...the exterior action signals our interior righteousness only if the spirit...is one of love."

Levering's point here is that natural law is a necessary component of Christian morality, yet it is still not enough for the constitution of a fully Christian ethic. The same point can be made by Jewish natural law theory, viz., that natural law is a necessary component of Jewish morality (though that is as arguable in the Jewish tradition as it is in the Christian tradition), yet it is still not enough to constitute a fully Jewish ethic. The task for both of us becomes how to separate the demands of the outward observance of natural law as the basic norm of doing justice from the demands of the interior attitude of love, but without setting up an irresolvable antinomy between the two of them.

In the Jewish tradition, there are two norms that are considered to be foundational in the sphere of what Levering calls "human-to-human" relations. The first is the scriptural commandment: "You shall love your neighbor as yourself" (Leviticus 19:18) which, in the second century, Rabbi Akiba ben Joseph asserted to be "the greatest, most all-inclusive [*kellal gadol*] commandment in the Torah."[5] The second norm was formulated by the first century rabbi, Hillel, as: "What is hateful to you, do not do to your fellow human," which he then declared to be "the essence of the Torah" (*kol ha-torah kullah*).[6] Now there have been those who have seen these two norms to be two sides of the same coin: the first being the positive formulation of the basic norm; the second being the negative formulation of it.[7] In this view, there doesn't seem to be any difference between the demands of love and the demands of justice. Justice is not having done to you what you don't want done to you; love is treating others the way you like to treat yourself. Nevertheless, there have been those who see an essential divide between the two norms.[8]

Hillel's dictum clearly refers to any other human being. That is indicated not only by the word he uses, i.e., "fellow human" (*haverakh* in Aramaic), but also from the fact that Hillel's dictum is in response to a request from a Gentile about Judaism. Though there is much more to Judaism than this universal norm, it is where Hillel wisely begins, telling the Gentile to begin by practicing a norm everybody should know already. It is good pedagogy to begin with what the pupil already knows, then gradually showing him how that leads to what he doesn't already know, but what he is going to know if he doesn't stop there. The dictum thus ends with this admonition: "Go learn [the rest of the Torah]!"

---

[5] *Palestinian Talmud*: Nedarim 9.3/41c.

[6] *Babylonian Talmud* [hereafter "B."]: Shabbat 31a.

[7] See e.g., *Targum Jonathan ben Uziel* to Lev. 19:18; Maimonides, *Book of the Commandments*, pos. no. 206; Maimonides, MT: Mourning, 14.1; MT: Gifts to the Poor; *Midrash Leqah Tov*: Qedoshim to Lev. 19:18, ed. Buber, 54a.

[8] See David Novak, *Covenantal Rights* (Princeton, NJ: Princeton University Press, 2000), 117ff.

Whereas it is obvious that Hillel's "fellow human" refers to any other human person, many have argued that the "neighbor" who is the object of what Rabbi Akiba designated to be *the* great commandment only refers to one's fellow Jews.[9] In other words, not only is a Jew clearly the subject of the commandment since the section it is part of is addressed to "the whole congregation of the children of Israel" (Leviticus 19:2), but one's fellow Jew (in this view anyway) is also the object of the commandment. But what makes one's fellow Jew, one's fellow covenant member (*ben berit*), loveable, whereas a gentile is only the object of justice to be universally applied? The answer, it seems to me, lies in how one interprets the words of Leviticus 19:18. For if one interprets the commandment to be saying that one should extend his or her self-love to others, then just as self-love is a universal fact, why shouldn't its extension to others also become a universal imperative? However, if one follows the great German translation/ interpretation of Martin Buber and Franz Rosenzweig (i.e., if I understand it correctly), then the commandment is to *love your neighbor as you yourself are loved by God.*[10] Accordingly, the verse concludes: "I am the Lord" (Y*HWH*), the tetragrammaton being the name of God, which in rabbinic theology, denotes God as loving and compassionate.[11] Therefore, a Jew is loveable because God loves him or her, and a Jew is to love his or her fellow Jew for the same reason. Nevertheless, the love commandment and what might be called the "no harm commandment" are not at loggerheads.[12] The love commandment deepens the no harm commandment; it doesn't contradict it. For it not

---

[9] See MT: Virtues, 6.3.

[10] Their German text reads: *Halte lieb deinen Genossen, dir gleich, ICH bins,* in *Die Fünf Bücher der Weisung* (Köln: Jakob Hegner, 1954), p. 326. Also, their term *Genossen* for the Hebrew *re'akha* is less universal than the term *Nächsten* used in Luther's famous German translation of the Bible. Along these lines, see Franz Rosenzweig, *The Star of Redemption*, trans. B. E. Galli (Madison, WI: University of Wisconsin Press, 2005), 257. For a more universalistic view, cf. Rosenzeig's teacher (and Buber's adversary), Hermann Cohen, *Religion of Reason Out of the Sources of Judaism*, trans. S. Kaplan (New York: Frederick Unger, 1972), 127; Cohen, "Die Nächstenliebe im Talmud," *Jüdische Schriften* I (Berlin: C. A. Schwetschke, 1924), 145ff. (This essay was based on Cohen's testimony in a trial in 1888, when he defended the Jewish tradition against charges that it teaches hostility to gentiles.)

[11] See A. Marmorstein, *The Old Rabbinic Doctrine of God* I (New York: KTAV, 1968/ reprint), 41ff.

[12] The no-harm precept is expressed as a principle of justice in Ulpian, *Digest*, 1.1.10.1): *Iustitia est…alterum non laedere* (" Justice is…an other person is not to be harmed").

only makes the ethical act more proactive, it also makes the ethical act a deed of body-and-soul, not just a deed done by the body, which is all the no harm commandment prescribes.

Furthermore, this interpretation of the commandment answers the question, most famously posed by Kant: How can one be commanded to feel a certain emotion, love being the most powerful emotion humans are capable of? Aren't our feelings simply given, as distinct from our deeds that are freely chosen?[13] Nevertheless, by emphasizing that the Lord God is the direct source of the commandment, God is not so much ordering us to love our neighbor; rather, God is eliciting our response to the experience of God's love for us by asking us to lovingly respond to that divine love—"You shall love the Lord your God" (Deuteronomy 6:5)—and then becoming God's agents in sharing that love with our fellow covenant members, just as they are asked to be God's agents in sharing that love with us. Love itself cannot be commanded; but we can be commanded to remove from our hearts impediments to our reception of God's love for us and for our neighbors and our imitation of that love.[14]

This love for God, and along with it our love for our covenanted neighbor, though, is not our attraction to God as the most perfect Being we could imagine (as it is for Plato and Aristotle).[15] Instead, that love for God and our covenanted neighbor is our response to God's love for us and for our neighbor together with us. That divine love we do experience through revelation, even though for most of us that experience is mediated, i.e., we have to learn it from the scriptural narrative and then internalize it. Our love is our response to God's attraction to us; it is not the expression of our attraction to a God whose presence we have not experienced. It is not our attraction to God as the End of all ends, the means thereto being devised by us. Instead, this love is our response to God's attraction to us, the means thereto being revealed to us by God in the Torah.

However, where in the world is God's love for us directly experienced? We Jews cannot say that our knowledge of God's love comes

---

[13] See *Critique of Practical Reason*, PA5:83, trans. W. S. Pluhar (Indianapolis, IN: Hackett, 2002), 107–08; also, *Religion Within the Boundaries of Mere Reason*, PA6:161–62, trans. A. Wood and G. di Giovanni (Cambridge: Cambridge University Press, 1998), 158.

[14] See Nahmanides, *Commentary on the Torah*, Deut. 10:16.

[15] See Plato, *Symposium*, 211Bff.; Aristotle, *Metaphysics*, 12.7/1072a20ff.

from our human experience of universal beneficence in created nature, from which we then infer a divine Benefactor as its cause. (In fact, both the experience and the causal inference from it are often quite doubtful.[16]) Instead, that knowledge comes from our particularly intimate, historical experience of God's love, whereby God makes us His covenanted partners. That is the supernatural relationship with God we enjoy with God, even in this world, through our keeping the commandments of the Torah.[17] The reaction to our experience of created nature, whether beneficial or detrimental, is not spontaneous; rather, it is how we are commanded through revelation to respond to what God is doing to us in the world.[18]

This experience of intimate covenantal love, though, is not exclusive ethnocentricity. Any Gentile who wants to be permanently included in it can present himself or herself for conversion to Judaism and full membership in the Jewish people. These converts too can become the objects of God's love for Israel. They are "born again" into Israel.[19] Indeed, even Gentiles who only want to be temporarily included in our covenantal life can become "sojourners" or our transient guests (like *gerei toshav* or "resident aliens") rather than becoming "full converts" (*gerei tsedeq*).[20] They too become the objects of this covenantal love. However impermanent their sojourn in our midst, they too are to be included in the extension of covenantal peace (*shalom*) involved in such intimate acts as attending to the needs of the sick and providing the dead with decent burial, acts which are only meaningful when performed with proper intention and personal attention known as "deeds of loving kindness" or "charity" (*gemilut hasadim*).[21]

---

[16] Cf. Maimonides, *Guide of the Perplexed*, 3.12, who does argue for inferring God's beneficence towards created nature from nature itself, though he is careful to point out that this general benificence is not always evident to humans in their individual circumstances.

[17] The full enjoyment of God's company, though, will have to wait for the world-beyond (*ha`olam ha-ba*). See B. Berakhot 31a re Ps. 127:2

[18] See Isa. 45:7; M. Berakhot 9.5. For the notion that anything one can say about God's relation to nature is retrospective from the vantage point of revelation, see David Novak, "Creation" in *The Cambridge History of Jewish Philosophy: The Modern Era*, ed. M. Kavka, Z. Braiterman, D. Novak (Cambridge: Cambridge University Press, 2012), 384ff.

[19] B. Yevamot 22a, 47a-b.

[20] See B. Avodah Zarah 64b.

[21] See B. Gittin 61a; also, Nahmanides, *Commentary on the Torah*, Num. 21:21.

The point in common with Levering's first conclusion noted above is that natural law can only command us to do justice to one another as fellow human persons, which largely means not to harm them. In the Jewish tradition, doing such minimal, ethically significant acts doesn't require one to cultivate an inner attitude or affective intention (*kavvanah*). The cultivation of that inner affective intention can only come from the experience of God's love for us as the recipients of revelation.[22] That is why, it seems, the Talmud states that one who does an act because it is what God has directly and lovingly commanded is on a higher level than one who simply does something because he or she thinks it is the right or just thing to do.[23]

> 2. "Grace is not limited to the time after Christ. God cares for all humans, and not just for the people of God. Those who are not members of the visible people of God (Israel/Church) are cared for by God in various ways, including natural law that enables them to distinguish right from wrong."

Here Levering makes the point that natural law qua natural law is not truly knowable in a secular way, i.e., natural law cannot be taken to be anything less than explicitly divine law. But how can anybody be expected to know natural law as divine law if that person is not the direct recipient of divine revelation, or is not a member of a traditional community whose original members received divine revelation directly and then transmitted a written and oral record of their revelatory experience to posterity? This issue is what is at stake in a famous text from Maimonides' great compendium of the Law, *Mishneh Torah*, from a section where he discusses at length (and at much greater length and depth than anybody else theretofore) the moral obligations of Gentiles, whether they are living under Jewish auspices or not.

This is how I translate words in this text of Maimonides:

> Whoever accepts the seven Noahide commandments as authoritative and is personally obligated to do what they command [*ve-nizhar la`asotan*], this person is considered to be one of the pious gentiles

---

[22] Whereas the direct object of *kavvanah* is God (see e.g., *Mishnah* [herafter "M."]: Berakhot 2.1, Rosh Hashanah 3.7–8, Menahot 13.11), that *kavvanah* can also be part of a covenantal act towards another human person. So, one is to pray (which is emotive and well as cognitive; see B. Taanit 2a re Deut. 11:13) both for and with a sick person as part of one's duty to personally care for the sick. See B. Nedarim 40a; B. Moed Qatan 5a re Lev. 13:45; Maimonides, MT: Mourning, 14.4.

[23] B. Kiddushin 31a.

[*me-hasidei ummot ha`olam*] and has a share in the world-beyond [*l`olam ha-ba*]. That is, when one accepts them and does them because of what was commanded concerning them [*mipnei she-tsivah bahen*] by God in the Torah. It is what was made known to us in the Torah through Moses our master, that the Noahides were so commanded earlier [*mi-qodem*]. However, if somebody did them because reason compels them to do so, that person is not a resident-alien [*ger toshav*] nor one of the pious gentiles, but only one of their [gentile] sages [*ela me-hakhmeihem*].[24]

Now almost every word in this text has been subjected to much scrutiny and much debate.[25] For our purposes, though, the first key phrase is "because of what was commanded concerning them by God." But where and when did God command these universally valid commandments? That depends on how one understands the next key phrase, "and what was made known to us through Moses our master." Most interpreters have assumed this means that the *prescription* of these commandments was first made known to "us" (the Jews) in the Torah given to Moses directly by God and written down as Scripture (*torah she-bi-khtav*). In other words, even though these commandments are universally valid, they can only be known as divine commandments when their source in the Mosaic Torah is confirmed. This, then, would mean that the only non-Jews who would qualify as "pious gentiles" would be Christians who accept the Mosaic Torah as being totally divine revelation (Muslims, though, only regarding some parts of it to be actual divine revelation, the rest being mere human invention).[26] And they are the Christians who regard the moral norms of the Mosaic Torah to still be binding on all humankind because they are from Mosaic revelation.[27]

---

[24] MT: Kings, 8.11. For Maimonides, "the world-beyond" (*ha`olam ha-ba*) is the transcendent and eternal realm (see MT: Repentance, 8.8). "This world" (*ha`olam ha-zeh*) is only a finite temporal island in an infinite eternity (cf. Plato, *Timaeus*, 37Dff.) Accordingly, when one observes a commandment as a divine norm, that person is participating in the eternal realm, however partially.

[25] See David Novak, *The Image of the Non-Jew in Judaism*, 2nd ed. (Oxford: Littman Library, 2011), 172ff.

[26] See David Novak, "Maimonides' Treatment of Christians and Its Normative Implications" in *Jewish Theology and World Religions*, ed. A. Goshen-Gottstein and E. Korn (Oxford: Littman Library, 2112), 217ff.

[27] According to this interpretation anyway, it seems that Thomas Aquinas' view that Christians are to observe the moral precepts of the Old Testament (*Summa theologiae*, I-II, q. 98, a. 5) only because they are natural law, but not because of the Old Covenant (i.e., Mosaic revelation), wouldn't enable Christians who followed him to be candidates for the world-beyond.

Nevertheless, where does the Mosaic Torah actually *prescribe* the Noahide commandments? The fact is, one can only look to the Mosaic Torah for *descriptions* of what are assumed to be norms every human person is expected to know from time immemorial. Thus they are what could be called "normative descriptions." That is the force of the phrase "that the Noahides were so commanded earlier (*mi-qodem*)." Clearly, the Mosaic Torah is not where the children of Noah (i.e., humankind who survived the Flood) actually learned the commandments addressed to them. Since the Mosaic Torah had not yet been given, it couldn't have been the source of the universal normative validity of these commandments. And, to emphasize the prehistoricity of these commandments, Maimonides designates six of the seven commandments to be "Adamic," i.e., they are coeval with creation.[28] Before any original prescription of them could possibly be located, humans have always understood what God basically requires of them in their life together with each other. (Only the prohibition of eating a limb torn from a living animal is derived from a seemingly prescriptive statement actually made to Noah and his family.[29]) So, what Maimonides means when he says these commandments are "commanded by God in the Torah" could be: All these commandments are reiterated in the Mosaic Torah, or the "Torah" where they are originally commanded is the primordial Noahide Torah, which Maimonides sees as having been perfected or brought to completion by the subsequent Mosaic Torah. In relation to the Mosaic Torah, the Noahide Torah is proto-Torah.[30]

The Noahides (originally the family of Noah) seem to have been saved by God from the Flood, precisely because they kept the commandments for which the rest of humankind was destroyed by God in the Flood for violating so outrageously. In other words, the binding moral force of these commandments is what the Mosaic Torah *presupposes* has already been morally valid ever since the beginnings of humankind; hence they are *valid and known to be valid whenever wherever*. In fact, these descriptions are all found in texts describing situations that took place *before* the revelation to Israel of the perpetually binding laws of the Mosaic Torah, which are binding on Israel alone. Furthermore, all these laws were considered to be divine

---

[28] MT: Kings, 9.1.   [29] See B. Sanhedrin 57a re Gen. 9:4.
[30] MT: Kings, 9.1.

commandments.[31] So, for example, when Joseph resists the sexual advances of Potiphar's wife, he states his reasons in the form of a rhetorical query: "How can I do this great evil, and [how can I] sin against God?!" (Genesis 39:9)[32]

Our last question about the Maimonidean text above is why doing something because it is "rationally compelling" is not fully sufficient to qualify as a fully valid fulfillment of Noahide law. If what *reason compels or that* "towards which reason inclines [*noteh lahen*]" (another term used by Maimonides) seems to be different from Noahide law, is natural law not divine law, but humanly devised law?[33] A positive answer to this question has been given by several opponents of natural law, who argue that Judaism does not, could not, and should not have a natural law doctrine.[34] And they imply that nobody should take natural law seriously, because it is an illusion.

Nevertheless, the position above can be successfully contested. That is because its first premise is wrong. Natural law is more than what is just "reasonable." For what is reasonable could simply mean the type of conventional, pragmatic morality that seems to work well, i.e., as long as there are stable conditions in societies that haven't experienced much political disruption (and where foundational questions are much less likely to be raised). Yet, by practicing this kind of morality, one doesn't intend (and therefore doesn't attain) the transcendent "world-beyond" (*olam ha-ba*), because the source of this morality is not seen to be transcendent, and it doesn't intend anything transcendent either. This kind of morality is not grounded metaphysically. In fact, its proponents are usually anti-metaphysical, not only denying that the political

---

[31] Maimonides says (MT: Kings, 9.1): "Generally [*mi-khlal*] from the words of the Torah it is evident that they [humankind] were commanded these laws."

[32] See David Novak, *Natural Law in Judaism* (Cambridge: Cambridge University Press, 1998), 27ff.

[33] MT: Kings, 9.1. Perhaps, in order to counter the opinion that these laws are not only knowable by humans, but that they are also devised by humans, Maimonides says here: "We have a tradition [*kabbalah*] about all of them." These "traditions" are considered to be a lesser form of revelation, but revelation nonetheless. See *Mishnah*: Avot 1.1. In other words, what is known through reason and what is received from revelation are not at odds with one another.

[34] See Marvin Fox, "Maimonides and Aquinas on Natural Law," *Interpreting Maimonides* (Chicago: University of Chicago Press, 1990), 124ff. For a critique of Fox's view, cf. David Novak, "Maimonides and Aquinas on Natural Law," *Talking with Christians* (Grand Rapids, MI: Eerdmans, 2005), 67ff.; Novak, *Jewish Social Ethics* (New York: Oxford University Press, 1992), 25ff.

procedures they devise have any cosmic significance, but implying that nothing pertaining to humans in this world has any cosmic significance. But, certainly for Maimonides, being the metaphysician he surely was, Noahide law has a transcendent origin and end, who is the same Creator God. Thus Noahide law is divine law. It is the result of the same type of divine command whereby God created the universe *ex nihilo* (meaning without any preconditions or prior limits). And this law is rationally knowable, and not just reasonable, when it is taken to be rooted in more than moral sensibilities or in custom. Though the kind of procedural pragmatism that only looks to what is reasonable is necessary legally, it is inadequate philosophically, nonetheless.

I think Matthew Levering would agree that the ability of humans to apprehend the basic percepts of natural law is the result of divine grace, the same divine grace that created an orderly, intelligible world. That apprehension can be attained by philosophical reflection.[35] Yet this grace is a smaller, preliminary grace that only prepares us to receive a much greater grace, one that can only be given to us through revelation. To paraphrase one of the ancient Rabbis, one must prepare oneself in the anteroom before one can enter the palace.[36]

3. "Part of the task of Christian natural law doctrine, then, is to remind Christians of what Christians should be doing, rather than solely to call upon others to value the dignity of all human persons."

I have always held (quite arguably to be sure) that Noahide law is the Jewish version of natural law; hence I use the two terms interchangeably. Now Noahide or natural law has had a double function in Jewish philosophical speculation: functioning one way when Jews have speculated about our relation to other peoples; functioning another way when Jews have speculated about our relation to ourselves. What the relation to other peoples means is obvious, since it deals with the interaction *between* two separate and distinct entities in the world. But, as we shall soon see, Noahide law is an important factor when Jews in the present speculate on how the normativity that was operative in our collective pre-Jewish past history prepared us for our present covenantal life, and how the normativity that operated in our

---

[35] See Russell Hittinger, *The First Grace* (Wilmington, DE: ISI Books, 2003).
[36] M. Avot 4.16.

pre-Jewish past has still been functioning as a normative criterion in and for our present covenantal life. That is how we relate to ourselves, i.e., looking back to our past from the vantage point of our present. Since Jews should have a high degree of self-understanding of our past before engaging the non-Jewish world in the present, let us start this discussion by dealing with the normative relation of the Jewish present and the pre-Jewish past.

Though the Jews assumed a distinct ethnic identity at the time of Abraham, separate from that of "the nations of the world," they were still essentially Noahides, according to the Rabbis, i.e., in the sense of being bound by Noahide law until the covenant at Sinai was instituted.[37] Nevertheless, the move from being bound by Noahide law to being bound by Torah law should not be taken to be the kind of abrupt quantum leap that would make any relation between the two separate entities impossible to constitute. Just as the Jews did not cease to be part of humankind because of their covenantal election, so Jews haven't left their being bound by natural law behind because of being bound by the new law of the Mosaic Torah.[38] Rather, the new law built upon the older law like the builder of an attic builds it upon the foundation in the basement. And, to continue the metaphor, the wise builder of the attic periodically looks to see that the attic's structure is consistent with that of the foundation, especially when the attic becomes shaky and thus needs to be rebuilt.

Along these lines, the Talmud formulates a principle: "Nothing permitted to the Jews is prohibited to the Gentiles."[39] The obverse of this principle is: *Anything prohibited to the Gentiles is also prohibited to the Jews.* But, surely, that doesn't mean anything any group of Gentiles considers to be prohibited, even if they consider it to be prohibited to all humankind, is therefore prohibited to the Jews too. In fact, there are numerous prohibitions in various non-Jewish cultures which the Rabbis deemed to be superstition, and Jews who follow them are judged to be practicing forbidden quasi-idolatry.[40] In fact, the only Gentile prohibitions Jews are obligated to observe are

---

[37] See M. Nedarim 3.11; Nahmanides, *Commentary on the Torah*, Gen. 26:5.

[38] See Cohen, *Religion of Reason Out of the Sources of Judaism*, 118f. But this is not so in kabbalistic theology, whose acosmic ontology has no place for natural law. See Novak, *The Image of the Non-Jew in Judaism*, 151f.

[39] B. Sanhedrin 59a.

[40] See M. Shabbat 6.10; Maimonides, *Guide of the Perplexed*, 3.37 re Lev. 18:3 and 20:23.

the Noahide laws, all of which are essentially prohibitions (even the commandment to establish justice in society, because it means rectifying violations of the other six prohibitions, a negation of a negation as it were). This indicates that unlike Gentile idolaters (and other Gentile violators of Noahide or natural law) who have removed themselves from what is meant to be universal normativity (i.e., they aren't natural-law-abiding), the Jewish tradition keeps the Jews within this universal normativity. To paraphrase the Talmud: one should not go from a higher moral level to a lower one.[41] And that would indeed be the case were Jews to try to transcend the limits of natural law in the name of "religion." That would be, as the Talmud puts it, a "profanation of God's name" (*hillul ha-shem*).[42]

In actual legal practice, Jewish jurists have employed the precepts of natural law as principles or criteria for correcting cases where, if only the specifics of Jewish law were to be applied, gross injustice would be the result. So, for example, there are cases where persons who have committed obviously criminal acts could escape punishment were the specifics of Jewish law to be literally applied. Nonetheless, Maimonides encapsulates the whole thrust of the rabbinic tradition when he states that judges should see to it that those obviously guilty of crimes should not escape punishment because of what we now call legal "loopholes." Moreover, judges should be doing this "for God's sake [*le-shem shamayim*], and not taking human dignity [*kvod ha-beriyot*] lightly."[43] Now, if I understand Maimonides correctly, it seems that "for God's sake" and "human dignity" are logically connected, i.e., for God's sake human dignity is to be respected, for humans are dignified because they are created [*beriyot*] according to the image of God (*be-tselem elohim*). But human dignity is not taken seriously when crimes against humans that could be rectified go unpunished, especially when that is because the judges are the type of legal positivists who are either ignorant of natural right or dismissive of it, or even contemptuous of it.

When it comes to how recognition of natural law by the Jewish tradition enables Jews (in Levering's words) "to value the dignity of all human persons," one needs to differentiate between what the

---

[41] B. Yevamot 22a.

[42] See B. Baba Kama 113b.

[43] MT: Sanhedrin 24.10. Re human dignity (*kvod ha-beriyot*), see e.g., B. Berakhot 19b.

tradition has to say about all human persons as the subjects of natural law precepts and what it has to say about all human persons as the objects of natural law precepts. Sometimes the two are not identical. So, whereas all those who are the subjects of natural law precepts are also the objects of natural law precepts, there are some who are objects but not subjects of the law. For example, the fourteenth-century theologian, Rabbi Menahem ha-Meiri, talked about Gentiles committed to living under a divine law, which he certainly meant to be a law both universal in scope and rationally knowable.[44] They regard themselves to be the subjects of its precepts, thus they are to be recognized as such by any Jewish society having the power to extend and enforce their legal recognition. And, by accepting these basic, universal duties upon themselves as subjects of the law, these righteous Gentiles thereby gain the rights and privileges of all objects of this law. (Meiri is silent about whether somebody who only accepted Noahide law, not being either a Christian or a Muslim, would qualify as such a law-abiding person, which is probably because there were no such "secular" people in his time; hence that was a moot point then.)

The question now is whether there are any human persons who are the objects of the law, and thus to be protected by the law, but who could not be considered to be its subjects as well. And, as such, they could not be required to uphold the duties the law requires. One such example is mentioned in the Talmud as follows:

> A Noahide is liable for the death penalty...according to Rabbi Ismael, even for the killing of the fetus [*ha ʿubrin*]...What is Rabbi Ismael's source for this legal opinion? Scripture states: "Whoever sheds the blood of a human within a human [*baʾadam*], his blood shall be shed." (Genesis 9:6) Now who is "a human *within* a[nother] human"? It is a fetus in his [or her] mother's womb.[45]

Actually, the ostensive meaning of the scriptural verse invoked here is "Whoever sheds the blood of a human, by humans [*baʾadam*] shall his [or her] blood be shed." Then the verse concludes "because in the image of God He made humans." Now the verse is clearly prescribing capital punishment for murderers because they deserve it. And this death penalty is to be executed through the due process of law

---

[44] See *Bet ha-Behirah*: Baba Kama 38a, ed. Schulsinger, p. 122. On Meiri, see Jacob Katz, *Exclusiveness and Tolerance* (Oxford: Oxford University Press, 1961), 114ff.

[45] B. Sanhedrin 57b.

by official human judgment. The proscription of murder, though, is already assumed to be known. In fact, it is assumed to be known when God holds Cain liable for the murder of his brother Abel, which is the first murder in human experience. And how was Cain expected to know the prohibition? It would seem that he was to know that his brother, like any other human person, is created by God according to the divine image. Thus those who are that close to God so as to somehow reflect God's glory directly, being the unique pinnacle of creation, they must certainly be objects of God's special concern.[46] As such, they are the objects of God's law that rules they are not to be harmed. Surely, God will be greatly angered if the objects of His concern are so completely violated. So, God will either punish their murderers Himself, or God will delegate that punishment to those who are the subjects of His commandments, in this case human officials who are themselves the subjects of divine law having special tasks designated by God.[47]

Clearly, the subjects of God's law are those persons who are capable of exercising intellect and free choice, hence their responsibility to fulfill the duties the law enjoins upon them. But what the interpretation of Rabbi Ishmael does is to extend the law's protection to those who are the least likely to be able to exercise intellect and free choice, namely, the unborn. Hence there is the universal prohibition of abortion as a gross violation of the rights of the most vulnerable humans, those least able to advocate for their own rights. They too are objects of the law, though they are the farthest from being the subjects of the law (except, perhaps, the irreversibly comatose). And, here is where a theistic natural law theory is needed politically, because of its doctrine of the inviolable dignity of every human person created according to God's image. Yet, for most secular versions of natural or human rights (which, as we have seen, is the modern version of natural law), humans gain their dignity and their rights primarily because they are moral subjects or agents, who are able to advocate for their own rights. But in these versions of natural law, there is no provision for protecting those who cannot be these subjects or agents; there is no provision for including them among the objects of the law. Furthermore, though the early natural rights theorists (like

---

[46] See Novak, *Natural Law in Judaism*, 167ff.
[47] See B. Sanhedrin 6b; *Palestinian Talmud*: Megillah 3.6/74d re M. Avot 1.18 (re Zech. 8:16).

Kant, for example) didn't explicitly exclude these non-subjects from the protection of the law, today we see increasingly that advocates of human rights do exclude these non-subjects of the law from the law's protection of its objects by denying their humanity. That is because, in this modern version of natural law/rights, it is our fellow citizens in society who determine whatever rights and duties anybody has or doesn't have. That is contrary to theistic natural law, where it is God who *endows* (in the words of the US Declaration of Independence) the objects of the law with their rights and the subjects of the law with their duties.

Since Matthew Levering and I are both advocates of what is now called a "prolife" political position, coming from our respective traditions, but for the same universally valid reasons, this is a good place to conclude my response to his essay. For it shows that our theoretical commonality is not only an academic exercise, but that it informs our political activism in the world (but not vice versa).

3

Islamic Natural Law Theories

Anver M. Emon

This essay provides an introductory overview of key natural law approaches in Islamic legal history. In doing so, it shows how the distinct vantage point of law and legal theory posits important questions about reason and authority that differ in salient ways from related questions that are framed by the well-studied field of Islamic philosophy. While the two fields of research and inquiry certainly overlap in various respects, attention to their difference reveals how pre-modern Muslim jurists conceptualized issues that might broadly be conceived as addressing Islamic law and morality.[1]

This is an opportune moment to explore these questions in Islamic legal thought in collaboration with scholars from the Christian and Jewish traditions, for at least two reasons. The first reason has to do with the resurgence in Islamic studies of research on *usul al-fiqh*, a genre of pre-modern Islamic legal literature often translated as jurisprudence or legal theory.[2] This resurgence is evident in the various efforts by scholars of Islam and Islamic law to move beyond examining the interstices of doctrinal rules, and instead to examine epistemic and hermeneutic possibilities at a time when Islamic law has assumed

---

[1] Anver M. Emon, *Islamic Natural Law Theories* (Oxford: Oxford University Press, 2010).

[2] See for instance, Ahmad Atif Ahmad, *Structural Interrelations of Theory and Practice in Islamic Law: A Study of Six Works of Medieval Islamic Jurisprudence* (Leiden: Brill, 2006); Rumee Ahmed, *Narratives of Islamic Legal Theory* (Oxford: Oxford University Press, 2012); David R. Vishanoff, *The Formation of Islamic Hermeneutics: How Sunni Legal Theorists Imagined a Revealed Law* (New Haven: American Oriental Society, 2011).

greater prominence in public discourse, whether in the Muslim world or outside of it. All too often, contemporary debates on Islam draw upon a particularly rarified image of the tradition (inflexible, rigorous, divine, unchanging) that serves as a backdrop to more general, and sometimes polemical, debates of identity politics across regions as diverse as North America, Europe (both Western and Eastern), Africa, and Asia. The turn to *usul al-fiqh* can be understood as a remedy to this phenomenon.

The second reason has to do with the increased efforts among religious communities, particularly the Abrahamic faith communities, to search for common ground and shared values at a time of increased tensions, even hostilities, between religious groups in an increasingly contested public sphere.[3] Correlatively, to dialogue about natural law with, for instance, Jews, Christians, and Muslims also allows us to inquire about the relationship between religion and what is often posited as a secular public sphere.[4] In particular, such dialogue may reveal important questions about religion and public life: to what extent do religious traditions themselves anticipate and make room for the kinds of arguments and logics that inform disputes about how to order and manage our affairs, or in other words, about how to govern?[5]

More often than not, those who write about religion in the public sphere do so from the perspective of a particular liberal theory of politics (e.g., Rawlsian), and using that liberal structure raise questions about whether religious traditions (or other comprehensive doctrines, to use Rawls' phrase), can *fit* in *our* society (leaving aside for now what "fit" and "our" means).[6] This essay changes the frame of

---

[3] Miroslav Volf, *Allah: A Christian Response* (New York: Harper Collins, 2011). International Theological Commission, "In Search of a Universal Ethic: A New Look at the Natural Law," Official Vatican Site for the International Theological Commission, http://www.vatican.va/roman_curia/congregations/cfaith/cti_documents/rc_con_cfaith_doc_20090520_legge-naturale_en.html (accessed June 20, 2013).

[4] Courtney Bender and Pamela Klassen, eds., *After Pluralism: Reimagining Religious Engagement* (New York: Columbia University Press, 2010).

[5] See for instance, José Casanova, *Public Religions in the Modern World* (Chicago: University of Chicago Press, 1994).

[6] See for instance, John Rawls, *Political Liberalism* (1993; reprint, New York: Columbia University Press, 1996); Will Kymlicka, *Multicultural Citizenship: A Liberal Theory of Minority Rights* (Oxford: Clarendon Press, 1995); Andrew March, *Islam and Liberal Citizenship: The Search for an Overlapping Consensus* (Oxford: Oxford University Press, 2011).

analysis to explore whether and how natural law offers insights into the Islamic tradition, and thereby enable further reflection about the range of arguments and logics that are legitimate (from an Islamic perspective) for purposes of law and governance. A principal conclusion drawn from this analysis will show how further research into Islamic natural law theories not only exposes the limits of those same natural law theories, but also gestures to further research questions concerning the nature and scope of legitimate authority and agency in Islamic law.

This essay will proceed in four sections. Section 3.1 will outline the major theories of Islamic natural law, drawing principally from my earlier scholarship on the topic. Section 3.2 will explore the significance of the term *tabi'a*—a term that occurs in Islamic natural philosophy and can mean quite literally nature. Exploring the implications of *tabi'a* on our understanding of the natural world contributes to the analysis in Section 3.3 of (a) the disciplinary difference between Islamic legal philosophy and Islamic natural philosophy, and (b) the epistemic limits of any Islamic natural law theory. Central to the discussion of limits are certain presumptions in competing Islamic natural law theories that may actually over-determine what is otherwise a more ambiguous and complex world. By tracing the move from the ambiguity of the world as it is to the determinacy that makes different Islamic natural law theories possible, I confess a certain skepticism about the juxtaposition of nature and law in "natural law," and thereby some dissatisfaction with the competing Islamic natural law theories outlined in Section 3.1. That skepticism and dissatisfaction, though, makes possible a deep appreciation for both how and why competing Islamic natural law theories conceptualize nature in ways that, for the historian but perhaps not for the lawyer, too neatly cover the complex conditions of authority, whether of God or the human agent, in light of the contingency of human existence in both time and space. As will be suggested, however skeptical one may be of natural law generally, or Islamic natural law specifically, the inquiry herein gestures to a central set of themes that cut across Islamic intellectual trends, namely authority and agency. To illustrate the central significance of these two concepts across the Islamic intellectual tradition, Section 3.4 explores a pre-modern theological debate about the Qur'an. Addressing this narrowly theological debate at the end of the essay emphasizes the central importance of authority and agency in so much of Islamic legal and theological thought. The juxtaposition of debates in legal philosophy, natural philosophy, and theology reveals how the themes of authority and agency not only unite different fields of inquiry, but also take distinct shape across them, and thus constitute important focal points for further research in the Islamic intellectual tradition.

3.1 ISLAMIC NATURAL LAW THEORIES

This section provides an overview of competing Islamic natural law theories[7] based on close readings of *usul al-fiqh* treatises by pre-modern jurists living roughly from the ninth to the fourteenth centuries. There were two principal theories, within which differences arose between jurists of each theoretical camp. For the purposes of this essay, the two theoretical approaches will be addressed generally in order to facilitate an understanding of the competing trends, their limits, and their contribution to the more global discourse of natural law, to which this volume is also directed.[8]

Pre-modern Muslim jurists recognized that reason serves important *epistemic* purposes in legal interpretation. Moreover, since the late nineteenth century, much of the debate about reason in Islamic legal studies has focused on whether, how, and to what extent Muslims can perform *ijtihad*, or renewed interpretation, on matters already addressed by historical precedent. In both the scholarly and popular literature, *ijtihad* offers theorists and reformists alike an important doctrinal site to address the scope of moral agency; the nature

---

[7] The use of the phrase "Islamic natural law" theories might strike some as loaded given how "natural law" has assumed an important place in Western intellectual history. The use of the phrase "Islamic natural law" is not meant to ellide the Islamic and Western trajectories of jurisprudence. Rather, the use of the phrase is based in part upon the way in which jurists tied the authority of reason to a particular view of the created world as fused with fact and value. As will be shown below, they used terms like *maslaha, manfa'a, and fa'ida* to designate the beneficial quality of the natural world, from which they could reason to the good and the bad, the lawful and the prohibited. As such, reason and nature become fused in these terms, and thereby contributed to designating the theories I describe as Islamic natural law theories.

[8] Readers interested in a more detailed account of both theories and their different exponents can consult my prior study from which this general overview is drawn: Emon, *Islamic Natural Law Theories.*

of epistemic authority; and the relationship between law, reform, and modernity.[9]

Importantly, a natural law inquiry frames the role of reason in a manner that is distinct from, though certainly not unrelated to, the question of *ijtihad*. A key distinction is that an Islamic natural law inquiry concerns the *ontological* authority of reason as a source of law, as opposed to its *epistemic* authority in legal reasoning. By *ontological role* I mean to inquire into whether and to what extent reason is or can be an authoritative *source* for law in those instances when source-texts such as the Qur'an or *hadith* are silent.

Pre-modern jurists were somewhat nervous to grant reason ontological authority in Islamic law, and for good reason. The Islamic legal tradition is often described as one that is drawn from the Qur'an and traditions of the Prophet Muhammad (*hadith*), or in other words textual authorities (*nusus*) that ground and delimit the scope of legal inquiry. To grant reason ontological authority, separate and distinct from the textual sources, might lead to unrestrained deliberation about Islamic law without due regard for the will of God. Indeed, such lack of restraint could be viewed as a challenge to the primacy of God's authority, as manifested by the primacy of the Qur'an and the *hadith* as sources of authority. Though jurists developed other sources of legal authority (e.g., rule by consensus or *ijma'*), the popular image of Islamic law is that it is a highly textual tradition in which reason is not an independent source of law.

However, Muslim jurists knew that the world of lived experience could not be captured between the Qur'an's two covers or by the large body of *hadith*. Consequently, their caution about reason did not mean the preclusion of any ontological role for reason. Rather, they held that reason could have an ontological role to play in the law. Where they differed, though, was what that grant of ontological authority implied about their theology and the relationship of that theology to the authority of the law derived through the operation of reason. In the Sunni *usul al-fiqh* literature, pre-modern jurists phrased the question as follows: in the absence of some scriptural source-text (*min qabla wurud al-shar'*) such as the Qur'an or the

---

[9] For scholarly works on *ijtihad,* see Shaista P. Ali-Karamali and F. Dunne, "The Ijtihad Controversy," *Arab Law Quarterly* 9, no. 3 (1994): 238–57; Wael B. Hallaq, "Was the Gate of Ijtihad Closed?" *International Journal of Middle East Studies* 16, no. 1 (1984): 3–41.

hadith, can jurists utilize reason as a source of law? There were those who said yes, and others who said, in lawyerly fashion, "it depends."

3.1.1 Hard Natural Law

Those who said yes—the Hard Natural Law jurists—believed that God creates all things for the purpose of good and benefit. Any other option would mean that God might do something for evil purposes, which they rejected as a theologically unacceptable possibility. If God only acts with goodness and justice, they argued, then all of His creation must also be vested with that goodness. To what end, they then asked, was this bountiful world created? Perhaps it might be for God's use and enjoyment. But since, in their theology, God is omnipotent and needs nothing, that option was theologically unacceptable. Instead the created world, they argued, must be for the benefit and enjoyment of God's creatures, in particular human beings. Indeed, they held, God did not create the world to cause pain and suffering for others, since that would be unfair and unjust to those adversely affected. As God is only just, creation must therefore pose a benefit to us. In their own technical vocabulary, Hard Natural Law jurists rendered the natural world "permissible" (*ibaha*), which was the technical term by which they infused the natural world with a normative content stemming from God's justice and will. Put simply, the "is" was also the "ought" for Hard Natural Law jurists. According to their theory, nature is objectively good for humanity given the assumption of a just Creator who only does the good and needs nothing. By fusing fact and value in the created world, Hard Natural Law jurists granted reason the ontological authority to analyze and investigate the world around them, and thereby derive new norms. For them, one could rationally deduce the good from nature, and transform that finding into a normative Shari'a-based value, since the empirical goodness of nature also contains normative content stemming from the will of God.[10]

[10] Throughout this essay, I utilize the phrase "fusion of fact and value" to convey how pre-modern Muslim jurists provided a theoretical foundation for reason's ontological authority. They did so by investing the created world with a presumably decipherable normative content, which stemmed from their belief in God as the Creator who created the world for good (though they disagreed about what this implied about God's nature). The phrase itself appears throughout the essay, and some of the anonymous reviewers raised further inquiries about what lay behind that apparent fusion. Moreover, the use of the phrase throughout the essay may strike some readers as

3.1.2 The Voluntarist Critique

Against the Hard Natural Law jurists were those who, for theological reasons, disagreed with the views (a) that God only does the good, and (b) that one could infer legal norms by observing the natural world. For nature to be a bounty and source of goodness, one must assume that God only does good with the purpose of benefiting humanity.[11] Voluntarist theologians rejected this theology of God, especially since it potentially undermined God's omnipotence. If God can only do the good for humanity's benefit, and human reason can determine the good (and thereby delineate obligations and prohibitions), then effectively humans can require God to reward and punish certain behavior as obligatory or prohibited. This possibility undermined the Voluntarists' belief that God is omnipotent and not subservient to anyone or anything. For Voluntarist theologians, the question about whether God can do only good or also evil fundamentally confused human nature with God's nature. Human nature may be subjected to reasoned deliberation about the good and the bad, but no one can presume to impose upon God any obligation to do the good. Jurists such as Abu Ishaq al-Shirazi (d. 476/1083) argued vociferously that God was not limited in any way. There is no standard of justice that precedes God or in any way limits His omnipotence. As al-Shirazi wrote: "God does as He wishes and rules as He desires" (*yaf'alu Allah ma yasha' wa yahkumu ma yuridu*).[12] For Voluntarist theologians, God does as He wishes; whatever He does is by definition good.

To justify their opposition to any fusion of fact and value, Voluntarists cited Q. 17:15, which states: "We do not punish until We send a messenger." This verse enshrines the idea that divine sanction requires an express statement of will, not a reasoned inquiry into the good and the bad. To reason from nature, they argued, assumes too

---

formulaic and insufficiently unpacked. The pre-modern jurists surveyed did not, to my knowledge, further elaborate on what they meant by their fusion beyond what I have elaborated, and so further analysis of what lay behind this fusion is not possible in the scope of this study. The consistent usage of the phrase in this essay, though perhaps not necessarily artful, is meant to ensure clarity for the reader.

[11] For Hard Natural Law sources relying on this assumption, see Abu Bakr al-Jassas, *Usul al-Jassas: al-Fusul fi al-Usul*, ed. Muhammad Muhammad Tamir, 2 vols. (Beirut: Dar al-Kutub al-'Ilmiyya, 2000), 2:100; Abu al-Husayn al-Basri, *al-Mu'tamad fi Usul al-Fiqh* (Beirut: Dar al-Kutub al-'Ilmiyya, n.d.), 2:320.

[12] Abu Ishaq al-Shirazi, *Sharh al-Lum'a*, ed. 'Abd al-Majid Turki (Beirut: Dar al-Gharb al-Islami, 1988), 2:983–84.

much of both God and human understanding of the divine will. For instance, the eleventh century jurist Ibn Hazm, never one to mince words, argued that the Hard Naturalists' fusion of fact and value in nature was "plain pomposity" (*makabirat al-ʿiyan*).[13] By their very nature, human beings are prone to sexual licentiousness, drunken debauchery, and lapses in religious observance. These are all potentially natural dispositions, he argued, all of which God has expressly prohibited. Consequently, one cannot infer from the facts of nature any moral norms and obligations that enjoy the imprint of the divine. For Voluntarists, where no source-text addresses an issue, no one can assert a divine rule of law. Voluntarists did not deny that a rule of God exists; they argued instead that humans are not in an epistemic position to determine what the law is.[14] Consequently in situations where there is no source-text, Voluntarists held that the divine law is in a state of suspension (*tawaqquf, waqf*), such that one cannot authoritatively assert a rule of obligation or prohibition.[15]

3.1.3 The Voluntarist Approach: Soft Natural Law

Nonetheless, the Voluntarists could not ignore the fact that as much as they looked to God for guidance in His sacred scriptures, those texts were limited. Consequently they could not deny the need to engage in legal reasoning. In fact, they could not deny that at times, reason would have to be a source of the law itself. To theorize reason's ontological authority, some Voluntarist theologians, in their role as legal theorists, developed a natural law theory that both fused fact and value in the created world, and preserved their Voluntarist commitment to God's omnipotence. Their natural law theory shall be called Soft Natural Law.[16] Like the Hard Natural Law jurists, Soft Natural

---

[13] Ibn Hazm, *al-Ihkam fi Usul al-Ahkam* (Cairo: Dar al-Hadith, 1984), 1:54.

[14] On human epistemic weakness, see Abu ʿAbd Allah al-Asfahani, *al-Kashif ʿan al-Mahsul fi ʿIlm al-Usul*, eds. ʿAdil Ahmad ʿAbd al-Mawjud and ʿAli Muhammad Muʿawwad (Beirut: Dar al-Kutub al-ʿIlmiyya, 1998), 1:370–71.

[15] Al-Khatib al-Baghdadi, *Kitab al-Faqih waʾl-Mutafaqqih* (n.p.: Matbaʿat al-Imtiyaz, 1977), 192–94; Ibn Hazm, *al-Ihkam*, 1:52; Abu al-Muzaffar al-Samʿani, *Qawatiʿ al-Adilla fi al-Usul*, ed. Muhammad Hasan Ismaʿil al-Shafiʿi (Beirut: Dar al-Kutub al-ʿIlmiyya, 1997), 2:46–47, 52; al-Shirazi, *Sharh al-Lumʿa*, 2:977. Ibn al-Farikan, *Sharh al-Waraqat*, ed. Sarah Shafi al-Hajiri (Beirut: Dar al-Bashaʾir al-Islamiyya, 2001), 347–50, stated that this position was adopted by the majority of Ashʿarites.

[16] The use of the phrases "hard natural law" and "soft natural law" in the Islamic context are terms that I have introduced into the narrow field of Islamic legal studies. However, through the dialogic process of this project and the expanded research

Law jurists argued that nature is fused with fact and value, thereby reflecting a presumption of the goodness of nature. But they argued that the fusion is not because God only does the good and cannot do evil. Rather, the good in nature results from God's *grace* (*tafaddul*). God chose to be gracious when creating the world, and the world has persisted in that fashion. In other words, the natural world has a certain determinacy that also reflects a divine goodness for humanity. With this theologically informed legal philosophy, they could thereby render reason an ontologically authoritative source of law.

Their theory of grace allowed them to preserve their Voluntarist theology while also allowing reason to play an important authoritative role in their philosophy of law.[17] *Theologically speaking*, since God can choose to change His grace anytime, Soft Natural Law is consistent with Voluntarist theology. *Jurisprudentially speaking*, after God created the world as a benefit, it does not seem that God has changed His mind; consequently, it is appropriate to grant reason ontological authority to investigate the created world and derive norms therefrom.

3.1.4 Soft Natural Law and the *Maqasid* Model: Limiting Reason's Scope

The Soft Natural Law jurists, having granted reason ontological authority, could not just leave it at that, though. They were worried about reason holding an unchecked ontological authority as a source of Shari'a—the so-called "slippery slope" concern, in other words. To let reason hold such authority, they worried, would make them seem like the Hard Natural Law adherents, who they disagreed with on theological grounds, but not necessarily on jurisprudential ones. So they devised a model of reasoning to limit the scope of reasoned

---

ambit of this essay, it is clear that the different approaches to determinacy captured by the adjectives "hard" and "soft" are not unique to the Islamic legal context. For example, in the field of natural philosophy and Aristotelian studies, as discussed below, the same adjectives are used to delineate competing notions of causal determinism. See for instance, Richard Sorabji, *Necessity, Cause and Blame: Perspectives on Aristotle's Theory* (Chicago: Chicago University Press, 1980), 244, 252. The family resemblances across these fields reveal a common theme across distinct disciplines and arguably help situate Islamic natural law theories within a larger set of philosophical debates.

[17] Because they believed that God's grace could change, though, their commitment to the fusion of fact and value was not nearly as hard and fast as the view held by the Hard Natural Law, which explains why I call this second group *Soft* Natural Law jurists.

deliberation. They held that there are various issues and interests that work to the benefit and detriment of society. Those issues may not be the subject of any source text. In cases where no source-text governs, those interests (i.e., *maslaha*) can be subjected to reasoned deliberation and relied upon to generate a norm of legal significance. As long as the interest at stake neither confirms nor negates a source-text, relates to one of the aims and purposes of the Shari'a (i.e., *maqasid*), and concerns a social necessity (as opposed to any lesser value), then it can be the source of law.

The terms *maslaha* and *maqasid* are significant for appreciating how Soft Natural Law jurists narrowed the scope of reason's ontological authority. For purposes of illustration, the views of the well-known Sunni jurist Abu Hamid al-Ghazali (d. 1111) will be examined here. For al-Ghazali, before discussing any method of generating rules by reference to benefits or *maslaha*, one must first know what a *maslaha* is. Generally, the term can refer to anything that allows one to obtain a benefit (*jalb manfa'a*) or to repel a harm (*daf' madarra*).[18] But al-Ghazali's use of the term had a more technical meaning than this general linguistic understanding. For him, *maslaha* as a technical term of art referred to any interest that upholds and preserves the purposes of the divine law (*al-muhafiza 'ala maqsud al-shar'*).[19] These purposes or basic aims of the law consist of preserving religion (*din*), life (*nafs*), reason (*'aql*), lineage (*nasl*), and property (*mal*). "Whatever involves the preservation of these five fundamental values is a *maslaha*, and whatever neglects these fundamental values is corrupt, and so repelling it is a *maslaha*."[20] Al-Ghazali illustrated these five values by referring to various scriptural examples. For instance, punishing an unbeliever who leads others astray upholds and protects the value of religion.[21] The value of life is upheld by the punishment of execution for murder or retribution for causing a physical injury.[22] The punishment for consuming alcohol upholds the virtue of having

---

[18] Abu Hamid al-Ghazali, *al-Mustasfa min 'Ilm al-Usul*, ed. Ibrahim M. Ramadan (Beirut: Dar al-Arqam, n.d.), 1:636. Ibn Manzur and al-Zabidi defined the term as the good or *salah*. Ibn Manzur, *Lisan al-'Arab*, 6th ed. (Beirut: Dar Sadir, 1997), 2:517; Muhibb al-Din al-Zabidi, *Taj al-'Urus min Jawahir al-Qamus*, ed. Ali Shiri (Beirut: Dar al-Fikr, 1994), 4:125–26.

[19] Al-Ghazali, *al-Mustasfa*, 1:636.

[20] Al-Ghazali, *al-Mustasfa*, 1:636.

[21] Al-Ghazali, *al-Mustasfa*, 1:637.

[22] Al-Ghazali, *al-Mustasfa*, 1:637.

a sound mind,[23] while the punishments for fornication and adultery protect the integrity of family and lineage.[24] Finally, the punishments for theft and usurpation maintain the basic aim of upholding property interests.[25]

Importantly, these values are not derived from scripture, although scriptural rules and provisions can and do corroborate these values. Rather, al-Ghazali considered these values to be intuitively known. They are the kinds of values that any society or legal tradition would uphold if it values the preservation and flourishing of society. As he said: "It is impossible that any society (*milla min al-milal*) or any legal system (*shari'a min al-shara'i'*), which aims to benefit creation (*islah al-khalq*) would not include prohibitions against neglect of and restraint from these five values."[26] These five aims provide the telos to which any *maslaha* must pose a nexus before it can be utilized as a foundation for a Shari'a rule.

Not every *maslaha* can enjoy such legal authority. To determine the legal authority of a *maslaha* requires examining (1) its relationship to scriptural sources and (2) the strength of its nexus to the basic aims noted above as measured in terms of the importance of the social good it is designed to achieve. For instance, scriptural sources may positively affirm a *maslaha* (*maslaha mu'tabar*).[27] However, for al-Ghazali, this type of *maslaha* was not appropriate for his *maslaha-maqasid* model of reasoning since a source text substantiates the *maslaha* already. On the other hand, scriptural sources might expressly repudiate or reject a particular *maslaha*.[28] Again, however,

---

[23] Al-Ghazali, *al-Mustasfa,* 1:637.

[24] Al-Ghazali, *al-Mustasfa,* 1:637.

[25] Al-Ghazali, *al-Mustasfa,* 1:637.

[26] Al-Ghazali, *al-Mustasfa,* 1:637.

[27] An example of this kind of *maslaha* would be the prohibition of any intoxicant. Certainly there is Qur'anic scripture that condemns the consumption of wine. One can use this textual reference to wine as a basis for creating other prohibitions against any and all intoxicating substances on the ground that they protect the integrity of the mind. Although the scriptural provision is not express on intoxicants generally, nonetheless, a rule by prior precedent (*qiyas*) can extend the ban on wine to include a ban on all intoxicants. Al-Ghazali, *al-Mustasfa,* 1:634–35.

[28] Al-Ghazali mentioned as an example the case of the king who has sex during the day in the month of Ramadan. Jurists debated how he should expiate the sin of deliberately breaking his fast in this fashion. The Qur'an stipulates as expiation that one should free a slave. But if one cannot do so, he should fast for two consecutive months. If that is not possible, he should feed sixty indigent people. Some jurists argued that a king should fast two consecutive months and not free a slave, despite the latter being mentioned first in the Qur'anic verse, and presumably taking priority over the other

this particular type of *maslaha* was not central to al-Ghazali's Soft Natural Law model of reasoning. Rather both forms of *maslaha* illustrate the enduring importance and centrality of source-texts (*nusus*) in al-Ghazali's legal method, and are arguably offered to circumscribe the extent to which extra-textual sources can be incorporated into the law. The last category of *maslaha* is the one where no specific textual indicator (*nass mu'ayyan*) expressly adopts or rejects it.[29] This type of *maslaha* is the one that can be the basis for generating *de novo* rules of law, and thereby is central to al-Ghazali's Soft Natural Law model of legal reasoning. It represents the site where a jurist utilizes greatest interpretive agency.

The second nexus that al-Ghazali addressed concerns the relationship between the silent *maslaha* and the five goals or aims of the legal system (*maqasid*). A silent *maslaha* can pose a nexus to the basic aims of the Shari'a in three different ways. First it may present a necessary interest (*darura*), in which case the *maslaha* is of the highest order. Necessary interests, according to al-Ghazali, are so central to society that no disagreement about them can be imagined.[30] Second, a *maslaha* can pose only a basic need (*haja*), where the *maslaha* is deemed important, but does not rise to the highest level of social interest. And lastly, a silent *maslaha* can present an edificatory interest (*tazyina, tahsina*).[31] These three categories reflect the varying strength (*quwwa*) of the nexus between the silent *maslaha* and the five *maqasid* values.[32] While Soft Natural Law jurists would give examples to demarcate and distinguish between these levels of significance, the

---

forms of expiation. They argued that since the king has such great wealth, freeing a slave does not pose a significant deterrence to him. Consequently, in order to deter him from breaking his fast, he should be required to fast two consecutive months instead. But for al-Ghazali, this view is invalid despite being based on a reasonable *maslaha*. He believed that this rationale contradicts the text of the Qur'an, which provides a clear indication of the order in which the expiations should be applied to the wrongdoer. To open the door to this kind of *maslaha*, argued al-Ghazali, would lead to a change in all the limits of the law (*hudud al-shara'i'*) because of changes in circumstance or context. Such interpretations would undermine determinacy in the law and diminish the integrity of jurists among the people. Al-Ghazali, *al-Mustasfa*, 1:635.

[29] Al-Ghazali, *al-Mustasfa*, 1:635–36.

[30] Al-Ghazali, *al-Mustasfa*, 1:638.

[31] Al-Ghazali, *al-Mustasfa*, 1:636.

[32] Al-Ghazali, *al-Mustasfa*, 1:635–36. Underlying each of these categories of interests are subsidiary interests that supplement or perfect the primary rules of these categories.

fact remains that they are not well defined.[33] That is perhaps part of the draw they provide, and the flexibility they offer.

Importantly, al-Ghazali posited the nexus between the *maslaha*, and scriptural sources on the one hand, and the *maslaha* and *maqasid* values on the other to make a significant and central point for his Soft Natural Law model of reasoning: a silent *maslaha* that only poses a need (*haja*) or vindicates an edificatory interest (*tahsin/tazyin*) cannot be the basis for creating new Shariʿa rules.[34] In other words, only the category posing the strongest nexus to the basic values, namely the *darura*, can provide an authoritative basis by which to determine the law in the absence of any scriptural source (i.e., *min qabla wurud al-sharʿ*). As al-Ghazali stated, "it is not farfetched that the interpretation of a jurist would lead to such a [*darura*-based] rule although no specific source of law exists as evidence for it" (*fa la buʿd fi an yuʿdi ilayhi ijtihad mujtahid wa an lam yashhad lahu asl muʿayyan*).[35] Soft Natural Law jurists such as Abu Hamid al-Ghazali held that only the silent *maslaha* that addresses a social necessity (*darura*) could be a basis for Shariʿa norms. A *maslaha* that falls into the other two categories cannot constitute a basis for legal norms that reflect the divine will. Certainly they may provide a basis for some normative, regulatory ordering, but they do not assume the authority of a Shariʿa norm.

3.1.5 Nature and Contingency in Hard and Soft Natural Law

The close examination of the *maqasid* model of reasoning is meant to illustrate one important point: despite granting ontological authority to reason, Soft Natural Law jurists nonetheless limited the scope of reasoned deliberation in their philosophy of law. More generally, though, this section has highlighted the fact that both Hard and Soft Natural Law jurists resorted to nature as a source of evidence for the

---

[33] For other jurists who adopt this hierarchy of *maslaha*, see Anver M. Emon, *Islamic Natural Law Theories* (Oxford: Oxford University Press, 2010), ch. 4.

[34] Al-Ghazali, *al-Mustasfa*, 1:640.

[35] Al-Ghazali, *al-Mustasfa*, 1:640–41. Notably, in his earlier work, *Shifaʾ al-Ghalil*, al-Ghazali stated that one could rely on both the *haja* and the *darura* for independent analysis, as long as they inductively pose a nexus to the body of Shariʿa (*kana mulaʾiman li tasarrufat al-sharʿ*). However, the third weakest category could not be used for such analysis. Abu Hamid al-Ghazali, *Shifaʾ al-Ghalil fi Bayan al-Shabh wa al-Mukhil wa Masalik al-Taʿlil*, ed. Muhammad al-Kubaysi (Baghdad: Raʾasa Diwan al-Awqaf, 1971), 208–09.

divine will. Even though Soft and Hard Natural Law theorists disagreed *theologically* about the nature of God's justice, jurists from both camps generally agreed, *jurisprudentially* speaking, that the natural order of the world provides an authoritative basis for reasoning about the law.

One principal concern that both models of legal philosophy evoke is that their reliance on a determinate natural order give the natural law inquiry the appearance of objective determinacy, when in fact the natural world and our experience of it is complex and contingent.[36] Soft Natural Law jurists such as al-Ghazali seemed to make a similar point when they rebuked Hard Natural Law jurists for thinking that an individual can determine values like the good and the bad, as if they could be "found" or "discovered" in some objectively true or correct fashion. Such values, al-Ghazali argued, are so embedded in who we are that we cannot escape our own context to find an objective position outside ourselves. Ideas of the good and the bad, according to al-Ghazali, are ideas to which we are conditioned at a young age. One accepts something as good or bad as a result of various factors (*asbab kathira*) that cannot be fully determined. But to assert the value as true with objective certainty would require disassociating the truth claim from any contextual considerations in order to discover the essence of the thing. But such disassociation, he suggested, is impossible. "It is possible that extensive investigation may fashion a sense of truth about [these moral values]. And perhaps they are true determinations. But [they can be known as objectively true] only through minute [analysis] (*shart daqiqa*), which the mind cannot satisfy."[37]

Ironically, we can apply al-Ghazali's critique to his own theory of Soft Natural Law. His theological resort to God's grace to fuse fact and value in nature for jurisprudential purposes led him to presume a determinacy in the natural order, and thereby made possible the

---

[36] On a related note, contemporary theorists critique the natural sciences as a model of evaluation in the human sciences, see Hans-Georg Gadamer, *Truth and Method*, trans. Joel Weinsheimer and Donald G. Marshall, 2nd ed. (New York: Continuum, 1989), 284; Charles Taylor, *Sources of the Self: The Making of the Modern Identity* (Cambridge, MA: Harvard University Press 1989), 20. The above concern with Islamic natural law theories raises concerns about how the world of human experience is framed and understood for purposes of law as opposed to other social science or humanistic endeavors.

[37] Al-Ghazali, *al-Mustasfa*, 1:117.

kind of reasoning he outlined in his *maqasid-maslaha* model. Both Soft and Hard Natural Law jurists rendered nature determinate so as to provide an ontological anchor for reasoned deliberation where source-texts are otherwise silent. Consequently, whether one prefers one or the other natural law theory is arguably less interesting than further exploring what nature and determinacy imply about the law and its claim to authority. And it is to this topic that we now turn.

3.2 *TABI'A* AND THE METAPHYSICS OF KNOWING

Examining how Muslim philosophers reflected on nature in their philosophies of the natural sciences will reveal the contours and limits of the presumption of determinacy in Islamic natural law theories.[38] The starting point for such an inquiry must begin with an analysis of the term *tabi'a*, which is often understood to refer to nature. The term itself comes from the trilateral root *t-b-'* and can refer to various features of the natural world. For instance the pre-modern lexicographer Ibn Manzur defined *tabi'a* in the following words: "the traits and dispositions to which humans are inclined" (*al-khaliqa wa al-sajiyya allati jubila 'alayha al-insan*). So for instance, one might say: "God imprinted (*taba'a*) upon the created world (*al-khalq*) characteristics (*taba'i'*) that He created. He brought forth [humanity] pursuant to [those characteristics, which are] their natural dispositions."[39] This definition certainly offers an enticing way to think about nature and human dispositions, and as such seems a tempting starting point to reflect on natural law in Islam. However, pre-modern jurists did not start or depart from the term *tabi'a* when devising their natural law theories. Instead, they situated the natural law inquiry in the context of debates about reason and what I have identified as the fusion of fact and value in nature. The Arabic terms of art they used to represent

---

[38] Some reviewers of my book asked why my approach to Islamic natural law theories does not begin with a discussion of *tabi'a*. See, for example, Andrew March, "[Review] *Islamic Natural Law Theories,*" *Journal of Law and Religion* 26 (2011): 101–09. This essay offers an initial effort to address that issue and thereby pose new questions to the pre-modern natural law account.

[39] Ibn Manzur, *Lisan al-'Arab*, 8:232.

the fusion of fact and value are not related to *tabi'a*. Instead, they are terms like *fa'ida* (bounty), *manfa'a* (benefit), *ibaha* (permissible), or *maslaha* (a good). The *usul al-fiqh* sources relied upon to ascertain competing Islamic natural law theories discuss the ontological authority of reason in terms that are not drawn from the trilateral root *t-b-'*.

The expectation that there would be a necessary link between what is called "natural law" in contemporary Western terminology, and the Arabic term *tabi'a*, might on first glance be understood as giving priority to philology or lexicography as the appropriate methodology for framing a study of Islamic natural law. That approach, though, does not pay heed to the way in which legal philosophy is a separate and distinct discipline that does not necessarily depart from nor build upon a philological methodology.

A more circumspect response, however, will show that an inquiry into *tabi'a* is neither irrelevant nor unnecessary to thinking about the "natural" in natural law, though in ways that reveal the distinct aims and purposes of legal philosophy and natural philosophy. As shown below, an inquiry into the salience and significance of *tabi'a* illustrates how it was a term of art in the field of Islamic philosophy (*falsafa*), a discipline that was albeit distinguishable from *usul al-fiqh*, but not so distinguishable as to be inappropriate for our discussion here. Indeed, even though *tabi'a* was a term of art in Islamic philosophical circles, those circles included Muslim jurists who also wrote treatises on *usul al-fiqh*. Presumably they would have known the term *tabi'a*. Yet, in their move from the philosophical to the jurisprudential, they avoided reference to it. This of course raises the question of why they did so. By analyzing how Muslim jurist-philosophers addressed *tabi'a* in terms of natural philosophy (as opposed to legal philosophy), this section will offer an answer. In doing so, this section will showcase how the two disciplinary approaches to nature (the legal philosophical and the natural philosophical) posit determinacy as a key issue in working through more foundational issues of authority, agency, and legitimacy in the Islamic intellectual tradition more broadly.

For Muslim jurists also writing in and about philosophy, *tabi'a* offered an important entry point for delimiting the scope to which the natural sciences (*tabi'iyat*) and their theories of causation could explain the world. For instance, Aristotle, writing in his *Physics*, outlined the ambit of the natural sciences. Importantly, the natural sciences offered Aristotle an opportunity to expound in both *Physics* and *Metaphysics* his theory of causation, and its implications on what can be known with certitude. In *Physics*, he inquired into nature and motion, setting forth through the natural sciences "all there is to know about the world."[40] For Aristotle, "nature" refers to animals, plants, and basic elements such as earth, air, wind, and fire. But most notably, all the things that fall within the ambit of nature are characterized as being either in motion or stationary—they have an innate nature that allows them to change or remain static (*Physics*, II.1). Causation was a central feature of Aristotle's approach to nature, whereby a thing or state of affairs is an effect of some cause. Consequently, a key question concerned the basis by which something changes. Given a particular thing in the world, what brings it into being? In other words, what causes it?

For Aristotle, a state of affairs may have multiple causes; something might come about for different reasons. Nonetheless, each is a causal explanation for the thing being considered. As such, Aristotle offered four different accounts of causation. Two of the causes are matter and form, or the things from which an entity is made.[41] Both form and matter are linked to one another in a relationship of dependency, as Bodnar explains: "As a rule there is a collaboration between these causes: matter provides the potentialities which are actualised by the form...These features, then, are on the one hand the contribution of the matter, and as such the matter is the (material) cause of these features of the composite entity, whereas on the other hand they are indispensable presuppositions for the realisation of the form, and to that extent their presence is prompted by the form."[42] Aristotle called this relationship of dependency "hypothetical necessity," such that the one does not make the other necessary but only hypothetically so. For instance, if lumber is the matter and the house is a form, the house may presume the existence of wood, but the presence of wood does

---

[40] Istvan Bodnar, "Aristotle's Natural Philosophy", *The Stanford Encyclopedia of Philosophy* (Spring 2010 Edition), Edward N. Zalta (ed.), <http://plato.stanford.edu/archives/spr2010/entries/aristotle-natphil/>.

[41] Istvan Bodnar, "Aristotle's Natural Philosophy", *The Stanford Encyclopedia of Philosophy* (Spring 2010 Edition), Edward N. Zalta (ed.), <http://plato.stanford.edu/archives/spr2010/entries/aristotle-natphil/>.

[42] Istvan Bodnar, "Aristotle's Natural Philosophy", *The Stanford Encyclopedia of Philosophy* (Spring 2010 Edition), Edward N. Zalta (ed.), <http://plato.stanford.edu/archives/spr2010/entries/aristotle-natphil/>.

not necessitate the existence of the house. The house is a possibility that inheres in the wood.[43]

Aristotle called his last two causes "efficient cause" and "final cause." Efficient causes operate by "initiating processes and bringing about their effects, whereas final causes account for processes and entities by being what these processes and entities are for, what they objectively intend to attain."[44] Notably, Aristotle held that form and final cause might coincide, such as matter like wood contributing to the form of a house, which is also the final cause. The wood bears within it a potentiality that the form (e.g., the house) actualizes. That potentiality manifests as the final cause or the house, which is the aim or purpose of this particular piece of wood.

Aristotle's theory of causation relates directly to our capacity to claim to know anything about the world. For instance, in *Physics* II.3, he wrote: "Knowledge is the object of our inquiry, and men do not think they know a thing till they have grasped 'why', that is to say its cause."[45] Any aspect of physical change in the world, therefore, is to be understood, at least in part, in terms of a theory of causation. Given his theory of four causes, Aristotle was able to account for the various ways in which something could come to be, and thereby be known. For instance, Andrea Falcon writes about Aristotle's theory of causality as it pertains to explaining the world and all that exists within it: "the science of nature is concerned with natural bodies insofar as they are subject to change, and the job of the student of nature is to provide the explanation of their natural change. The factors that are involved in the explanation of natural change turn out to be matter, form, that which produces change, and the end of this change,"[46] or in other words Aristotle's four causes.

---

[43] For this example, see Istvan Bodnar, "Aristotle's Natural Philosophy", *The Stanford Encyclopedia of Philosophy* (Spring 2010 Edition), Edward N. Zalta (ed.), <http://plato.stanford.edu/archives/spr2010/entries/aristotle-natphil/>.

[44] Istvan Bodnar, "Aristotle's Natural Philosophy", *The Stanford Encyclopedia of Philosophy* (Spring 2010 Edition), Edward N. Zalta (ed.), <http://plato.stanford.edu/archives/spr2010/entries/aristotle-natphil/>.

[45] See also, Andrea Falcon, "Aristotle on Causality", *The Stanford Encyclopedia of Philosophy* (Fall 2011 Edition), Edward N. Zalta (ed.), <http://plato.stanford.edu/archives/fall2011/entries/aristotle-causality/>.

[46] Andrea Falcon, "Aristotle on Causality", *The Stanford Encyclopedia of Philosophy* (Fall 2011 Edition), Edward N. Zalta (ed.), <http://plato.stanford.edu/archives/fall2011/entries/aristotle-causality/>.

Of particular interest to this analysis is the concern of Muslim
jurists and theologians about the implication of any theory of causation on their theistic commitments to an omnipotent God. Muslim
jurist-theologians wrote about natural philosophy and causation in
the shadow of Classical Greek philosophy, as preserved and commented upon by Muslim philosophers, such as Ibn Sina, al-Farabi,
and others. As in the case of their legal philosophy, these Muslim
jurists writing on philosophy were poignantly attentive to how any
philosophical account of causation could impinge upon their theological commitment to an omnipotent God who can enter history
and alter our natural order. One jurist of particular note, known in
the Latin West as Algazel, was al-Ghazali (d. 1111), who was already
addressed at length above. A highly respected jurist and theologian,
he was no stranger to the Greek philosophical tradition, though he
came to it by way of al-Farabi and particularly Ibn Sina.[47]

Interestingly, al-Ghazali accepted the conclusion that causation
theories hold explanatory power about the world. He did not rebuke
the power of natural philosophy to help explain the world; in that
sense, al-Ghazali was not against the sciences of nature, for which he
used a derivative of the term *tabi'a*. For instance, in his *Deliverance
from Error*, al-Ghazali wrote:

> Knowledge of the natural sciences (*'ilm al-tabi'iyat*) consists of examin-
> ing the world of the heavens and the stars, and the distinct substances
> that lie beneath them such as water, air, dirt, and fire, and the contin-
> gent substances such as animals, vegetation, and minerals, and the
> causes that alter them, transform them, and blend them. That is like
> the doctor's examination of the human body—its primary and second-
> ary parts—and the causes of the change in its disposition. Just as it is
> not a condition of faith to reject the knowledge of medicine, it is not
> a condition of [faith] as well to reject that knowledge [of the natural

[47] Michael E. Marmura, "al-Ghazali," in the *Cambridge Companion to Arabic
Philosophy*, eds. Peter Adamson and Richard C. Taylor (Cambridge: Cambridge
University Press, 2005), 137–54, 44. Though Ibn Sina was certainly working within an
Aristotelian tradition, Avicennian scholarship notes how his approach was not some
sort of pure Aristotelianism, but rather a reworking of many features of Aristotle's phi-
losophy in light of his Neoplatonic commitments. Amos Bertolacci, "The Doctrine of
Material and Formal Causality in the 'Ilahiyyat' of Avicenna's 'Kitab al-Šifa,'" *Quaestio*
2 (2002): 125–54, 126; Robert Wisnovsky, "Avicenna and the Avicennian Tradition," in
The Cambridge Companion to Arabic Philosophy, eds. Peter Adamson and Richard C.
Taylor (Cambridge: Cambridge University Press, 2005), 92–136; Wisnovsky, "Final and
efficient causality in Avicenna's cosmology and theology," *Quaestio* 2 (2002): 97–123.

sciences], except on specific issues, which we mentioned in the book *The Incoherence of the Philosophers,* and others on which disagreement is required.[48]

He concluded by stating: "nature is subservient to God, most high, and does not act by itself, but rather it is put into motion by means of its creator. The sun, the moon, the stars, and natural dispositions are subservient to His command. There is nothing from among them that moves on its own."[49]

Importantly, al-Ghazali did not reject the various approaches to the natural sciences. Rather, his caution had more to do with whether or not theories of causation allowed for or undermined theistic presumptions that permit alternative explanations for how the world works. While accepting the natural sciences' explanatory power, al-Ghazali limited their explanatory power for theistic reasons, namely to maintain room for an omnipotent God who, through the performance of miracles, has "violated" what philosophers might consider the steady laws of nature and causation. As al-Ghazali argued, any theory of causation must also permit God to enter the world of human affairs and disrupt what might otherwise be understood as hard and fast expectations and predictions about how the natural world works.

In his *The Incoherence of the Philosophers,* al-Ghazali took up the very specific issue of causation and the place of miracles in any theory of knowledge. To do so, he first outlined the scope and types of knowledge available through the natural sciences. Making reference to Aristotle (though actually implicitly through Ibn Sina), al-Ghazali divided the natural sciences into foundational sciences and practical ones. Foundational sciences concern different qualities of matter, such as divisibility, motion, and change (*al-inqisam wa al-haraka wa al-taghayyur*), as well as time, space, and the idea of absence or void. Practical sciences have more functional significance, such as medicine and magic.[50] According to al-Ghazali, the foundational and practical natural sciences are not necessarily contrary to anything in the

---

[48] Abu Hamid al-Ghazali, "al-Munqidh min al-dalal," in *Majmu'a rasa'il al-Imam al-Ghazali,* ed. Ahmad Shams al-Din (Beirut: Dar al-Kutub al-'Ilmiyya, 1988), 8:3–84, 41–42.

[49] Al-Ghazali, "al-Munqidh min al-dalal," 42.

[50] Al-Ghazali, *The Incoherence of the Philosophers: A Parallel English-Arabic Text,* trans. Michael Marmura (Salt Lake City: Brigham Young University Press, 1997), 164. All translations are principally drawn from Marmura's with various modifications by the author.

revealed law. Indeed, he wrote: "There is no necessity to oppose [the philosophers] as a matter of revealed law concerning anything from among these sciences."[51]

To the extent he had objections to the natural sciences, he defined them narrowly. Specifically he issued four objections about the natural sciences, of which the first is particularly important to this analysis as it concerns causation. The first objection, he wrote, concerned the philosophers' view of causation, which he characterized as follows:

> [T]heir judgment that this connection between causes and effects that one observes in existence is a connection of necessary concomitance, and so that it is within neither [the realm of] power nor within [that of] possibility to bring about the cause without the effect or the effect without the cause.[52]

Al-Ghazali's critique of causation concerned its implication of a necessary, determinist, connection between cause and effect so as to preclude the theistically informed possibility that God can enter history and subvert the laws of nature. He framed this critique by reference to both Qur'anic accounts about God's miracles and concerns about the implications of causation on the Qur'an's veracity.

For instance, in the Qur'an, the Pharaoh of Egypt challenges Moses to bring forth a sign that would attest to the truth of Moses' claims about God and his demand for his people to be set free. "If you have come with a sign, then produce it, if you are among the truthful."[53] Standing only with his staff in hand, Moses threw it down and it transformed into a plainly visible snake (*thu'ban mubin*).[54] If one adopts the causation theories of Aristotelian natural philosophy, the transformation of the staff to a snake would either raise serious doubts about the laws of nature or alternatively the veracity of the Qur'an. Al-Ghazali did not necessarily take issue with natural philosophy—he quite clearly indicated that he was not opposed to natural philosophy in general. He could not, however, go so far as to adhere to natural philosophical foundational principles at the expense of the truth of the Qur'an's message.

One way to appreciate al-Ghazali's critique of causation is to explore what "miracle" implies about God and the natural world. In Arabic,

[51] Al-Ghazali, *Incoherence*, 166.
[52] Al-Ghazali, *Incoherence*, 166.
[53] Qur'an, 7:106.
[54] Qur'an, 7:107.

the term for miracle is *mu'jiza;* it refers to something that violates the normal course of events and, thereby, attests to the prophecy of those who perform them. According to A. J. Wensinck, a miracle is "a thing deviating from the usual course of things, appearing at the hands of him who pretends to be a prophet, as a challenge to those who deny this, of such a nature that it makes it impossible for them to produce the like of it. It is God's testimony to the sincerity of His apostles."[55] Miracles, in other words, are products of God that occur in the hands of those whose sincerity God wishes to showcase for others to witness in order "to realise His will...[I]t produces, in accordance with God's custom, in those who witness it, the conviction of the apostle's being sincere."[56]

Importantly, the power of a miracle rests in part upon its *violation* of the natural order, thereby implying that there is, presumptively, a stable, predictable natural order. If there were no natural order, then the occurrence of a miracle would not be out of the ordinary; it would not violate anything, and in that sense, would not be "miraculous." Consequently, any critique of the natural sciences and its theory of causation cannot so undermine the natural sciences lest such a critique render the category of "miracle" null or devoid of salience. Yet on the other hand, if veracity and truth are tied to the constancy, predictability, and verifiability that comes from the natural science's methods of causal analysis, then the claim that a miracle has occurred would not necessarily lead one to assume the truth or veracity of the claimant. Therefore, to critique the natural sciences and the causal mode of explaining the world, jurists such as al-Ghazali had to chart a careful course so as to uphold the explanatory power of the natural sciences, while also making room for miracles to offer their own explanatory power in accordance with certain theistic assumptions.

To chart this middle course, al-Ghazali had to limit the scope of causal explanatory power of the material world. For al-Ghazali, such a limit on the scope of causal explanation was necessary "in as much as [on this limitation] rests the affirmation of miracles (*ithbat al-mu'jizat*) that violate the habitual [course of nature] (*al-khariqa li al-'adat*) such as changing the staff into a snake...Whoever renders

---

[55] A.J. Wensinck, "Mu'djiza," *Encyclopaedia of Islam, Second Edition*, eds. P. Bearman, Th. Bianquis, C. E. Bosworth, E. van Donzel, and W. P. Heinrichs (Brill, September 6, 2011. *Brill Online*).

[56] Wensinck, "Mu'djiza."

the habitual courses [of nature] a necessary constant makes all those [miracles] impossible."[57] The impossibility of miracles was unacceptable to al-Ghazali because of what it would imply about both the truth of the Qur'anic message and a theological commitment to an omnipotent God. Consequently, for al-Ghazali, it was not necessary to challenge any and all features of the natural sciences. His concern was really only to affirm the truth of miracles, and thereby "to support what all Muslims agree on, to the effect that God has power over all things."[58]

But if God has power over all things, what can and does natural causation actually explain? Al-Ghazali addressed this question in Chapter 17 of *The Incoherence*. He acknowledged that there are obvious connections between decapitation and death, or between the presence of fire and things being burned. For him, though, the question was how to understand that connection. Those who embrace a determinist causal theory of nature will say, for instance, that the fire causes burning. But al-Ghazali asked: "For what proof is there that [the fire] is the agent [of burning]? They have no proof other than observing the occurrence of the burning at the [juncture of] contact with the fire."[59] In other words, while one can observe that where there is fire there is something that is burned, to hold that the fire thereby caused the burning is only an inference. At most, he argued, natural philosophers can say that there is a correlation between fire and burning. As he wrote: "It has thus become clear that existence with a thing (*'inda al-shay'*) does not prove that it exists because of it (*la yudillu 'ala annahu mawjud bi-hi*)."[60] The key distinction in this sentence has to do with the prepositions translated as "with" (*'inda*) and "because" (*bi*). The former connotes correlation while the latter connotes causation. For al-Ghazali, natural science can certainly demonstrate the correlation between fire and burning, but without more, it can only infer (with all the epistemic limitations inherent therein) that the fire caused the burning. Rather, he wrote that the causal nexus between things "is due to the prior decree of God, who creates them side by side, not to its being necessary in itself."[61] Importantly for this analysis,

[57] Al-Ghazali, *Incoherence*, 166.
[58] Al-Ghazali, *Incoherence*, 169.
[59] Al-Ghazali, *Incoherence*, 171.
[60] Al-Ghazali, *Incoherence*, 171.
[61] Al-Ghazali, *Incoherence*, 170.

though, the epistemic limits inherent to any such inference are all al-Ghazali needed to make miracles both possible and salient without also undermining the explanatory power of the natural sciences.

Al-Ghazali's opponents might retort that if there is no necessary connection between cause and effect, and if God can intervene when He so chooses, then what allows any of us to know anything about the world in which we live. In an entertaining passage, al-Ghazali recounted his opponents' possible argument:

> For if one denies that the effects follow necessarily from their causes and relates them to the will of their Creator, they will have no specific designated course but [a course that] can vary and change in kind, then let each of us allow the possibility of there being in front of him ferocious beasts, raging fires, high mountains, or enemies ready with their weapons [to kill him], but [also the possibility] that he does not see them because God does not create for him [a vision of them]. And if someone leaves a book in the house, let him allow as possible its change on his returning home into a beardless slave boy...or into an animal; or if he leaves a boy in his house, let him allow the possibility of his changing into a dog...If asked about any of this, he ought to say: "I do not know what is at the house at present. All I know is that I have left a book in the house, which is perhaps now a horse that has defiled the library with its urine and its dung, and that I have left in the house a jar of water, which may well have turned into an apple tree. For God is capable of everything."[62]

With this challenge, al-Ghazali had to reconcile his embrace of both the explanatory power of the natural sciences, and his theistic commitments to an omnipotent deity. He already held that the natural sciences permit us to make correlations, from which we can infer causation. To suggest that such casual nexuses are necessary would preclude any space for divine miracles. However, to deny the necessity of causation is not to deny that inferences of causation have considerable strength. Indeed, it is the strength of those causal inferences that makes the wonder of miracles possible. Consequently, al-Ghazali offered an important nuance to his critique of causation in the natural sciences. He did not mean to suggest that allowing space for divine intervention would make possible the fantastical transformation of a book into a horse. Rather, what he argued was that the strength of a causal inference from a correlation between two things is based on

---

[62] Al-Ghazali, *Incoherence*, 174.

habit: these correlations happen repeatedly in such a way as to support the inference of causation. He wrote: "the continuous habit (*istimrar al-'ada*) of their occurrence repeatedly, one time after another, fixes unshakeably in our mind (*yarsakhu fi adhhanina...tarassakhan la tanfakku 'anhu*)...their occurrence according to past habit."[63]

Nearly a century later, Ibn Rushd (d. 1198) challenged al-Ghazali's critique of philosophy, point by point, in his *Tahafut al-Tahafut*. However, Ibn Rushd did not challenge al-Ghazali's approach to causation and miracles. On these specific issues, Ibn Rushd was more interested in salvaging the legacy of Greek philosophy at the expense of Ibn Sina. Moreover his principal critique in this area of al-Ghazali's thought was that the latter confused the ambit of the practical religious sciences with the theoretical natural sciences. Despite the narrowness of Ibn Rushd's critique, his analysis of nature and causation is worth examining to appreciate how jurist-philosophers framed *tabi'a* philosophically, and to better understand the implications of their philosophies of nature on any study of Islamic natural law theory.

Like al-Ghazali, Ibn Rushd used the term *tabi'a*, and in particular its related adjectival term *tabi'i*, to designate the natural sciences along the lines of Aristotle's *Physics* (*al-'ilm al-tabi'i*).[64] While he took issue with al-Ghazali's enumeration of the different fields of the natural sciences, of particular interest here is Ibn Rushd's discussion of causation, determinacy, and the appropriate distinction between theoretical philosophical subjects and the more practical religious sciences.

Ibn Rushd began his critique of al-Ghazali by addressing the issue of causation. As noted above, al-Ghazali was concerned that a robust account of causation in the natural sciences would lead to a hard determinism of the sort that would exclude God from the world of

---

[63] Al-Ghazali, *Incoherence*, 174. Marmura translates this passage as "fixes unshakeably in our mind the belief in their occurrence according to past habit." The Arabic may or may not imply the incorporation of "belief." I have excluded it from the above translation, while allowing for the possibility that implicit in al-Ghazali's usage is a recognition that what is fixed in the mind is a belief or the truth of the inference drawn from the correlation. The point, therefore, is to emphasize that what is understood to be a necessary feature of the world is simply an inference, or in Marmura's words, "belief".

[64] Ibn Rushd, *Tahafut al-Tahafut*, ed. Muhammad al-'Arabi (Beirut: Dar al-Fikr al-Libnani, 1993), 2:285. For the English translation, see Simon Van Den Bergh, trans., *Averroes' Tahafut al-Tahafut (The Incoherence of the Incoherence)* (1987; reprint, Cambridge: EJW Gibb Memorial Trust, 1954), 312, who translates the phrase *'ilm tabi'i* as "physical" science.

humanity. Theologically, a hard determinism would preclude the possibility of miracles, and thereby undermine the veracity of the Qur'anic revelation and its authority. In his response to al-Ghazali, Ibn Rushd posited two distinct domains of inquiry and knowledge, the domain of the natural sciences and the domain of what Van Den Bergh translates as "religions."[65] The Arabic term translated as "religions," though, is *shara'i*, the plural form of *shari'a*, which for Ibn Rushd could refer to Islamic law, but more likely in this context refers to the Islamic religious sciences of which Islamic legal doctrines and jurisprudence form a part. Ibn Rushd used the term *shara'i* to situate the discussion of miracles outside the realm of the natural sciences. He wrote:

> The ancient philosophers had no position on the discussion of miracles. That is so because [miracles], in their opinion, are among the things of which it is not necessary to undertake an investigation or pose questions since they are among the principles of religious traditions (*mabadi' al-shara'i*). One who investigates them and harbors doubts about them deserves punishment in their opinion, just as one who investigates the rest of the general principles of religious traditions (*sa'ir mabadi' al-shara'i al-'amma*), such as whether God exists...There is no doubt about [God's] existence, although the nature of [God's] existence is a divine matter outside of human rational comprehension.[66]

Later, Ibn Rushd retorted that to attribute to the philosophers a denial of miracles is simply wrong. Rather, he held that those who doubt such matters are heretics (*zanadiqa*).[67] In defense of the ancient Greek philosophers, Ibn Rushd argued that they did not encourage debate, doubt, or dispute in fundamental matters of religion. Rather, they required religious adherents to abide by the principles of their religious tradition.[68]

The above analysis illustrates how Ibn Rushd's critique of al-Ghazali focused on how the latter went too far by applying insights derived from the theoretical natural sciences to the more practical religious sciences. For Ibn Rushd, the issue of miracles was not the proper subject of the natural sciences, and thus was insulated from the concerns about causation that al-Ghazali

---

[65] Van Den Bergh, *Incoherence*, 315.
[66] Ibn Rushd, *Tahafut*, 2:287–88.
[67] Ibn Rushd, *Tahafut*, 2:294.
[68] Ibn Rushd, *Tahafut*, 2:294.

articulated. For Ibn Rushd, the discussion of miracles provided a means by which he could distinguish natural philosophy (designated by the term *tabi'a*) from the religious sciences within which debates about theology and perhaps even jurisprudence (i.e., *usul al-fiqh*) properly take place. Though Ibn Rushd did not define in this section what he meant by *shari'a* or its general principles, he nonetheless adopted the term in order to contrast it with the natural philosophy associated with the term *tabi'a*.

The above analysis of natural philosophy and causation illuminates how jurists such as al-Ghazali and Ibn Rushd understood the term *tabi'a* and its implications on whether and to what extent the natural world could be known and explained. It also allows us to appreciate how for some jurist-philosophers, such as Ibn Rushd, the realm of *shari'a* and the realm of philosophy represented distinct fields of inquiry with their own principles. To blend the two, as al-Ghazali did, might be an undue elision that did not adequately appreciate how the register of one did not match, fit, or otherwise coincide with the register of the other. Alternatively, whereas Ibn Rushd was more concerned with issues of method and approach, al-Ghazali seemed particularly concerned about how the content of one method or discipline might nonetheless impinge upon the other. Al-Ghazali's principal aim in the discussion above was to make space in a philosophy of nature for theistic commitments to miracles despite their violation of principles of natural causation. For al-Ghazali, the conceptual significance of *tabi'a* is best appreciated when the term is juxtaposed with *mu'jiza*. When understood in terms of this juxtaposition, implicit in the term *tabi'a* is a philosophical discourse about what can and cannot be known about the world *as it is*. Ibn Rushd, however, would much rather juxtapose *shari'a* and *falsafa* as distinct disciplines that operate on their own principles and internal logics. *Shari'a* as Ibn Rushd understood it was distinct from philosophy, and thus did not require him to respond to the substance or merits of al-Ghazali's theologically oriented critiques against philosophy.

3.3 NATURE, CONTINGENCY, AND AUTHORITY

The contrast between Ibn Rushd and al-Ghazali reveals how the term *tabi'a* became a site of both philosophical and theological significance as jurist-philosophers contended with whether and to what extent we can claim to know the world as it is. To the extent *tabiʿa* reflects the world as it is, the term and its philosophical implications are not irrelevant to an inquiry into Islamic natural law theories. Given that Islamic natural law theories are premised upon a fusion of fact and value, any assessment of the facts (i.e., of what is) cannot be appreciated without also understanding the philosophy of knowledge that is prior to any assessment of the way the world *is*. In this narrow sense, *tabiʿa* contributes both directly to a theory of knowledge about what *is*, and indirectly to normative assessments of what *ought to be*.

For instance, in al-Ghazali's treatise of legal theory or *usul al-fiqh*, *al-Mustasfa*, he delineated seven different categories that contribute to the premises of a syllogism. The syllogism occupied an important place in al-Ghazali's approach to knowledge since it provided him with a method by which we can claim to know something. These seven categories of knowledge, because of their contribution to the content of any premise in a syllogism, not only affect the veracity and truthfulness of each premise, but also the truth of the syllogistic conclusion, and thereby the authority of norms derived therefrom. Of his seven categories, the one of particular interest to this study is what he called *al-tajribiyyat* or experiential, which can refer to unchanging features of our experience in the world (*ittirad al-ʿadat*).

> That is like your determination that fire burns, that bread satiates [an appetite], or that a rock falls to the lowest point (*asfal*), and that fire rises to the top, that wine is intoxicating, and Seammony is a purgative laxative. Experiential knowledge is clear (*yaqiniyya*) according to those who experience it. People disagree on this knowledge in light of their differences in experience. So the knowledge of the doctor that Seammony is a laxative is like...the determination that magnets (*al-maghnatis*) attract iron according to those who know [that]. This is not a matter of sensory perception (*al-mahsusat*), because sensory perceptions know that this stone falls to the ground. But the judgment (*al-hukm*) that every stone falls is a general judgment, and not a judgement [only] for a specific instance. Sensory perceptions only have the capacity to make specific determinations (*qadiyya fi ʿayn*). Likewise if one sees some liquid and drinks it, and then becomes intoxicated, he determines that this category of liquid is intoxicating. By way of sensory perception, he only knows a drink and a single instance of intoxication. The determination on all [such drinks] is on the basis of reason but through the mediating role of sensory perceptions or by recurring perceptions, one after another. Knowledge does not come about from a single instance...When [something] occurs repeatedly many times in

different circumstances...certainty [about the experience] sinks into someone, and he knows it is the influencing factor (*mu'aththir*), just as it is [clear] that seeking warmth by fire gets rid of coldness, and that bread removes the pain of hunger...It is as if reason says: 'if it were not for this cause effecting [the matter], it would not recur in most cases. Even if there were agreement on the matter, there would be divergence. This, now, instantiates a major element in the meaning of the necessity of cause and effect (*tulazim al-asbab wa al-musabbabat*), by which [something] is designated as an unchanging feature of [our] experience. We addressed in depth [the meaning of necessity of cause and effect] in the book *The Incoherence of the Philosophers*.[69]

Notably, when evaluating the veracity of truth claims, al-Ghazali subtly shifted registers from a descriptive natural philosophy to a prescriptive natural law. He accomplished this shift, in part, by focusing on the syllogism as a method of generating knowledge. For instance, when writing about how and what we can know, he used two examples. For the first, he wrote:

Every substance is formed, and every formed thing exists, so it necessarily follows that every substance exists. [70]

Switching to a legal register (*min al-fiqh*), al-Ghazali then followed up with his second example

Any date wine (*nabidh*) is intoxicating. Any intoxicating substance is prohibited. It follows necessarily that any wine is prohibited.[71]

Al-Ghazali held that, assuming the premises to be true, it necessarily follows (*lazama bi al-darura*) that, for instance, wine is prohibited.

Abstracting from these two examples, al-Ghazali recognized that as our confidence in the truth of the premises in a syllogism waxes and wanes, the authority of the syllogism's conclusion also waxes and wanes. If the premises are known to be true with certainty, then the syllogism is considered a *burhan*, or the ideal notion of the logical syllogism. If the premises are uncontested (but not known with certainty), then the logical proof is known as a disputable analogy (*qiyas*

---

    [69] Al-Ghazali, *al-Mustasfa*, 1: 109–11.

    [70] Al-Ghazali, *al-Mustasfa*, 1:93.

    [71] Al-Ghazali, *al-Mustasfa*, 1:93. Al-Ghazali, later in that passage, clarifies that the prohibition is premised upon an analogy between date wine (*nabidh*), and grape wine (*khamr*), which is specifically mentioned in the Qur'an.

jadali). If the premises are only probably or likely true (*maznuna*), the result is what al-Ghazali called a legal analogy (*qiyas fiqhi*).[72] This is not the place to address what al-Ghazali means by these three types of analogy. For the purposes of this discussion, what is important is to recognize that by juxtaposing the two examples and distinguishing between different types of syllogism based on the veracity of their premises, al-Ghazali used the syllogism to move from natural philosophy to legal philosophy, and thereby shifted registers from the task of explanation (the is) to the task of normative judgment (the ought).

Moving from what "is" to what "ought to be" is indeed the move that pre-modern Muslim jurists theorized in their natural law theories noted above. In their legal philosophy, though, they were less interested in whether and how one can know what "is." Instead, presuming that a determinate (or sufficiently determinate) "is" exists, their debate principally concerned how one moves from the "is" to the "ought" given pre-existing theological commitments about God's omnipotence and justice. This presumption helps to explain why pre-modern jurists did not invoke *tabi'a* when devising their distinct approaches to natural law. Indeed, as suggested earlier, Muslim jurists of either the Soft or Hard Natural Law theories uncritically held presumptions about nature and its determinacy for purposes of law and legal determinations. In other words, for them, understanding the "is" of natural philosophy and the "ought" of pre-modern Islamic natural law theory were two analytically distinct inquiries. While both might be linked in terms of their reference to some conception of nature, nature was principally a conceptual vehicle by which Islamic natural law theories grounded the authority of an ought statement. Pre-modern Muslim theorists of natural law grounded their normative claims by setting out a theological framework that either fixed the stability of what *is* (i.e., Hard Natural Law), or gave nature enough determinacy on which to rest reason's ontological authority (i.e., Soft Natural Law).

The natural law presumption of a determinate (or determinate enough) nature is of particular interest given natural philosophical debates on causation and necessity. Richard Sorabji notes how Aristotle's distinction between cause and necessity allowed for a degree of indeterminacy in the natural order of things, which in turn

---

[72] Al-Ghazali, *al-Mustasfa*, 1:93.

made moral responsibility and blame philosophically intelligible.[73] As Sorabji and others have suggested, the more one considers events to be determined by necessity, the less room there is for moral responsibility. The less one views the world as determinate in this fashion, the more room there is for moral agency. As Sorabji writes: "If it had all along been necessary that a person should act as he did, this would be incompatible, I believe, with an important part of our thinking about conduct and morality."[74]

This is not the place to offer an extensive analysis of determinacy in Islamic natural philosophy. Nor is the present author necessarily the person to offer such a study.[75] But it is important to recognize that jurist-philosophers such as al-Ghazali embraced some version of indeterminism in their natural philosophy.[76] But more to the point, for the purposes of this study, whether Muslim philosophers adopted

---

[73] Richard Sorabji, *Necessity, Cause, and Blame: Perspectives on Aristotle's Theory* (Chicago: University of Chicago Press, 1980).

[74] Sorabji, *Necessity, Cause and Blame*, 251.

[75] For scholars who have researched this topic in the field of Islamic philosophy, see Catarina Belo, Richard Frank, Len Goodman, Frank Griffel, Michael Marmura, Jon McGinnis, and Robert Wisnovsky

[76] Given that Ibn Rushd wrote a summary treatment of al-Ghazali's *al-Mustasfa,* the focus here will be on al-Ghazali. Nonetheless, it is noteworthy that Ibn Rushd's natural philosophy reflected his commitment to indeterminism. In her in-depth study of Ibn Rushd's commentaries on Aristotle's *Physics,* Ruth Glasner argues that Ibn Rushd presented Aristotle as upholding an indeterminist view of nature. She reviews both his middle and long commentaries on *The Physics,* including two different versions of the middle commentary. While her discussion of Ibn Rushd's view on determinism is an account of his intellectual development, her analysis reveals his commitment to a thesis of indeterminism. Indeed, she writes that "Averroes' agenda was to offer a scientific natural interpretation of indeterminism as an alternative to Kalam's theological one." Ruth Glasner, *Averroes' Physics: A Turning Point in Medieval Natural Philosophy* (Oxford: Oxford University Press, 2009), 63. In his critique of al-Ghazali, Ibn Rushd also raised doubts about the determinist thesis. He wrote: "are the acts which proceed from all things absolutely necessary (*mawjud daruriyya al-fi'l*) for those in whose nature it lies to perform them, or are they only performed in most cases or in half the cases? This is a question which must be investigated (*yastahaqqu al-fahs 'anhu*)... [I]t is not absolutely certain that fire acts when it is brought near a sensitive body, for surely it is not improbable that there should be something which stands in such a relation to the sensitive thing as to hinder the action of the fire... But one need not deny fire its burning power so long as fire keeps its name and definition." Van Den Bergh, *Averroes'* Tahafut al-Tahafut, 318–19; Ibn Rushd, *Tahafut al-Tahafut,* ed. Muhamad al-'Arabi (Beirut: Dar al-Fikr al-Libnani, 1993), 1:291. Though he considered the world eternal, according to Glasner, Ibn Rushd was careful to ensure against a determinist view of the world. In doing so, he implicitly avoided the entanglements with agency and morality that Sorabji and others associated with different forms of determinism.

a determinate or indeterminate conception of causation and nature is not of central interest. Rather, of greater interest herein is that competing natural law theorists argued for, at the very least, *just enough* determinacy in nature to grant reason ontological authority in the law.

Al-Ghazali, for example, was committed to a degree of causal indeterminacy in the world.[77] As Frank Griffel shows, al-Ghazali utilized a theory of divine habit to establish a suitable degree of constancy and consistency in the natural order. Griffel writes: "The 'laws of nature' that, according to the *falasifa*, govern God's creation may be understood as habitual courses of action subject to suspension, at least in principle. Our human experience, however, has shown us that God does not frivolously break His habit. This insight allows us to equate God's habit with the laws of nature, for all practical purposes."[78]

The constancy in the divine habit, though, should not be mistaken as suggesting a purely determinist view of the world. Indeed, to do so would run counter to al-Ghazali's critique of natural causation for the purpose of ensuring the veracity of miracles, as already addressed above.[79] Rather, positing a divine habit permitted enough determinacy for al-Ghazali's natural philosophy to ground al-Ghazali's Soft Natural Law theory, without at the same time preventing God from entering history and intervening in the course of world events. Consequently, even though he preserved God's omnipotence for theological purposes in his natural law theory, al-Ghazali's approach to causation allowed for sufficient causal indeterminacy to make moral agency possible. Even if we assume al-Ghazali espoused implicitly a degree of causal determinacy for purposes of his natural law theory, we already know that he did not embrace in his natural philosophy what some philosophers might call "hard determinism"—"the view that not only is determinism true, but that also, because of it, there is no such thing as moral responsibility or voluntary action."[80]

---

[77] Jules Janssens, "[Review] *Al-Ghazali's Philosophical Theology*," *The Muslim World* 101 (January 2011): 115–19, 117, who situates Frank Griffel's impressive study of al-Ghazali within the existing scholarship on al-Ghazali, in particular the work of Michael Marmura and Richard Frank.

[78] Frank Griffel, *Al-Ghazali's Philosophical Theology* (Oxford: Oxford University Press, 2009), 175.

[79] See also, Griffel, *Al-Ghazali's Philosophical Theology*, ch. 6.

[80] Sorabji, *Necessity, Cause and Blame*, 244.

Consequently, al-Ghazali's approach to causal determinacy allowed him to be theoretically coherent across his theology, natural law theory, and natural philosophy. Al-Ghazali granted ontological authority to reason by fusing fact and value in a natural order whose goodness was a function of God's grace (*tafaddul*). That divine grace was deemed determinate enough to provide a foundation for the ontological authority of reason as a matter of law. But that grace allowed for a certain degree of causal indeterminacy given the possibility that God could change the divine mind. That causal indeterminacy allowed him to remain steadfast in his theological commitment to an omnipotent God.

Of course, his argument about grace begs various questions. For instance, how real is the possibility that God may change God's mind? Or, we might ask the more epistemic question of how anyone can ever really know that God has in fact changed God's mind? As intriguing as these questions may be, they were irrelevant to al-Ghazali's natural law approach, given his main interest, namely to distinguish his Soft Natural Law theory from Hard Natural Law. The argument of divine grace emphasizes al-Ghazali's concern to provide a sufficiently determinate nature upon which to base reason's ontological authority, and thereby proffer a jurisprudence of natural law.

Muslim jurist-philosophers such as al-Ghazali required a degree of causal indeterminacy for purposes of their theology. That indeterminacy, though, was not so indeterminate as to undermine al-Ghazali's commitment to a natural law theory. Indeed, for purposes of natural law, jurists such as al-Ghazali and other Soft Natural Law exponents only needed a sufficiently determinate natural order to legitimately grant reason ontological authority in the law.

Appreciating how and why al-Ghazali shifted analytic registers from natural philosophy to legal philosophy reveals that what is at stake in legal philosophy has less to do with knowing what "is" and more on establishing the conditions for the authority of the "ought." This enduring interest in authority despite the focus on causal indeterminacy is evident in the work of not just al-Ghazali, but other pre-modern Soft Natural Law jurists. For instance, Abu Ishaq al-Shatibi (d. 790/1388) theorized about the norms "good" and "bad." He recognized that things and events in the world are complex. There is no way of saying that X is purely beneficial or Y is purely harmful. Things in the world have dispositions or tendencies toward one or the other. In fact, he wrote: "Good and corrupt acts in the world are

understood in terms of the [aspect] that is predominant (*ghalaba*)."[81]
X is perhaps mostly beneficial, but has some harm *as a matter of fact*.
Likewise, Y is mostly harmful, but perhaps has some benefit *as a matter of fact*. Things that are *predominantly* beneficial or harmful *as a matter of fact* will be presumed to be *purely* beneficial or harmful *as a matter of law* (*fi al-haqiqa al-shar'iyya*).[82] For purposes of law, the "good" and the "bad" are normative values that, given the pursuit of normative authority, cover or hide the unavoidable indeterminacy in the world by imagining the world as determinate enough to sustain the authority of the law.

3.4 (IN)DETERMINACY AND MORAL AGENCY: A QUR'ANIC POSTLUDE

For pre-modern jurist-philosophers, such as al-Ghazali, debates about nature provided the backdrop to thinking about larger questions of authority and agency in temporal and spatial terms. They preserved a degree of indeterminacy in their natural philosophies to allow God to interfere with our expectations and experience of the laws of nature by way of miracles. But that indeterminacy was not so great as to undermine the testamentary character of miracles, which depended on a sufficient determinacy in nature. They posited a determinate (or determinate enough) nature in their natural law theories, however theologically justified, as a necessary condition for granting reason ontological authority. In both natural philosophy and natural law, they framed their debates about determinacy in terms of theological commitments about divine justice and omnipotence. Theology, therefore, provided an important vehicle by which pre-modern jurist-philosophers addressed profound questions about how humans make sense of their world and order their affairs in it legitimately. Indeed, as has thus far been shown, as much as theology, philosophy, and law were distinct disciplines for pre-modern jurists, they shared key concerns about moral agency and authority in the Islamic tradition.

---

[81]　Abu Ishaq al-Shatibi, *al-Muwafaqat fi Usul al-Shari'a*, ed. 'Abd Allah Daraz et al (Beirut: Dar al-Kutub al-'Ilmiyya, n.d.), 2:20; Emon, *Islamic Natural Law Theories*, 171.
[82]　Al-Shatibi, *al-Muwafaqat*, 2:21; Emon, *Islamic Natural Law Theories*, 171.

Thus far, we have examined these concerns from the vantage point of Islamic natural philosophy and Islamic natural law. These concerns, though, were not limited to these two fields of inquiry; indeed they were part of disputes that are often considered purely theological. As much as these disciplines may be distinct, this section suggests that the questions about determinacy, moral agency, and authority pervade all three disciplines, each of which provides a different angle on the same set of questions. The discussion that follows concentrates on a particular theological debate in pre-modern Islam concerning the Qur'an. The reason this debate is addressed here is as follows. First, throughout this essay, the analysis has revealed that even when addressing issues of law or philosophy in Islam, Muslim jurists' theological commitments infused their analysis. Consequently, it is fitting to close this essay with a specific discussion of a squarely theological debate. Second, the specific theological debate on the Qur'an provides a different but related angle on the concerns about determinacy discussed already, and thereby on the broader topics of moral agency and authority in the Islamic tradition.

The particular theological debate concerns whether the Qur'an either is an eternal text that is outside of time and space, or rather was revealed by God in a specific time and place. In the language of pre-modern theologians, those who held that the Qur'an is an eternal text (i.e., outside history) adopted what Islamic intellectual history labels as the "uncreated" (*ghayr makhluq*) position. This group, which at that time seemed to consist of leading scholars of law and *hadith*, denied that the Qur'an was created by God in history, and therefore did not suffer from the indeterminacy of our contingent human existence. Those who held that God revealed the Qur'an in time and space (i.e., in history) adopted what has been called the "created" position (*makhluq*), and thus situated the text in the contextual, indeterminate world of human history.[83] Both groups presumed that the Qur'an was divinely revealed. They disagreed, though, on whether the Qur'an lay outside or inside history. If the former, we can imagine that the Qur'an occupies a plane of existence separate from our indeterminate world (whether moderately indeterminate or not). If the latter, the Qur'an is a constitutive feature of our experience, and like all other features of our experience, its normative implications are embedded within (and perhaps even delimited by) the complex world of human experience.

[83] Michael Cooperson, *Al Ma'mun* (Oxford: Oneworld Publications, 2005), 115.

This particular theological dispute was not merely an academic one. It assumed political dimensions during the reign of the ʿAbbasid caliph al-Maʾmun (r. 813–33 CE), who proclaimed in 827 CE that, despite the plausible variety of theological positions, the view that the Qurʾan is created (*makhluq*) was right and true. Furthermore, in 833 he went so far as to demand that leading *hadith* scholars publicly proclaim their adherence to the theology of the Qurʾan's createdness, thus instituting what historians call the *mihna* or inquisition. Michael Cooperson and John Nawas suggest that the most likely explanation for al-Maʾmun's official action had to do with claiming for the caliphate a religious authority that the scholars of law and *hadith* claimed for themselves.[84] Nawas states that "[c]ommon to all the men subjected to the *mihna*... is that they all had something to do with *shariʿa* and the legal establishment which it signifies....[T]he caliph ordered the *mihna* in order to acquire the authority of the *shariʿa,* to secure for himself and future caliphs unquestioned supremacy on issues of faith."[85]

A theoretical implication drawn from this history is that the more we frame the Qurʾan in terms of history—and the indeterminacy of its meaning that arises from a contextualized reading of the text—the more we enable its readers to claim the moral authority to determine its meaning in different times and places. Indeed, al-Maʾmun's letter, as preserved by the historian al-Tabari (d. 923 CE), suggests as much. In it, he worried that the masses were uneducated and easily led astray, and that the caliph had the responsibility (and by implication the moral authority) to uphold the religion of God (*din Allah*).[86] An example of the masses being led astray was how they equate God with God's revelation of the Qurʾan (*sawu bayna Allah tabaruk wa taʿala wa bayna ma anzala min al-Qurʾan*), or in other words they adhere to the uncreatedness of the Qurʾan.[87]

Ultimately, those holding that the Qurʾan was uncreated were victorious in the battle over theological orthodoxy. Their victory is still felt today; anyone who opposes the inherited orthodox view on the

---

[84] Cooperson, *Al Maʾmun,* 115; John A. Nawas, "A Reexamination of Three Current Explanations for al-Maʾmun's Introduction of the *Mihna,*" *International Journal of Middle East Studies* 26 (1994): 615–29; John A. Nawas, "The *Mihna* of 218 AH/833 AD Revisited: An Empirical Study," *Journal of the American Oriental Society* 116, no. 4 (1996): 698–708.

[85] Nawas, "The *Mihna*" 708.

[86] Al-Tabari, *Taʾrikh al-Tabari,* 5:186.

[87] Al-Tabari, *Taʾrikh al-Tabari,* 5:186.

Qur'an, and promotes approaches that even approximate theological views deemed heterodox runs the risk of being deemed heterodox. The apostasy case of the late Nasr Hamid Abu Zayd, an Egyptian intellectual deemed to have apostatized from Islam through his writings on the Qur'an, is a well known case of an intellectual whose ideas were viewed by some as heterodox, and thereby contrary to prevailing Islamic norms.[88]

Beyond the particular circumstances of al-Ma'mun, the debate also had broader theological implications on the nature of God in light of the polemics between Christians and Muslims, particularly given Christian doctrines about Christ's divinity and the Trinity.[89] To suggest that the Qur'an is co-eternal with God might be construed as associating with the eternal God another eternal entity, which could be viewed as undermining a monotheistic theology of God. Yet to suggest that God revealed the Qur'an in time and space could be construed as demeaning its standing and stature as the direct word of God, given the interpretive distance between God's revelatory act, and the more contingent moment of reading and interpretation.

One might argue that the significance of the created/uncreated Qur'an controversy has little to do with authority and agency. It may have theological ramifications on the nature of God and monotheism, and have political implications for defining the outer limits of a religious community, but has little to do with issues of agency and authority. On the contrary, this theological dispute raises important questions about moral agency and authority that were significant in the debates on natural law and natural philosophy addressed above.

---

[88] Richard C. Martin, Mark R. Woodward, and Dwi S. Atmaja, *Defenders of Reason in Islam: Mu'tazilism from Medieval School to Modern Symbol* (Oxford: Oneworld Publications, 1997), 166–67. For an overview of the relationship between intellectual freedom and apostasy cases, and the Abu Zayd case, see Baber Johansen, "Apostasy as objective and depersonalized fact: two recent Egyptian court judgments," *Social Research* 70, no. 3 (Fall 2003): 687–710; Susanne Olsson, "Apostasy in Egypt: Contemporary Cases of *Hisbah*," *The Muslim World* 98 (2008): 95–115. For a comparative study of Mu'tazilite ideas and those of Abu Zayd, see Thomas Hildebrandt, "Between Mu'tazilism and Mysticism: How much of a Mu'tazilite is Nasr Hamid Abu Zayd?" in *A Common Rationality: Mu'tazilism in Islam and Judaism*, eds. Camilla Adang, Sabine Schmidtke, and David Sklare, 495–512 (Würzburg: Ergon in Kommission, 2007).

[89] Harry Austryn Wolfson, *The Philosophy of the Kalam* (Cambridge: Harvard University Press, 1976), 112–32.

One the one hand, to consider the Qur'an created or *makhluq* is to embed it in time and space, subject it to scrutiny, and empower the reader, whether as an individual or as a ruler, to assess the salience of the text, its meaning, and its normative implications given changed circumstances. Situating the text in time and space enables new meanings to be generated across the different temporal and spatial contexts within which the text is read. In that sense, what renders a reading authoritative is not simply whether and how it accords with God's will, but also whether and how the reading speaks to the particular place and moment that the reader inhabits, which will change as each reader changes. The authority of any given reading, therefore, has less to do with an archaeology of God's will, and instead with the construction of meaning in terms of a temporal and spatial point of reference.

On the other hand, to consider the Qur'an uncreated and eternal with God is to remove it from both time and space entirely, leaving it and its meaning in the realm of the perfect and infallible divine. An uncreated Qur'an is both ontologically real, and epistemically out of reach, thereby limiting the moral agency and authority that one can claim for a particular reading or generated meaning. Indeed, the very notion of "generating" meaning raises the fear of trespassing on God's authority by invoking His words for something He did not intend. This is not to suggest that a reader can claim no legitimacy or authority for his or her Qur'anic reading on this theology. Rather, this is simply to suggest that the quality of legitimacy and authority that can be attributed to the interpretation must be limited by virtue of the indeterminacy that characterizes the reader's existence but not the Qur'an's.

Notably, if we look beneath the surface of the theological debate, we find that both positions are concerned about the related issues of authority, agency, and legitimacy. Both positions are concerned with the legitimate authority of a historically situated reader to create meaning from the Qur'an. For instance, if we approach the *created* Qur'an from the vantage point of moral agency and authority, we can appreciate how any given reader is in a different position from the moment(s) of God's revelatory act. To appreciate the temporal and spatial distance between those two positions both legitimates Qur'anic interpretation, and qualifies the authority of any such interpretation at one and the same time. The temporal and spatial distance between a created Qur'an and a subsequent reader makes possible an interpretive authority that is albeit different and distinct from God's authority at the moment of the revelatory act. Likewise, if we approach the *uncreated* Qur'an in terms of moral agency and authority, we soon become aware that the reader's position in both time and space is in stark contrast to the Qur'an's position outside time and space. The reader and the Qur'an are in different ontological positions. As much as the reader may legitimately interpret the Qur'an, any authority his or her interpretation may have is limited by the distance between the reader (who exists in history, which contributes to an indeterminate range of possible readings) and the Qur'an, which is not embedded in the contingencies of human experience.

Ironically (again), both theological starting points lead to similar conclusions on the significance of indeterminacy for the authority to generate meaning from the Qur'an. The irony is that both grant the human agent an authority circumscribed by his or her own temporal and spatial position in relation to the revelatory act (whether considered in time and space, or not). The temporal and spatial contingencies of our existence both allow for and delimit the authority we can claim when generating Qur'anic meaning. Just as the conditions of our existence provide the basis for our claim to authority, so too do they limit the scope of authority we can claim when pronouncing on the meaning and normative significance of the Qur'anic message.

This dual implication of our temporal and spatial existence on our authority is perhaps better appreciated if we consider what might follow if we fail to acknowledge or embrace the contingencies of our existence, and their implication on the indeterminacy of meaning that can be generated from reading the Qur'an. Failure to acknowledge our temporal and spatial conditions runs the risk of eliding God's authority with our own. If one adopts the created position without a sufficient regard for his or her temporal and spatial embeddedness, it is not unimaginable that when readers interpret the text, they will not appreciate the temporal and spatial distance between the divine revelatory act and their contingent selves. Likewise, if one adopts the uncreated position without due awareness of being in time and space (in contrast to the Qur'an, which is not in time or space), the reader may not appreciate the difference in his position relative to the Qur'an. Therefore when expounding on the meaning of the text, the reader may represent his interpretation as sufficiently immanent in the text so as to emanate from God, and thus eliding once again the reader's interpretive authority with God's.[90]

CONCLUSION

As an introduction to Islamic approaches to natural law, this essay has outlined two competing trends drawn from an analysis of pre-modern Islamic legal sources. Those two trends—called herein Hard Natural Law and Soft Natural Law—start from competing theological perspectives, but end at jurisprudentially similar positions. Hard Natural Law theorists began with a theology of a just God who created the natural world as a good for humans to enjoy. As a divinely created thing, the natural world therefore is not just a set of facts—an "is" so to speak—but holds within it normative insights, or in other words, clues about how things "ought" to be. The natural world reflects both an "is" and an "ought," and as such is the site where fact and value are fused. On this basis, the natural world provides the necessary foundation for Hard Natural Law jurists to justify granting reason ontological authority for purposes of law and legal ordering.

Soft Natural Law jurists, though, started from a different theological position. As theological voluntarists, they did not share the same view of God's justice as the Hard Natural Law jurists. They believed in an omnipotent God who was not bound or limited in any way whatsoever, including by some notion of the good or just. However, while they held firm to this theological position, they could not deny that, *as a matter of law*, there were some issues on which God seemed to

[90] The danger posed by a lack of historical consciousness is not lost on those concerned with the hermeneutics of the Qur'an and the legal tradition. See for instance, Ebrahim Moosa, "The Debts and Burdens of Critical Islam," in *Progressive Muslims: On Justice, Gender, and Pluralism*, ed. Omid Safi (Oxford: Oneworld Publications, 2003), 111–27; Fatima Mernissi, *The Veil and the Male Elite: A Feminist Interpretation of Women's Rights in Islam* (New York: Basic Books, 1992); Abou El Fadl, *Speaking in God's Name*. The danger of eliding the authority of the reader with the authority of God arguably animates scholars of Islamic law who take special pains to distinguish between shari'a as the perfected law of God, and the *fiqh*, or legal doctrines developed by jurists over centuries. See, Anver M. Emon, "To Most Likely Know the Law: Objectivity, Authority, and Interpretation in Islamic Law," *Hebraic Political Studies* 4, no. 4 (2009): 415–40, 418–19.

express no will. In the absence of some indicator of God's will, and the presence of a real legal issue that required resolution, they could not avoid altogether empowering reason as a source of law in some limited cases. They too developed a natural law theory, one that also fused fact and value in nature. But that fusion was a function of God's grace (*tafaddul*). By invoking God's grace, Soft Natural Law jurists both granted reason ontological authority as a source of law, and upheld their voluntarist commitment to an omnipotent God. They argued that God, by His grace, created the world as a good, as a matter of fact, and by virtue of the normative content of His will, as a matter of normative value. Consequently, one could rationally infer substantive norms from the natural world, and in some limited cases impute to those norms the authority of divinely sanctioned law. None of this precluded the possibility, though, that God might alter God's grace. Nonetheless in the absence of evidence to the contrary, they presumed a fusion of fact and value, and thereby developed what has been called herein Soft Natural Law theory.

Those who read this discussion of an Islamic natural law tradition might find fault with the very venture of reading into the Islamic tradition a "natural law" tradition, as I have done. They might argue that a more appropriate place to begin such an inquiry is in the field of Islamic natural philosophy, where jurist-philosophers defined and addressed the scope of knowledge that could be derived through the natural sciences. In this vein, the argument goes, the real focus should be on the term *tabi'a* as a more appropriate starting point in the Islamic tradition.

As I have suggested, though, such an argument confuses legal philosophy and natural philosophy, without suitably accounting for how both disciplines have different and distinct aims. This is not to say that an analysis of *tabi'a* is irrelevant to any discussion of natural law. Rather it is to say that when pre-modern jurists addressed *tabi'a* in more philosophical terms, the issues that were central to them were different than when they were addressing what I have identified as different theories of natural law in the Islamic legal tradition.

In the context of natural philosophy, jurist-philosophers such as al-Ghazali did not deny that the natural sciences can help explain the world. As shown above, al-Ghazali was well aware of the explanatory power of the natural sciences. His concern, though, was with the extent to which natural philosophical theories of causation precluded God from entering the world to perform miracles. He did not deny that causation could explain things in the world. For him, the natural sciences and causation are important modes of explanation and description. He simply wanted to introduce a sufficient degree of *indeterminacy* so as to permit God to perform miracles in the world. Indeed in order for miracles to have their miraculous aura, al-Ghazali needed the natural sciences and natural causation to hold considerable explanatory and descriptive power. When a jurist-philosopher such as al-Ghazali addressed *tabiʿa*, therefore, his principal aim was to ensure sufficient indeterminacy in the natural order so as to permit God to enter history, and support his Prophets in the world by performing miracles that would attest to their veracity.

Notably, though, the term *tabiʿa* was used in the context of the natural sciences to reflect the world as it is. The natural law theories outlined above, however, start with a presumption about the world as it is, in order to derive normative principles to claim how things ought to be. The absence of *tabiʿa* as a term of art in natural law debates, therefore, is not surprising given the different questions animating pre-modern Islamic debates about the natural sciences as opposed to natural law.

Attending to the absence, though, raises certain questions about the analytic work done by the natural law presumption about the world as it is. For instance, a focus on *tabiʿa* permits a recognition that preserving causal indeterminacy in the world is important. The natural law presumption about the world as it is, though, presumes either a determinate or determinate enough natural order to ground the authority of reason and enable reasoned deliberation about what the law can and should be. A concern, though, might be whether the natural law presumption over-determines the world as it is. Or in other words, an attention to the absence of *tabiʿa* in pre-modern Islamic natural law debates raises the question of whether nature is truly as determinate as Hard and Soft Natural Law jurists presumed for purposes of their natural law theories. Indeed, a more skeptical critique might suggest that to cover the indeterminacy of the world in this fashion runs the risk of covering too much. To draw upon Robert Cover's important critique of the law, the natural law presumption about determinacy, as described above, reflects a tendency in law to over-determine a complex state of affairs, and poses the danger of unduly justifying the marginalization of some narratives of identity and value as against others.[91]

---

[91] Robert Cover, "Foreword: *Nomos* and Narrative," *Harvard Law Review*, 97, no. 4 (1983): 4–68.

Perhaps the law is the kind of enterprise that demands this sort of generalization. The exceptions and particularities that characterize our highly contingent world are often too great to manage for a legal system that must speak to a wide range of people, on a wide range of issues. Perhaps it is too much to expect of the law, natural law or otherwise, to regulate across this wide spectrum of people and issues without presuming a certain state of affairs, without utilizing generalizations. This kind of generality and presumptiveness is not unique to the Islamic legal tradition. The Common Law is replete with doctrines that presume more than some think it should. Common Law Tort doctrine, for example, espouses the doctrine of the reasonable person. Feminist scholars remind us, though, that who a reasonable person is might in fact differ, and problematically so, depending on whether one is a boy or a girl, a man or a woman.[92] The critique of this tendency toward the general does not undermine the coherence or importance of the legal endeavor. It simply renders it vulnerable to critique. That is hardly an indictment of law generally or Islamic law specifically. It is simply a reminder that the law, like so many other things, is not perfect. It carries authority and weight, but that authority is never absolute.

This final point about authority is arguably the key to understanding what is at stake in the debates on determinacy, whether in Islamic natural philosophy, Islamic natural law, or Islamic theology. As much as pre-modern Muslim jurists may have endowed the natural order with a high degree of determinacy for purposes of their natural law theories, they also attributed to it a degree of indeterminacy in their natural philosophies. On the surface, their reasons for their complex approach to nature and natural law had everything to do with theology. But this essay has argued that even these theological concerns were covers for more profound questions that cut across traditional disciplinary divisions. By juxtaposing the jurist-philosophers' competing views on the determinacy of nature in both natural philosophy and natural law, we can better appreciate that what was really at stake was a concern about authority and moral agency, as opposed to nature. Moreover, moral agency and authority were equally at stake in the theological dispute addressed at the end of this essay regarding

---

[92] Mayo Moran, *Rethinking the Reasonable Person: An Egalitarian Reconstruction of the Objective Standard* (New York: Oxford University Press, 2003).

the nature of the Qur'an itself. However one might regard the coherence of natural law, causation in the natural world, or the historicism of the Qur'an, this essay suggests that the substantive conclusions are less interesting than a recognition of the conditioned authority that attends any claim to knowledge or law. Our temporal and spatial existence need not negate the possibility of agency and authority in the context of a religious legal tradition such as Islamic law. Rather it reminds us that when we make normative claims within a tradition in which abiding by God's will is paramount, any claim must be couched so as not to exceed the limits of the human condition. That, in the end, seems to be the thematic undercurrent that characterizes the debates about *tabi'a* in Islamic natural philosophy, explains the dispute between the Hard and Soft Natural law theorists, and provides a potential salve for the fierce polemics that continue today about the nature of the Qur'an.

Response to Anver M. Emon's "Islamic Natural Law Theories"

Matthew Levering

Reading Anver Emon's essay was a fascinating experience not least because of the connections with Christian thinking on natural law that continually came to mind as I was reading. Emon is particularly concerned to show that human subjectivity and historical context cannot be excluded from any identification of moral norms. In this regard, the debate over whether the Qur'an is an eternal text or a text that was given in history (and thus with a particular historical context) interests him, because both sides of this debate highlight the interpreter's limited insight vis-à-vis God's speech. For the same reason, he appreciates al-Ghazali's challenge to the immanent causal framework of Aristotle, in which framework God arguably plays no role other than as final cause. Al-Ghazali's perspective destabilizes and historicizes such Aristotelian "nature" by means of an occasionalist account of causality, similar to accounts that one finds in medieval Christian thinkers such as William of Ockham (or, from a quite different theological perspective, in the Scottish philosopher David Hume). The result is that the appeal to "nature" is itself historicized. Along these lines, Emon suggests that "to cover the indeterminacy in the world in this fashion runs the risk of covering too much." He argues that there is "a tendency in law to over-determine what is otherwise a complex state of affairs," a tendency that "poses the danger of unduly justifying the marginalization of some narratives of identity and value as against other."

Yet, given that "some narratives of identity and value" will inevitably be privileged over against others, no matter what efforts we make to avoid this, then one question is how we might best ensure that human identity and value are recognized even in the face of adverse narratives. What is it for humans to have a "human" identity? What grounds and enhances human "value"? To my mind, this requires some account, however limited, of human flourishing, and thus some teleological language will be necessary. The account of human flourishing will entail a description of things that harm human flourishing, as well as reflection on the implications of human neediness and dependence.[1] If humans are to be identifiable as such and to have recognizable "value," then there must also be some defensible notion of what humans are (human nature) and why each human has value. This conceptual labor will necessarily involve universal claims about humanity, without concealing the particular standpoints of those who make such claims. Viewed in this light, the identification of "human nature," so long as the concept is properly limited, does not threaten particularity or difference, but instead stands as a vital defense of human beings against the tide of dehumanizing rhetoric and violence.[2]

At the same time, I share Emon's concern that our conclusions about nature and natural law retain epistemological awareness of the role of subjectivity in interpreting the world. We cannot construe the world outside ourselves as an uninterpreted given, although neither should we suppose that the being of the world does not manifest itself to us in a manner that shapes our interpretations. Emon also rightly reminds believers that we need to be aware of the limited character of our interpretations of God's inexhaustibly rich revelation, without however denying the possibility and indeed the actuality of true interpretation. Certainly, any interpretation either of the world or of revelation that refuses to see all other humans as fully human, possessed of intrinsic dignity and value, is an affront to God and humanity.

I also note that when Emon surveys the different options available in the Muslim jurisprudential and philosophical traditions for conceiving "fact and value in nature," these options have parallels within

---

[1] See Alasdair MacIntyre, *Dependent Rational Animals: Why Human Beings Need the Virtues* (Chicago: Open Court, 1999).

[2] I think that efforts to bracket belief in the Creator God from discussion of human identity and value are a mistake, as also are efforts to learn about human identity and value solely on the basis of God's revelation. Belief in a Creator God makes the concept of "human nature" and human dignity more plausible. See Charles Taylor, *A Secular Age* (Cambridge, MA: Harvard University Press, 2007), especially Part II.

Greco-Roman and Christian thought. Here Emon has opened up for me a new set of Muslim dialogue partners, and I wish to begin to think about the paths taken by these scholars first by recollecting broadly similar paths that Christians have taken. The historical contexts and concerns that animate the Christian scholars will inevitably be different from those that animate the Muslim scholars, even when a concrete historical connection can be traced—as is possible for the medieval period, when Christian thinkers learned conscientiously from Muslim scholars such as al-Ghazali, Ibn Sina, and Ibn Rushd.

Let me turn first to the jurists whom Emon terms advocates of "Hard Natural Law." These jurists are concerned about cases for which the Qur'an and the *hadith* do not provide explicit guidance. In such cases, how can one arrive at a determination of right behavior? Hard Natural Law jurists argue that one can use reason, because the good God created human reason for a good purpose, just as God created the whole creation good. Since the creation is good, we can reasonably discern orderly patterns in the natural world and rely upon their goodness. As Emon says, "Hard Natural Law jurists invested reason with the ontological authority to analyze and investigate the world around them, and thereby derive new norms."

This position seems similar to the Stoic effort, exhibited by Cicero in *On Duties*, to derive natural law from nature. Cicero discusses the natural inclinations of self-preservation, procreation and upbringing of children, life in society, and the search for truth and freedom. On this basis, Cicero concludes that just as humans have "a sense of beauty, loveliness, harmony in the visible world," so also "nature and reason, extending the analogy of this from the world of sense to the world of spirit, find that beauty, consistency, order are far more to be maintained in thought and deed."[3]

A broadly similar view about "nature and reason," including the natural inclinations, is advocated by Edward Feser in his recent study of Thomas Aquinas' philosophy. For Aquinas, says Feser, "Like the other, non-rational animals, we have various ends inherent in our nature, and these determine what is good for us."[4] All animals, like all created things, have ends or goals that constitute the perfection of their nature, that is to say their flourishing. It is correct to speak

---

[3] Cicero, *De officiis*, trans. Walter Miller (Cambridge, MA: Harvard University Press, 1913), I. iv, 15–17.

[4] Edward Feser, *Aquinas* (Oxford: Oneworld, 2009), 178.

of "nature's purposes" in this regard.[5] Our nature as rational animals orients us to certain kinds of actions, even though we often act upon our desires in disordered ways that undercut our flourishing.[6] What is "natural" cannot be determined by empirical study of all the things humans do, but "has instead to do with the final causes inherent in a thing by virtue of its essence."[7] The result is that by the operation of reason, we can discern certain goods that fulfill our nature—goods that are ordered hierarchically in relation to the highest good, God—and we can thereby recognize elements of morally good human behavior (natural law).

Other jurists surveyed by Emon hold to what he terms "Soft Natural Law." On this view, the sovereign and free God can command whatever he wishes (whether good or evil from our perspective), and our goodness consists in obeying him, because what God freely wills is what counts as "good." Thus we cannot know what is right without a divine command. This is especially so because human nature seems highly prone to sins that God has prohibited. To God's radical freedom, the Soft Natural Law jurists add the idea that by his "grace" (*tafaddul*), God freely willed that the created order be good. God can change this at any time, since the created order's goodness depends not on the created order but on God's grace. But so long as God does not will otherwise, we can assume that the created order is good, with the result that in the absence of revealed teaching, we can use our reason to arrive at moral precepts that are legally binding.

This position has similarities with that of the medieval theologian John Duns Scotus, whom the Catholic Church declared "blessed" in 1993. Scotus argues that the precepts of the first table of the Decalogue—"You shall not have other gods before me," "You shall not

---

[5] Feser, 179.

[6] As Alasdair MacIntyre says, "To have learned how to stand back in some measure from our present desires, so as to be able to evaluate them, is a necessary condition for engaging in sound reasoning about our reasons for action. Here one danger is that those who have failed to become sufficiently detached from their own immediate desires, for whom desire for their and the good has not become to a sufficient degree overriding, are unlikely to recognize this fact about themselves. And so what they present to themselves as a desire for their own good or for *the* good may in fact be and often enough is some unacknowledged form of infantile desire, a type of desire that has been protected from evaluative criticism" (MacIntyre, *Dependent Rational Animals*, 72–73).

[7] Feser, *Aquinas*, 180.

take the name of the Lord your God in vain," and "Remember the sabbath day, to keep it holy"—strictly belong to natural law, because God
must always be honored (although not necessarily on a particular day
of worship). But with respect to the precepts of the second table of the
Decalogue, which teach about how we should treat fellow humans,
Scotus considers that these precepts do not strictly belong to natural law, because God can command that they be different. However,
they are "exceedingly in harmony" with the natural law, so that God
only rarely, if ever, commands otherwise.[8] Scotus finds that "speaking
broadly" these precepts can be said to belong to natural law, but that
these precepts "contain no goodness such as is necessarily prescribed
for attaining the goodness of the ultimate end, nor in what is forbidden is there such malice as would turn one away necessarily from the
last end."[9] This is so because the attainment of union with God does
not strictly speaking depend upon how we relate to our neighbors.
Attainment of union with God only involves how we relate to our
neighbors because God has commanded that this be so.[10]

Al-Ghazali speaks of "five fundamental values" that law aims to
preserve: religion, life, reason, lineage, and property. He employs the
Qur'an to confirm the significance of each of these five fundamental values in law. But he also argues that these values can be known
by reason. Emon remarks that for al-Ghazali, "these values are *intuitively* known. They are the kinds of values that any society or legal
tradition would uphold if it values the preservation and flourishing
of society." These "five fundamental values" invite comparison to the
Jewish Noahide laws, but in recent Christian natural law theory they
also sound rather similar to the "primary or basic human goods"
set forth by John Finnis and others.[11] When Finnis lists the "basic
human goods," he identifies them as life, procreation and education
of children, knowing the truth about God, living in society, reasonableness or virtue, and harmony with the transcendent source. This
list is somewhat differ from al-Ghazali's—for instance, property is not
mentioned explicitly by Finnis—but the two sets seem similar in that

---

[8] See *Duns Scotus on the Will and Morality*, trans. Alan B. Wolter, O.F.M., ed.
William A. Frank (Washington, D.C.: Catholic University of America Press, 1997),
203 (from Scotus, *Ordinatio* III, suppl., dist. 37).

[9] *Scotus*, 202.

[10] I discuss and critique Scotus' view in my "God and Natural Law: Reflections on
Genesis 22," *Modern Theology* 24 (2008): 151–77.

[11] John Finnis, *Aquinas* (Oxford: Oxford University Press, 1998), 80.

they identify basic goods that stimulate non-scriptural legal reasoning about moral norms. For al-Ghazali, however, these fundamental values only come into play for the jurist when scripture is silent, and even then only when they involve interests "so central to society that no disagreement about them can be imagined."

As Emon notes, al-Ghazali also takes an interest in "*tabi'a*," a word that means "the traits and dispositions to which humans are inclined." The Aristotelian cosmological and teleological framework, and Aristotle's unmoved mover who knows himself but does not know humans or the cosmos, can obviously be detrimental to God's freedom and power (including his power to perform miracles and to reveal himself). Against Aristotle, therefore, al-Ghazali underscores that no created cause acts on its own; all actions by creatures originate in God's action, so much so that God for al-Ghazali should be in some sense conceived as the sole real cause.[12] In short, al-Ghazali fears that the concept of *tabi'a* leads to a strictly immanent understanding of the movement of created things. He therefore posits that the cause–effect connection that we perceive is not a necessary connection, but instead is something that we are habituated to assume to be present. God must sustain the cause–effect connection on every occasion, and if God does not do this then the cause–effect connection will not be present. For Ibn Rushd, who defended the Aristotelian framework against al-Ghazali's criticisms, *tabi'a* or nature is the "habit" present in the way things work and relate to each other, and *tabi'a* need not be prejudicial to God's freedom and power.

I think that once Aristotle's God has been freed from the limitations imposed by Aristotle's inability to handle the question of how Pure Act can know things other than itself, Aristotle's view of causality and teleology can be separated from a closed, deterministic cosmic causal framework. Aquinas argues in detail for how this is so, and I find his arguments persuasive.[13] For Emon, however, al-Ghazali's occasionalism

---

[12] For discussion see my "Providence and Predestination in Al-Ghazali," *New Blackfriars* 92 (2011): 55–70. On al-Ghazali's thought, see, e.g., Frank Griffel, *Al-Ghazali's Philosophical Theology* (Oxford: Oxford University Press, 2009); Richard M. Frank, *Al-Ghazali and the Ash'arite School* (Durham, NC: Duke University Press, 1994); Farouk Mitha, *Al-Ghazali and the Ismailis: A Debate on Reason and Authority in Medieval Islam* (London: The Institute of Ismaili Studies, 2001).

[13] See Rudi te Velde, *Aquinas on God: The 'Divine Science' of the Summa Theologiae* (Aldershot: Ashgate, 2006); David B. Burrell, C.S.C., *Faith and Freedom: An Interfaith Perspective* (Oxford: Blackwell, 2004). Burrell engages significantly with both Aquinas and al-Ghazali.

is valuable not least for its insistence that "we cannot escape our own context to find an objective position outside ourselves." For Emon a key issue is "whether nature is truly as determinate as Hard and Soft Natural Law jurists presumed for purposes of their natural law theories." He does not think that "nature" can provide a determinate basis for legal reasoning, insofar as "nature" is not a given that is then interpreted, but rather our interpretations of nature are bound up in our very perception of it (as Hans-Georg Gadamer argues).

We return, then, to the pressing question of whether humans, across cultures, can perceive certain defining elements of "human nature." It is a question that equally extends to the wide diversity of interpretations of revealed scriptural norms, as Emon recognizes. If we keep the question at the level of the perception of "human nature" outside of scriptural reasoning (though certainly not unrelated to scriptural reasoning), then the problem has been well articulated by Alasdair MacIntyre. MacIntyre observes that the "contemporary universe of discourse... has no place within it for any conception of fixed ends, of ends to be discovered rather than decided upon or invented... it has no place for the type of *telos* or *finis* which provides the activity of a particular kind of being with a goal to which it must order its purposes or fail to achieve its own specific perfection in its activity."[14] In response to this situation, MacIntyre foregrounds the work of practical reason, which is embedded in a set of practices, including a tradition-based practice of enquiry. Asking whether practical reasoning can encounter and sincerely entertain rival arguments, he finds that the preconditions of shared rational enquiry turn out to be none other than the "precepts that Aquinas identified as the precepts of the natural law."[15]

---

[14] Alasdair MacIntyre, *First Principles, Final Ends and Contemporary Philosophical Issues* (Milwaukee, WI: Marquette University Press, 1990), 6–7.

[15] Alasdair MacIntyre, "Intractable Moral Disagreements," in *Intractable Disputes about the Natural Law: Alasdair MacIntyre and Critics*, ed. Lawrence S. Cunningham (Notre Dame: University of Notre Dame Press, 2009), 1–52, at 23. MacIntyre concludes his essay by remarking, "What the defense of the precepts of the natural law therefore requires is not an attempt to demonstrate the falsity of the conclusions of the public defenders of those denials. For such an attempt is bound to fail. What is needed instead is attention to the premises from which they argue and an attempt to undermine belief in those premises by demonstrating the flaws and confusions that inform those premises, flaws and confusions exemplified, so I have suggested, by the utilitarian use of the concept of happiness and of cognate concepts" (MacIntyre, 52). This is an excellent description of MacIntyre's own philosophical project. See also the reflections of Gerald McKenny, "Moral Disagreement and the Limits of Reason: Reflections on MacIntyre and Ratzinger," in *Intractable Disputes about the Natural Law*, 195–226.

Reflection upon the conditions needed for shared rational enquiry in the face of rival commitments—conditions such as life, freedom, and truth—leads us, MacIntyre thinks, to natural law. This claim is particularly interesting for interreligious discussion of natural law.

It is also worth singling out for future discussion the work of Hadley Arkes, who has repeatedly and persuasively called attention to the insufficiency of legal positivism for accounting for why it is that, for example, murder and incest are illegal.[16] Arkes does this through fascinating and detailed attention to concrete case law. He also challenges certain legal reasoning as unjust, for instance the United States Supreme Court's decision in *Roe v. Wade*, with its unwarranted assumptions about when human life—otherwise protected by law— begins. Arkes insists that there must be something behind our positive law about murder that marks murder as wrong, and this something merits the name natural law. I think he is right.

Emon concludes his essay, "Our temporal and spatial existence need not negate the possibility of authority in the context of a religious legal tradition such as Islamic law. Rather it reminds us that when we make normative claims within a tradition in which abiding by God's will is paramount, any claim must be couched so as not to exceed the limits of the human condition." This point stands at the heart of his approach, which has to do as much with Islamic law as with natural law. To my mind, certain moral principles are in fact shared across cultures on the basis of natural law, whether or not natural law *doctrine* has plausibility in these cultures. But because serious disagreement will emerge when one begins to apply these principles in the complex circumstances of life, natural law doctrine alone cannot be counted upon to do all, or even most, of the work. Even so, both revealed and secular laws require an account of the human nature of those to whom the laws are or might be addressed, especially those who are presently outsiders. Certainly believers will find, and should expect to find, resources for such an account in revelation itself. But important resources are also found in the universal elements that pertain to basic human flourishing. In this way, natural law doctrine can help to safeguard human "identity and value."

---

[16] See, e.g., Hadley Arkes, *First Things: An Inquiry into the First Principles of Morals and Justice* (Princeton: Princeton University Press, 1986); Hadley Arkes, *Constitutional Illusions and Anchoring Truths: The Touchstone of the Natural Law* (Cambridge: Cambridge University Press, 2010).

Response to Anver M. Emon's
"Islamic Natural Law Theories"

David Novak

I. COMPARATIVE JURISPRUDENCE

In this response to Anver Emon's "Islamic Natural Law Theories," I would like to basically show analogies to the Jewish tradition on the main conceptual issues he locates in the Islamic tradition and ponders for his own promotion of that tradition here and now. Also, I want to show the value of what Emon teaches those who like myself have great respect for the Islamic tradition if, for no other reason, than those committed to the Islamic tradition act very much like those of us committed to the Jewish tradition. Moreover, we not only act alike, we also talk alike. Thus scholars and thinkers in both traditions face many of the same conceptual issues. So, perhaps this comparative study can be useful to Emon in his rethinking the question of natural law in Islam, since both Judaism and Islam are traditions based on the normative revelations of the God who most Jewish thinkers and most Muslim thinkers regard to be the same God.[1] This why the interactions of law and theology in both Judaism and Islam are quite similar, which is one of the main points I have learned from Emon's essay. Furthermore, it is of great social and political significance at this point in history that Judaism and Islam as systems of religious

[1] See David Novak, "The Treatment of Islam and Muslims in the Legal Writings of Maimonides," *Studies in Islamic and Judaic Traditions*, Brown Judaic Series 110, ed. W. M. Brinner and S. D. Ricks (Atlanta, GA: Scholars Press, 1986), 233ff.

ideas and norms face the same challenge of maintaining their integral identity in an increasing secular social and political world. Each of our traditions has to navigate between the Scylla of assimilation into that world and the Charybdis of sectarian flight from that world (or even war against that world).

One sees in Emon's essay a dialectical relation between law as discovered by humans through philosophical reason and law as presented to humans by theology through revelation. And by "theology," I mean the content of revelation as "God's word" (which could well be the meaning of the two Greek words *theos* and *logos* that make up the word "theology"). There are definite analogies to these dialectical relations in the Jewish tradition. Reading Emon's essay has enabled me to see these dialectical relations in my own tradition better, and I hope my showing Jewish analogues will enable him to see these dialectical relations more clearly in his own tradition. This is what the comparisons made in this book are, optimally, supposed to do for us and for our readers.

II. NATURAL LAW: THREE ISLAMIC APPROACHES

When discussing natural law in pre-modern Islam, Emon delineates three different positions. First, there are those whom Emon calls "Hard Natural Law jurists," who assign to human reason what he calls "ontological authority," which he distinguishes from the "epistemic authority" given to the exegesis of "textual sources." Whereas textual exegesis talks about a revealed datum, the human reason spoken of by the Hard Natural Law jurists talks about created nature in which "God creates all things for the purpose of good and benefit." This is "a particular view of the created world fused with fact and value." Here "the empirical goodness of nature also embodies the willful intent of God." Second, there are those whom Emon calls "Voluntarist theologians," according to whom "God does as He wishes; whatever He does is by definition good." For them, "humans are not in an epistemic position to determine what the law is." Third, there are those Emon calls "Soft Natural Law jurists," who see that "the fusion of fact and value in nature" results from God's grace, not from natural necessity. If I understand this view correctly, it seems to be saying that nature itself is the result of God's grace. As such, nature is not taken to be a totally independent, autonomous realm where fact and value are necessarily linked, which is contrary to the position of the Hard Natural Law jurists. According to the Soft Natural Law school of thought in Islam, however, nature is not so independent that it is impervious to miraculous divine intervention into its workings, which happens when God changes His mind from what He originally intended when creating the natural order. Nevertheless, Emon points out that "after God created the world as a benefit, it does not seem that God has changed His mind; consequently, it is appropriate to grant reason ontological authority." In other words, although God intervenes in some natural events, miraculously causing them to veer from their original course (what we would call the "laws of nature"), when it comes to God's law for humans (whether natural or revealed) God does not change His mind. Thus God's natural law becomes evident to humans when they ponder the purposes inherent in the regular natural order, purposes which are evidence of God's gracious creation in which fact and value are fused. (This explains why almost all Islamic—and Jewish and Christian—natural law theorists in the Middle Ages became so enamored of Aristotelian teleology.)

III. JEWISH ANALOGUES TO THE THREE ISLAMIC APPROACHES TO NATURAL LAW

There is little doubt in my mind that this third view of natural law is one that Emon himself identifies with, for he is not only a historian of Islamic law; he is a constructive Islamic thinker in his own right as well. I can very much resonate to this view of natural law since, *mutatis mutandis*, I identify with its analogue in Judaism. So let us now look at Jewish analogues to Hard Natural Law jurisprudence and Voluntarist theology, and then look at the analogue to the kind of Soft Natural Law jurisprudence I identify with in Judaism.

There are those in the Jewish tradition who very much correspond to the Voluntarist theologians Emon has described. They are rabbinic theologians who reject the idea of the "reasons of the commandments" (*ta`amei ha-mitsvot*).[2] For to assume God's commandments

---

[2] See *Babylonian Talmud*: Sanhedrin 21b re Deut. 17:16–17. See, also, E. E. Urbach, *The Sages* [Heb.] (Jerusalem: Magnes Press, 1971), 312ff.

have reasons, which are knowable when one thinks about nature's purposes (in their view anyway), presumes that either God is subject to an uncreated order higher than Himself, or that God the Creator of the natural order is subordinate to what He has created when making laws for humans to obey. So, it follows from this view of nature as a possible source of opposition to God's absolute freedom of will that nature has no independence at all, and that God's will directly revealed in Scripture and interpreted by inspired tradition is the only legitimate source of human action.[3] Thus a mediaeval text, having much earlier rabbinic teaching behind it, teaches: "God has made a law [*huqqah*]; you are not allowed to enquire why it says this and why it says that!"[4] Furthermore, an earlier rabbinic text argues that Scripture did not for the most part reveal the reasons of the commandments, because when reasons for a few of the commandments were revealed, those who believed themselves to be wiser than God the Lawgiver convinced themselves that understanding the reason of a commandment could actually exempt them from its observance.[5] They seem to have presumed that sometimes the observance of the commandment was only intended for those who, unlike themselves, couldn't understand its reason. In other words, intelligent humans could actually devise better means to the fulfillment of natural ends than God Himself could decree. But, if nature like humans has no inherent purposes, the only purpose of them both being to obey God's will that requires no reason itself for its own operation, then there is no point in talking about natural law at all. (Several prominent modern Jewish thinkers, who could be called "fideists" or "religious positivists," have brought this kind of ancient and mediaeval voluntarism up to date.[6])

---

[3] Cf. Maimonides, *Guide of the Perplexed*, transl. S. Pines (Chicago: University of Chicago Press, 1963), 3.25. For the argument that if attributing irrational activity to a human lawgiver makes him unworthy of our respect, how much more so does that make God unworthy of our respect.

[4] *Midrash Leqah Tov*: Huqqat, ed. Buber, 119b re Num. 19:2.

[5] *Babylonian Talmud*: Sanhedrin 21b.

[6] For their respective positions and my critique thereof, see David Novak, *Jewish Social Ethics* (New York: Oxford University Press, 1992), 22ff.

IV. HARD NATURAL LAW THEORY: MEDIAEVAL VERSUS MODERN

When it comes to those in the Jewish tradition who can be compared to those Emon calls "Hard Natural Law" theorists in his own tradition, one must distinguish the more radical modern Hard Natural Law theorists from the more conservative pre-modern Hard Natural Law theorists. Since what could be considered Hard Natural Law theory has definitely appeared in modern Judaism, it is important to characterize this theory and distinguish it from pre-modern Hard Natural Law so that the greater challenge it poses to the normative Jewish tradition not be confused with the lesser challenge posed by the pre-modern version, the version Emon and I are dealing with in our respective essays.

The great divide between modern natural law theory and pre-modern natural law theory is the presence of the idea of autonomy in the former and its absence in the latter. This modern idea of autonomy comes in two versions: (1) There is liberal autonomy by which humans come together as citizens to form a society *de novo*, thereby agreeing upon certain norms as the procedures any rational person in their original position would choose for themselves (to paraphrase the most influential recent liberal theorist, John Rawls).[7] (2) There is Kantian autonomy, by which rational humans formulate for themselves and all others like themselves norms whereby they will here and now (but without presuming complete success in history) an ideal world of human equality and common moral aspiration.[8] Here it is not so much that humans devise the law, rather the idea of law itself inspires the autonomous act of self-legislation. In modern Judaism, there have been both liberal and Kantian autonomists.

Both liberal and Kantian autonomists do affirm a universally valid morality. Unlike moral relativists who cannot challenge traditional morality because they have no alternative morality with which to challenge it, even the less rigorous liberal autonomists do have a rationally formulated morality (and the Kantians all the more so). As such, their challenge of the Jewish tradition is not over the

---

[7] See his *A Theory of Justice* (Cambridge, MA: Harvard University Press, 1971), 17ff.

[8] See Kant, *Groundwork of the Metaphysic of Morals* PA421ff., trans. H. J. Paton (New York: Harper and Row, 1964), 88ff.

existence of rational morality; their challenge to the Jewish tradition is over the existence of God. For the liberal autonomists, the existence of God is either a non-issue or something to be fought against. They either ignore the "God question" or they are hostile to it. Most contemporary Kantians (Jewish and non-Jewish) either ignore the question or decide that Kantianism, especially its idea of moral autonomy, is better off without any consideration of God and religion at all.[9] Yet, even when Jewish Kantians do take the God question seriously, like Kant they do not see God to be the Lawgiver, whether of natural law, and certainly not of revealed law.[10] That is probably why most contemporary Jewish Kantians, even those who might be privately religious, keep their Jewish faith and their Kantianism wholly apart in public.

All this is important to bear in mind when dealing with the pre-modern Hard Natural Law thinkers who, though taken by their contemporary opponents to be radicals, now look rather conservative when compared to the modern autonomists described above. Whether or not one agrees with them, those who still argue like the pre-modern Hard Natural Law theorists can still be included in normative Jewish discourse in a way that most Jewish autonomists cannot be included. That is because the autonomists have excluded themselves from normative Jewish discourse by their explicit or even implicit denial of the authority of God's law, whether in its "thicker" (i.e., more concrete) revealed form or even in its "thinner" (i.e., more abstract) natural form (to borrow terms of the cultural anthropologist Clifford Geertz which have become quite familiar). Certainly, there is the same problem with modern autonomists in Islam as well as in Christianity, though I suspect that they are much less of a problem in contemporary Islam, since autonomy is an idea developed in the European Enlightenment that immediately affected Christians and Jews, but not Muslims (except those Muslims who have recently adopted Enlightenment ideas and ideals).[11]

[9] For an influential presentation of this view, see James Rachels, "God and Human Attitudes" in *Divine Commands and Morality*, ed. P. Helm (Oxford: Oxford University Press, 1981), 34ff.

[10] See *Critique of Pure Reason* B847.

[11] See J. B. Schneewind, *The Invention of Autonomy* (Cambridge: Cambridge University Press, 1998).

V. CONSERVATIVE MEDIAEVAL HARD NATURAL
LAW THEORY

By contrast, the "hardest" of the pre-modern Hard Natural Law theorists among the Jews have still affirmed divinely given law, something
modern Jewish liberals seem to have denied, and something Jewish
Kantians have been rather ambivalent about. Nevertheless, they see
God's law to have already been revealed in created nature itself, and
that historical revelation only supplies certain secondary specifics.[12]
Now these specifically revealed subsets of the genus revelation in
nature are taken to be culturally necessary, since natural law alone
would be insufficient to order the life of any concrete historical community.[13] In other words, no traditional human community could
have its historically transmitted vision of human flourishing pene-
trate the lives of its members if it operated at an abstract, universal
level, which would indeed be the case if the community were only a
society governed according to natural law.

The subordination of theology (the content of revealed law) to
philosophy (that discovers the precepts of natural law) is noticeable
in the thought of Maimonides (d. 1204), considered by many to be
the greatest Jewish jurist-theologian-philosopher. Maimonides saw
prophecy, being the medium through which God's law is revealed
to humans, to have universal potential and even general manifestation in the world.[14] Prophecy is not confined to the Jews (or to any
other particular people, however singular they believe themselves to
be). God's law is not confined to any particular historical manifestation thereof. To be sure, Maimonides, as an "official" Jewish leader
(he had juridical authority in his Egyptian Jewish community and
beyond) needed to affirm the superiority of Jewish revelation over
its Christian and Islamic rivals. And that for no other reason than
Maimonides (like many of his contemporaries) needed to explain
why he hadn't converted to Islam, a religion he respected, and which
was the official religion of the polity in which he lived and worked and
where he was proactive politically. And he did this by arguing that
any true revelation of God's law in nature had to deal with the coherent intellectual relationship humans need to have with God, plus the

---

[12] See Maimonides, *Guide of the Perplexed*, 3.28.
[13] See *Guide of the Perplexed*, 3.43.
[14] See Maimonides, *Mishneh Torah*: Foundations, 7.1ff.

coherent practical or political relationship humans need to have with each other.[15] The qualitative difference between one revelation and another, making one preferable to the other, is about how well that specific revelation correlates these two overlapping spheres of intelligent human action. Obviously, for him at least, Judaism comes in first, being superior in degree, but not being of a different kind. (And, in fact, a Muslim or a Christian could make a similar argument for the specific superiority of their own tradition.)

There is little if any room in this Hard Natural Law theory, however, for the traditional doctrine of God's election of the people Israel who are the recipients of God's revealed law, which is much more than natural law (even for those non-voluntarist Jewish theologians who do recognize a role for natural law in the full covenantal reality constituted by the Torah, as we shall see shortly). For Maimonides, it seems that anyone with enough philosophical ability could become a prophet, i.e. to attain prophetic apprehension of God by means of proper development or actualization of his potential, especially through active membership in a community of prophets and would-be prophets.[16] (Prophecy is much more important than the ability to predict future events, which most people think is the essence of prophecy.)

Considering how ubiquitous the doctrine of the election of Israel is in Scripture and the rabbinic writings, it is noteworthy how little that doctrine is dealt with by Maimonides.[17] One notices this in his extensive treatment of Abraham, the prophet who founded the people Israel who accepted the Torah at Sinai. Maimonides doesn't present Abraham as the one chosen by God to found this new people, which the scriptural narrative emphasizes. Instead, he emphasizes how Abraham reasoned his way to the conclusion that the world must have a First Cause (a point having some rabbinic precedent), and then how Abraham founded a polity consisting of those members of his family who thought as he did, plus outsiders attracted to his monotheistic vision.[18] Thus this polity was to be devoted to making recognition of that indisputable truth the theological-political task of the people centered therein and therefor. Accordingly, election as an act

---

[15] See *Guide of the Perplexed*, 2.40.
[16] See *Guide of the Perplexed*, 3.32.
[17] See David Novak, *The Election of Israel* (Cambridge: Cambridge University Press, 1995), 225ff.
[18] See *Mishneh Torah*: Idolatry, 1.1ff.

of divine grace, which is always selective, is very much played down. Yet that to me seems to be theologically inadequate.

VI. SOFT NATURAL LAW THEORY

If I have read him correctly, it seems that Emon is most sympathetic to what he calls "Soft Natural Law" theory. I too am most sympathetic to what could be its analogue in the Jewish tradition. The essence of this theory could be succinctly stated in the following proposition: *Natural law, which is formulated philosophically, is the precondition but not the cause of a flourishing human life; that life is only fulfilled by revealed law, which is constituted theologically.* Let me now explain. And this will require making contrasts between Hard and Soft Natural Law theory, since the two can be easily confused in a way that Voluntaristic theology and any natural law theory cannot be confused. In fact, voluntarists today are usually dismissed as "fundamentalists," which is a term of condemnation. And, even though many secularists would like to lump Soft Natural Law thinkers and voluntarists together in this pejorative category, it has never been too difficult for Soft Natural Law thinkers to cogently escape the charge of "fundamentalism" whenever it has been levelled against them.

Natural law is formulated philosophically in the sense that its precepts can be argued for on the basis of a definite view of human nature. Human nature is what essentially characterizes human beings, what differentiates us from other beings in the world. To accept human nature in oneself is to accept its normative implications for oneself as the subject of natural law when it commands one to act towards other persons in a certain way or refrain from acting towards them in a certain way. And to accept oneself as the object of natural law is to require other persons to act towards oneself in a certain way or refrain from acting towards oneself in a certain way. The *certain way* in both cases, either when one is the subject or the object of natural law, is a mode of action that is true rather than false to essential human nature. And to be false to oneself and to others inevitably leads to existential incoherence or even madness (think of Lady Macbeth).[19]

---

[19] In his play, *Macbeth*, when describing how Lady Macbeth prepared herself and her husband for the murder of Macduff, Shakespeare shows how she "denaturalizes"

Moreover, since humans are basically social or communal beings, all their significant actions are always transactions, i.e., they always involve mutual relations with other human persons primarily, and relations with other nonhuman beings in the world only secondarily. Therefore, one can argue for natural law prescriptions (philosophy providing the most cogent forms of argumentation) because it affirms and enhances natural human community; and one can argue against what natural law proscribes because it denies and degrades human natural human community.

The notion of a common human nature, which functions despite the many differences among human persons and communities (though differences that may be more ontologically significant than this natural commonality), is quite intelligible and even attractive to the adherents of many different cultures in the world. It is the only "multiculturalism" that doesn't wind up in the dead end of relativism or nihilism. Indeed, without that ontological commonality, relations among various peoples could only be warlike. When one regards all those outside one's faith community (*faith* being a community's positive response to *revelation*) to be antinomians (if not actual savages), they can then only be regarded as ripe for subjugation, enslavement, or annihilation. Thus natural law when taken to be Noahide law (see my essay) has provided Jews with a coherent way of having morally significant reciprocal relations with those gentile individuals and gentile peoples who have a similar kind of natural law recognized by their own traditions.

Because it is formulated philosophically, the acceptance of natural law is not dependent on the acceptance of any particular, historically manifest, normative revelation, even though (as we shall soon see) it must not be hostile or even indifferent to historical revelations, just as these historical revelations must not be hostile or even indifferent to natural law. As such, even though one's acceptance of natural law might lead one to seek the thicker content of revealed law, nonetheless, natural law should not be used as a covert means of

herself by putting these words in her mouth: "I have given suck, and know how tender 'tis to love the babe that milks me: I would, while it was smiling in my face, have pluck'd my nipple from his boneless gums, and dash'd the brains out, had I sworn as you have done to this" (Act 1, Scene 7). Yet she admits: "These deeds must not be thought after these ways; so, it will make us mad" (Act 2, Scene 2). And, finally, after she does become mad, Shakespeare has her physician say: "Unnatural deeds do breed unnatural troubles" (Act 5, Scene 2).

proselytizing. The fact that natural law might well point to the need for a higher more content-laden law, and can even make acceptance of that higher law possible as an intelligent choice, does not mean acceptance of natural law is the potential for acceptance of that higher law. It is not potential that follows a necessary trajectory into its full actualization. (This, by the way, goes against the tendency of some religious natural law theorists to try to argue others into their faith, using natural law as the premise from which they deduce their conversionary conclusion.)

Natural law is the precondition but not the cause of a fulfilling human life. Many modern thinkers have assumed that natural law—as the body of natural rights or human rights—is sufficient for a flourishing human life. For them, nothing else is required. As for the content of revealed law, they consider it be a private matter, as trivial as individual taste (i.e., if one's bad taste is for cultural relics). And, for more radical modern thinkers of this stripe, the content of anybody's revealed law is taken to be antithetical to their notion of human rights; in fact, for many contemporary thinkers of this stripe, the chief human right seems to be the right to be *against* God, and against traditions that affirm the normative supremacy of God. But not even the pre-modern Hard Natural Law theorists (whether Islamic or Jewish) would have said that. Even for them, there was something provided by revelation that could not be discovered (let alone invented) by philosophy as the exercise of human wisdom.[20] Yet, as we saw above, they thought the difference between natural law and revealed law, or between philosophy and theology, is one of degree rather than one of kind. For some of them, revelation provided a more direct apprehension of God than ordinary philosophical ratiocination could provide. And, for some of them, revelation provided more specific content than the more general natural law could provide. Nevertheless, we could ask whether or not one could argue for a difference in kind between natural law and revealed law so that the lines between philosophy and theology are less blurred, and the relation between them is more mutually enriching. The relation *between* philosophy and theology should be one where the conjunction "and" rather than the disjunction "or" predominates; where the conjunction "and" rather than the reductionist "because of" predominates.

---

[20] See Maimonides, *Mishneh Torah*: Kings, 8.11.

A better way to make the difference between philosophy and theology sharper than has been done by the Hard Natural Law theorists is to remove the divine–human relationship from philosophy and more or less confine it to theology. (Thus one will have to stop seeing natural law as presupposing natural theology and its idea of "Nature's God," which is hardly evident since natural science long ago stopped seeing the universe as a teleological hierarchy with God at its apex.) This doesn't mean that philosophy should be atheistic in principle which would, of course, make it impossible to interrelate philosophy and theology at all. In fact, one's philosophy need not even be agnostic. Thus one could postulate (in the Kantian sense) the existence of God as Lawgiver without, however, requiring one to provide actual proof for such an assertion.[21] And, since postulating God as Lawgiver is not presented as a premise from which natural law is its necessary conclusion, theistic natural law thinkers of this kind need not and should not require their secularist interlocutors to accept theistic premises in order to engage in dialogue with them.

One sees such postulation of God in the United States Declaration of Independence, which talks about persons being "endowed by their Creator with certain unalienable rights"; and one sees it in the Canadian Charter of Rights and Freedoms, whose preamble begins with the words: "Whereas Canada is founded upon principles that recognize the supremacy of God and the rule of law" (which I read as two phrases in apposition, viz., the supremacy of God is affirmed when God is recognized as the source of all true law; or the rule of law is grounded in the recognition of the normative supremacy of God). Nevertheless, this postulation does not constitute a positive relationship with God. It doesn't provide us with any intimate communal experience of God's presence to us, for us, and with us. As such, it doesn't give us enough content for communal worship and individual prayer, which comprise the main content of a religious way of life. There is not enough here for us to be able to talk to God in the present about what God has done for us and with us in the past, which is for the sake of our ongoing relationship with God into the future.[22]

---

[21] See David Novak, *In Defense of Religious Liberty* (Wilmington, DE: ISI Books, 2009), 29ff.

[22] Even the decidedly non-theistic (former Christian) philosopher, Martin Heidegger, noted in *Identity and Difference*, trans. J. Stambaugh (Chicago: University of Chicago Press, 2002), 72–73: "The deity enters into philosophy... [as] Being as the generative ground... as *causa sui*. This is the right name for the god of philosophy. Man can neither pray nor sacrifice to this god. Before *causa sui*, man can neither fall to

That natural law doesn't provide a positive relationship with God is shown by the fact that the Noahide law in its rabbinic formulation, when taken to be natural law (see my essay), doesn't require non-Jews to actually affirm God's real relationship with them (which is more than the mere postulation of God's existence as the source of natural law). The two Noahide laws pertaining to God are negative precepts: the prohibition of idolatry and the prohibition of blasphemy (i.e., cursing God). Clearly, somebody who worships a god who is less than the Creator of heaven and earth, i.e., a superhuman entity who is not a singular deity, that person is a polytheistic idolater (even if no image is involved in their worship). This idolater is hardly in a position to have an exclusive, positive relationship with the One God, a relationship involving awe and love. For love and awe of God involve blessing God rather than cursing God, and love and awe involve not replacing the One and Only God with someone less than Him, or by even associating God with anyone else in some sort of pantheon. In fact, both blasphemy (which comes closest to the vehemence of modern atheism) and idolatry are manifest expressions of hatred of God. Human persons, both individually and collectively, have to get over this hatred of God before they can possibly be ready for a positive, awesome, affectionate relationship with God. That quest comes from the side of human nature that is oriented to God (and which is a side of human nature that can only be satisfied by a positive relationship with God that is constituted by an historical revelation).

The other side of human nature, which seeks to live in peace with one's fellow humans, requires humans to get over their propensity to act against each another violently, hence the prohibitions of murder and robbery. And it requires humans to get over their tendency to engage in actions that are destructive of family life, the foundation of true human community, which is necessarily rooted in a mutually faithful, procreative, exogamous, heterosexual relationship, hence the prohibitions of incest, homoeroticism, adultery, and bestiality.[23] Finally, it requires each member of a society, in one way or another, to support a political order that protects the rights of all its members, hence the admonition to establish courts where justice is sought through the due process of law. The importance of the cultivation

---

his knees in awe nor can he play music and dance before this god." Heidegger contrasts this god with *der göttlicher Gott* (Heidegger, 141).

[23] See *Babylonian Talmud*: Sanhedrin 58a re Gen. 2:24.

of the interpersonal side of human nature for the cultivation of the divine–human side of human nature is because God reveals His law to human communities, hence these communities must be properly ordered among their members so as to be open to the higher substantiation of their lives by God's revealed law. This in the end is what all humans created in the image of God ultimately seek, and they primarily seek it collectively.

All of these natural laws, when affirmed and formulated by those who hold a Soft Natural Law position, only make an intelligent acceptance of revealed law possible, but they do not necessitate it. This affirmation and formulation does not automatically make any human being or beings accept revelation; and it certainly did not force God to reveal His higher law to any human community. This comes out in a famous rabbinic legend, which tells of how God offered the full Torah to all the peoples of the world.[24] And when they ask what this Torah commands, God informs them of the prohibitions of murder, incest, and robbery—all of which they should have known already from universally evident Noahide law. (One would have expected God to have informed them of specifically Jewish laws such as the dietary prohibitions, just like candidates for conversion to Judaism are to be informed of them before their acceptance of the full Torah that is required for their full acceptance into the Jewish people.[25]) Yet each people refuses the divine offer by complaining that their cultural practices are contrary to these prohibitions, hence they couldn't accept the full Torah that reiterates them. Doing that would force them to give up their national cultural identity, which is something they feel they cannot do. The legend concludes with God saying that if they couldn't even accept the Noahide laws, how could they possibly accept the full Torah? Nevertheless, even if the peoples of the world had accepted the Noahide laws, they could have said that this is enough for them. In other words, acceptance of the Noahide laws only makes acceptance of the full Torah possible as an intelligent choice; but it doesn't require acceptance of the full Torah. In fact, the Talmud teaches that Israel's acceptance of the Torah was initially forced upon them by God, but that was because of the direct revelation of God at Mount Sinai, not because of any necessary conclusion from the natural necessity of

---

[24] *Sifre*: Ve-z'ot ha-berakhah, no. 343, ed. Finkelstein, 395ff.; also, *Babylonian Talmud*: Avodah Zarah 2b.

[25] See *Babylonian Talmud*: Yevamot 47a.

affirming natural or Noahide law.[26] There it seems to be implied that having already accepted the Noahide laws, the Jews wouldn't be told by God that they weren't ready yet to accept the full Torah.

Thinking out the most cogent correlation of law, theology, and philosophy—whether in Judaism or in Islam—could well lead one to prefer for good reasons one version of natural law over its rivals. I hope Anver Emon would agree that both he and I are Soft Natural Law theorists in our respective traditions.

---

[26] See *Babylonian Talmud*: Shabbat 88a; also, Maimonides, *Mishneh Torah*: Kings, 8.10.

Bibliography

Classical Jewish Sources

Albo, Joseph. *Book of Principles.* 5 vols. Edited and translated by I. Husik. Philadelphia: Jewish Publication Society of America, 1929–30.

Biblia Hebraica. 7th ed. Edited by R. Kittel. Stuttgart: Privilege Württ, Bibilanstadt, 1951.

Babylonian Talmud (Bavli). 20 vols. Vilna: Romm., 1898.

Buber, Martin and Franz Rosenzweig. *Die Fünf Bücher der Weisung.* Köln: Jakob Hegner, 1954.

Lifschuetz, Israel. *Tiferet Yishrael.* In *Mishnayot.* 12 vols. New York: M. P. Press, 1969.

Maimonides. *Guide of the Perplexed.* Translated by S. Pines. Chicago: University of Chicago Press, 1963.

—— *Book of the Commandments.* Edited by C. Heller, Jerusalem, n.p., 1946.

—— *Midrash Rabbah.* 2 vols. Edited by S. Buber. Jerusalem: n.p., 1964.

—— *Mishnah Torah.* 12 vols. Edited by S. Frankel. B'nai Brak: Shabse Frankel, 2001.

Midrash Leqah Tov. 2 vols. Edited by S. Buber. Vilna: Romm. 1884.

Mishnah. 6 vols. Edited by C. Albeck. Tel Aviv: Mosad Bialik and Dvir, 1957.

Nahmanides. *Commentary on the Torah.* 2 vols. Edited by C. B. Chavel. Jerusalem: Mosad ha-Rav Kok, 1959–63.

Palestinian Talmud. Edition Pietrkov. 7 vols. Jerusalem: n.p., 1959.

Rashi. *Commentary on the Torah.* Edited by C. B. Chavel. Jerusalem: Mosad ha-Rav Kook, 1982.

Sifra. Edited by I. H. Weiss. New York: Om, 1947.

Sifre: Devarim. Edited by Louis Finkelstein. New York: Jewish Theological Seminary of America, 1969.

Targum Jonathan ben Uziel. In *Miqraot Gedolot: Pentateuch.* 5 vols. New York: Otsan ha-Sefarim, 1953.

Tosefta. Edited by S. Zuckermandl. Jerusalem: Wahrmann, 1937.

Tosafot. In *Babylonian Talmud* (Bavli). 20 vols. Vilna: Romm., 1898.

Secondary Jewish Sources

Bleich, J. David. "Judaism and Natural Law." *Jewish Law Annual* 7 (1988): 5–42.

Cohen, Hermann. "Die Nächstenliebe im Talmud." *Jüdische Schriften* I. Berlin: C. A. Schwetschke, 1924.

——*Religion of Reason out of the Sources of Judaism.* Translated by S. Kaplan. New York: Frederich Ungar, 1972.

Collins, John J. *Jewish Wisdom in the Hellenistic Age.* Louisville, KY: Westminster John Knox Press, 1997.

Halivni, David Weiss. *Mishnah, Midrash, and Gemara.* Cambridge, MA: Harvard University Press, 1986.

Heschel, Abraham Joshua. *Heavenly Torah.* Translated by G. Tucker. New York: Continuum, 2005.

Katz, Jacob. *Exclusiveness and Tolerance: Studies in Jewish-Gentile Relations in Medieval and Modern Times.* Oxford: Oxford University Press, 1961.

Marmorstein, A. *The Old Rabbinic Doctrine of God* I. New York: KTAV, 1968.

Novak, David. "Can We Be Maimonideans Today?" In *Maimonides and His Heritage.* Edited by I. Dobbs-Weinstein, L. E. Goodman, and J. A. Grady. Albany, NY: SUNY Press, 2009.

—— *Covenantal Rights.* Princeton, NJ: Princeton University Press, 2000.

—— "Creation." In *The Cambridge History of Jewish Philosophy: The Modern Era.* Edited by M. Kavka, Z. Braiterman, and D. Novak. Cambridge: Cambridge University Press, 2012.

—— *The Election of Israel.* Cambridge: Cambridge University Press, 1995.

—— *The Image of the Non-Jew in Judaism.* New York: Edwin Mellen Press, 1983; 2nd ed., edited by M. LaGrone. Oxford: Littman Library of Jewish Civilization, 2011.

—— *In Defense of Religious Liberty.* Wilmington, DE: ISI Books, 2009.

—— *Jewish-Christian Dialogue: A Jewish Justification.* New York: Oxford University Press, 1989.

—— *The Jewish Social Contract.* Princeton, NJ: Princeton University Press, 2005.

—— *Jewish Social Ethics.* New York: Oxford University Press, 1992.

—— *Les Juifs et les chrétiens révèrent-ils le même Dieu?* In *Le Christianisme au miroir du judaïsme.* Edited by Shmuel Trigano. Paris: Revue Pardès, 2003.

—— "Maimonides' Treatment of Christians and Its Normative Implications." In *Jewish Theology and World Religions.* Edited by A. Goshen-Gottstein and E. Korn. Oxford: Littman Library, 2012.

—— *Natural Law in Judaism.* Cambridge: Cambridge University Press, 1998.

—— "Philosophy and the Possibility of Revelation: A Theological Response to the Challenge of Leo Strauss." In *Leo Strauss and Judaism.* Edited by D. Novak. Lanham, MD: Rowman and Littlefield, 1996.

—— *The Sanctity of Human Life.* Washington D.C.: Georgetown University Press, 2007.

—— *Talking With Christians: Musings of a Jewish Theologian.* Grand Rapids, MI: Eerdmans Publishing Co., 2005.

—— *Traditions in the Public Square: A David Novak Reader.* Edited by R. Rashkover and M. Kavka. Grand Rapids, MI: Eerdmans Publishing Co., 2008.

—— "The Universality of Jewish Ethics: A Rejoinder to Secularist Critics." *Journal of Religious Ethics* 36 (2008): 181–211.

Rosenzweig, Franz. *The Star of Redemption.* Translated by B. E. Galli. Madison, WI: University of Wisconsin Press, 2005.

Schechter, Solomon. *Some Aspects of Rabbinic Theology.* New York: Behrman House, 1936.

Classic Christian Sources

Ambrosiaster. *Commentaries on Romans and 1–2 Corinthians.* Translated and edited by Gerald L. Bray. Downers Grove, IL: InterVarsity Press, 2009.

—— *Quaestiones Veteris et Novi Testamenti.* Edited by A. Souter. CSEL 50. Vienna: 1908.

Aquinas, Thomas. *Summa theologica (Summa theologiae).* Translated by the English Dominican Fathers. Westminster, MD: Christian Classics, 1981.

Augustine. *Answer to Faustus, a Manichean.* Translated by Roland J. Teske, SJ. Hyde Park, NY: New City Press, 2007.

—— *City of God.* Translated by Henry Bettenson. New York: Penguin, 1984.

—— *On Free Will.* In Augustine, *Earlier Writings.* Edited and translated by J. H. S. Burleigh. Louisville, KY: Westminster John Knox Press, 2006.

—— *On the Spirit and the Letter.* In Augustine, *Anti-Pelagian Works.* Translated by Peter Holmes and Robert Ernest Wallis, revised by Benjamin B. Warfield. Nicene and Post-Nicene Fathers. First Series. Vol. 5. Peabody, MA: Hendrickson, 1995 (1887).

Chrysostom, John. *Homilies on the Epistle to the Romans.* Translated by J. B. Morris and W. H. Simcox, revised by George B. Stevens. In *Chrysostom: Homilies on the Acts of the Apostles and the Epistle to the Romans.* Edited by George B. Stevens. Nicene and Post-Nicene Fathers. First Series. Volume 11. Peabody, MA: Hendrickson, 1995 (1889).

Dun Scotus on the Will and Morality. Translated by Alan B. Wolter, O.F.M., ed. William A. Frank (Washington D.C.: Catholic University of America Press, 1997)

Origen. *Commentary on the Epistle to the Romans, Books 1–5.* Translated by Thomas P. Scheck. Washington D.C.: Catholic University of America Press, 2001.

Pelagius. *Pelagius's Commentary on St. Paul's Epistle to the Romans.* Translated by Theodore De Bruyn. Oxford: Oxford University Press, 1993.

Secondary Christian Sources

Bammel, Caroline Hammond. "Philocalia IX, Jerome, Epistle 121 and Origen's Exposition of Romans VII." *Journal of Theological Studies* 32 (1981): 51–81.

Banner, William. "Origen and the Tradition of Natural Law Concepts." *Dumbarton Oaks Papers* 12 (1958): 49–82.

Barr, James. *Biblical Faith and Natural Theology*. Oxford: Oxford University Press, 1993.

Barth, Karl. *Epistle to the Romans*. Translated from 6th ed. by Edwyn C. Hoskyns. Oxford: Oxford University Press, 1933.

Biggar, Nigel. *Behaving in Public: How to Do Christian Ethics*. Grand Rapids, MI: Eerdmans, 2011.

Bonner, Gerald. *Freedom and Necessity: St. Augustine's Teaching on Divine Power and Human Freedom*. Washington, D.C.: Catholic University of America Press, 2007.

Boyd, Craig A. *A Shared Morality: A Narrative Defense of Natural Law Ethics*. Grand Rapids, MI: Brazos Press, 2007.

Boyle, Joseph. "Natural Law and the Ethics of Tradition." In *Natural Law Theory: Contemporary Essays*. Edited by Robert P. George. Oxford: Clarendon, 1992: 3–30.

Braaten, Carl, E. "A Lutheran Affirmation of the Natural Law." In *Natural Law: A Lutheran Reappraisal*. St. Louis, MO: Concordia Publishing House, 2011: 3–16.

Bray, Gerald L. "Translator's Introduction" to Ambrosiaster, *Commentaries on Romans and 1–2 Corinthians*, translated and edited by Gerald L. Bray. Downers Grove, IL: InterVarsity Press, 2009.

Brock, Stephen L. "National Inclination and the Intelligibility of the Good in Thomistic Natural Law." *Vera Lex* 6 (2005): 57–78.

——"Natural Law, the Understanding of Principles, and Universal Good." *Nova et Vetera* 9 (2011): 671–706.

Budziszewski, J. "Diplomacy and Theology in the Dialogue on Universal Ethics." *Nova et Vetera* 9 (2011): 707–35.

—— *The Line Through the Heart: Natural Law as Fact, Theory, and Sign of Contradiction*. Wilmington, DE: ISI Books, 2009.

Burrell, David B., C.S.C. *Faith and Freedom: An Interfaith Perspective*. Oxford: Blackwell, 2004.

Bussiéres, Marie-Pierre. "Ambrosiaster's Method of Interpretation in the Questions on the Old and New Testament." In *Interpreting the Bible and Aristotle in Late Antiquity: The Alexandrian Commentary Tradition between Rome and Baghdad*. Edited by Josef Lössl and John W. Watt. Burlington, VT: Ashgate, 2011.

Campbell, Douglas A. *The Deliverance of God: An Apocalyptic Rereading of Justification in Paul*. Grand Rapids, MI: Eerdmans, 2009.

Cessario, Romanus, O.P. *Introduction to Moral Theology*. Washington, D.C.: Catholic University of America Press, 2001.

Chadwick, Henry. "Origen, Celsus and the Stoa." *Journal of Theological Studies* 48 (1947): 34–49.

Charles, J. Daryl. *Retrieving the Natural Law: A Return to Moral First Things.* Grand Rapids, MI: Eerdmans, 2008.

Daniélou, Jean, SJ. *God and the Ways of Knowing.* Translated by Walter Roberts. San Francisco: Ignatius Press, 2003.

Dewan, Lawrence, O.P. "St. Thomas, Natural Law, and Universal Ethics." *Nova et Vetera* 9 (2011): 737–62.

De Bruyn, Theodore. "Introduction" to *Pelagius's Commentary on St. Paul's Epistle to the Romans,* translated by Theodore De Bruyn. Oxford: Oxford University Press, 1993.

De Groot, Jean. "Teleology and Evidence: Reasoning about Human Nature." In *Natural Moral Law in Contemporary Society.* Edited by Holger Zaborowski. Washington D.C.: Catholic University of America Press, 2010: 141–69.

Di Blasi, Fulvio. *God and the Natural Law: A Rereading of Thomas Aquinas.* Translated by David Thunder. South Bend, IN: St. Augustine's Press, 2006.

Dougherty, Richard J. "Natural Law." In *Augustine Through the Ages: An Encyclopedia.* Edited by Allan D. Fitzgerald, O.S.A. Grand Rapids, MI: Eerdmans, 1999: 582–84.

Dulles, Avery, SJ. *Magisterium: Teacher and Guardian of the Faith.* Naples, FL: Sapientia Press, 2007.

—— "Who Can Be Saved?" In Dulles, *Church and Society: The Laurence J. McGinley Lectures, 1988–2007.* New York: Fordham University Press, 2008: 522–34.

Dunkle, Brian L., SJ. "A Development in Origen's View of the Natural Law." *Pro Ecclesia* 13 (2004): 337–51.

Evans, Robert F. *Pelagius: Inquiries and Reappraisals.* New York: Seabury Press, 1968.

Feser, Edward. *Aquinas.* Oxford: Oneworld, 2009.

Finnis, John. *Aquinas.* Oxford: Oxford University Press, 1998.

Fredriksen, Paula. *Augustine and the Jews: A Christian Defense of Jews and Judaism.* New York: Doubleday, 2008.

Fürst, Alfons. "Origen: Exegesis and Philosophy in Early Christian Alexandria." In *Interpreting the Bible and Aristotle in Late Antiquity: The Alexandrian Commentary Tradition between Rome and Baghdad.* Edited by Josef Lössl and John W. Watt. Burlington, VT: Ashgate, 2011: 13–32.

Gathercole, Simon J. "A conversion of Augustine: From Natural Law to Restored Nature in Romans 2:13–16." In *Engaging Augustine on Romans: Self, Context, and Theology in Interpretation.* Edited by Daniel Patte and Eugene TeSelle. Harrisburg, PA: Trinity Press International, 2002: 147–70.

George, Robert P. "Kelsen and Aquinas on the Natural Law Doctrine." In *St. Thomas Aquinas and the Natural Law Tradition.* Edited by John Goyette, Mark S. Latkovic, and Richard S. Myers. Washington D.C.: Catholic University of America Press, 2004: 237–59.

Grabill, Stephen J. *Rediscovering the Natural Law in Reformed Theological Ethics*. Grand Rapids, MI: Eerdmans, 2006.

Grisez, Germain. "The First Principle of Practical Reason: A Commentary on the *Summa Theologiae*, 1–2, Question 94, Article 2." *Natural Law Forum* 10 (1965): 168–201.

—— "Natural Law and Natural Inclinations: Some Comments and Clarifications." *New Scholasticism* 6 (1987): 307–20.

Guroian, Vigen. *Incarnate Love: Essays in Orthodox Ethics*. Notre Dame, IN: University of Notre Dame Press, 1987.

Harrison, Carol. *Rethinking Augustine's Early Theology: An Argument for Continuity*. Oxford: Oxford University Press, 2006.

Hart, David Bentley. *The Experience of God: Being, Consciousness, Bliss*. New Haven, CT: Yale University Press, 2013.

Hauerwas, Stanley. *The Peaceable Kingdom: A Primer in Christian Ethics*. Notre Dame: University of Notre Dame Press, 1983.

Heither, Theresia. *Origenes. Commentarii in epistulam ad Romanos/ Römerbriefkommentar*. Freiburg im Breisgau: Herder, 1990.

Hittinger, F. Russell. *A Critique of the New Natural Law Theory*. Notre Dame: University of Notre Dame Press, 1987.

—— *The First Grace: Rediscovering the Natural Law in a Post-Christian World*. Wilmington, DE: ISI Books, 2003.

—— "Human Nature and States of Nature in John Paul II's Theological Anthropology." In *Human Nature and Wholeness: A Roman Catholic Perspective*. Edited by Daniel N. Robinson, Gladys M. Sweeney, and Richard Gill. Washington D.C.: Catholic University of America Press, 2006: 9–33.

—— "The Situation of Natural Law in Catholic Theology." *Nova et Vetera* 9 (2011): 657–70.

Horsley, Richard A. "The Law of Nature in Philo and Cicero." *Harvard Theological Review* 71 (1978): 35–59.

Hughes, Kevin L. *Constructing Antichrist: Paul, Biblical Commentary, and the Development of Doctrine in the Early Middle Ages*. Washington, D.C.: Catholic University of America Press, 2005.

International Theological Commission. "In Search of a Universal Ethic: A New Look at the Natural Law." <http://www.vatican.va/roman_curia/ congregations/cfaith/cti_documents/rc_con_cfaith_doc_20090520_ legge-naturale_en.html>.

Johnson, Luke Timothy. *Among the Gentiles: Greco-Roman Religion and Christianity*. New Haven, CT: Yale University Press, 2009.

Kelly, J. N. D. *Golden Mouth: The Story of John Chrysostom—Ascetic, Preacher, Bishop*. Ithaca, NY: Cornell University Press, 1998.

Kolakowski, Leszek. *Is God Happy? Selected Essays*. New York: Basic Books, 2013.

Levering, Matthew. *Biblical Natural Law: A Theocentric and Teleological Approach.* Oxford: Oxford University Press, 2008.

——— "God and the Natural Law: Reflections on Genesis 22." *Modern Theology* 24 (2008): 151–77.

——— *Jewish-Christian Dialogue and the Life of Wisdom: Engagements with the Theology of David Novak.* London: Continuum, 2010.

——— "Knowing What is 'Natural': Thomas Aquinas and Luke Timothy Johnson on Romans 1–2." *Logos* 12 (2009): 117–42.

Long, Steven A. "Natural Law or Autonomous Practical Reason: Problems for the New Natural Law Theory." In *St. Thomas Aquinas and the Natural Law Tradition.* Edited by John Goyette, Mark S. Latkovic, and Richard S. Myers. Washington D.C.: Catholic University of America Press, 2004: 165–93.

——— "Teleology, Divine Governance, and the Common Good—Reflections on the ITC's *The Search for Universal Ethics: A New Look at Natural Law.*" *Nova et Vetera* 9 (2011): 775–89.

Lunn-Rockliffe, Sophie. *Ambrosiaster's Political Theology.* Oxford: Oxford University Press, 2007.

Martens, Peter W. *Origen and Scripture: The Contours of the Exegetical Life.* Oxford: Oxford University Press, 2011.

Martin, Ralph. *Will Many Be Saved? What Vatican II Actually Teaches and its Implications for the New Evangelization.* Grand Rapids, MI: Eerdmans, 2012.

McKenny, Gerald. "Moral Disagreements and the Limits of Reason: Reflections on MacIntyre and Ratzinger." In *Intractable Disputes about the Natural Law: Alasdair MacIntyre and Critics.* Edited by Lawrence S. Cunningham. Notre Dame: University of Notre Dame Press, 2009: 195–226.

McInerny, Ralph. *Implicit Moral Knowledge.* Edited by Fulvio Di Blasi. Rubbettino: Soveria Mannelli, 2006.

Mitchell, Margaret M. *The Heavenly Trumpet: John Chrysostom and the Art of Pauline Interpretation.* Louisville, KY: Westminster John Knox Press, 2002.

Oakes, Edward T., SJ. *Infinity Dwindled to Infancy: A Catholic and Evangelical Christology.* Grand Rapids, MI: Eerdmans, 2011.

Oderberg, David. "The Metaphysical Foundations of Natural Law." In *Natural Moral Law in Contemporary Society.* Edited by Holger Zaborowski. Washington D.C.: Catholic University of America Press, 2010: 44–75.

O'Donovan, Oliver and Joan Lockwood O'Donovan, *Bonds of Imperfection: Christian Politics, Past and Present.* Grand Rapids, MI: Eerdmans, 2004.

Papanikolaou, Aristotle. *The Mystical as Political: Democracy and Non-Radical Orthodoxy.* Notre Dame: University of Notre Dame Press, 2012.

Pinckaers, Servais, O.P. *The Sources of Christian Ethics.* Translated by Mary Thomas Noble, O.P. Washington, D.C.: Catholic University of America Press, 1995.

Porter, Jean. "Does the Natural Law Provide a Universally Valid Morality?" In *Intractable Disputes about the Natural Law: Alasdair MacIntyre and Critics*. Edited by Lawrence S. Cunningham. Notre Dame: University of Notre Dame Press, 2009: 53–95.

—— *Ministers of the Law: A Natural Law Theory of Legal Authority*. Grand Rapids, MI: Eerdmans, 2010.

—— *Natural and Divine Law: Reclaiming the Tradition for Christian Ethics*. Grand Rapids, MI: Eerdmans, 1999.

—— *Nature as Reason: A Thomistic Theory of the Natural Law*. Grand Rapids, MI: Eerdmans, 2005.

Ramsey, Paul. *Basic Christian Ethics*. Louisville, KY: Westminster John Knox Press, 1993.

—— *Nine Modern Moralists*. Englewood Cliffs, NJ: Prentice-Hall, 1962.

—— *War and the Christian Conscience: How Shall Modern War Be Conducted Justly?* Durham, NC: Duke University Press, 1961.

Ratzinger, Joseph. "That Which Holds the World Together: The Pre-political Moral Foundations of a Free State." In Jürgen Habermas and Joseph Ratzinger, *Dialectics of Secularization: On Reason and Religion*. Edited by Florian Schuller. Translated by Brian McNeil, C.R.V. San Francisco: Ignatius Press, 2006: 53–80.

Reasoner, Mark. *Romans in Full Circle: A History of Interpretation*. Louisville, KY: Westminster John Knox Press, 2005.

Rhonheimer, Martin. "The Cognitive Structure of the Natural Law and the Truth of Subjectivity." *The Thomist* 67 (2003): 1–44.

Rist, John M. *Real Ethics: Rethinking the Foundations of Morality*. Cambridge: Cambridge University Press, 2002.

Roukema, Riemer. *The Diversity of Laws in Origen's Commentary on Romans*. Amsterdam: Free University Press, 1988.

Rziha, John. *Perfecting Human Actions: St. Thomas Aquinas on Human Participation in Eternal Law*. Washington D.C.: Catholic University of America Press, 2009.

Scheck, Thomas P. "Introduction" to Origen, *Commentary on the Epistle to the Romans, Books 1–5*, translated by Thomas P. Scheck. Washington D.C.: Catholic University of America Press, 2001: 1–48.

—— *Origen and the History of Justification: The Legacy of Origen's Commentary on Romans*. Notre Dame: University of Notre Dame Press, 2008.

Slater, Peter. "Goodness as Order and Harmony in Augustine." In *Augustine: From Rhetor to Theologian*. Edited by Joanne McWilliam. Waterloo, Ontario: Wilfrid Laurier University Press, 1992.

Sokolowski, Robert. "Discovery and Obligation in Natural Law." In *Natural Moral Law in Contemporary Society*. Edited by Holger Zaborowski. Washington D.C.: Catholic University of America Press, 2010: 24–43.

Souter, Alexander. *Pelagius's Expositions of Thirteen Epistles of St Paul.* Cambridge: Cambridge University Press, 1922–1931.

Stoyanov, Yuri. *The Other God: Dualist Religions from Antiquity to the Cathar Heresy.* New Haven, CT: Yale University Press, 2000.

Taitslin, Anna. "The Competing Sources of Aquinas' Natural Law: Aristotle, Roman Law and the Early Christian Fathers." In *The Threads of Natural Law: Unravelling a Philosophical Tradition.* Edited by F. J. Contreras. New York: Springer, 2013: 47–63.

Troeltsch, Ernst. "Christian Natural Law." In Troeltsch, *Religion in History.* Translated by James Luther Adams and Walter F. Bense. Minneapolis, MN: Fortress Press, 1991: 159–67.

—— "Stoic-Christian Natural Law and Modern Secular Natural Law." In Troeltsch, *Religion in History.* Translated by James Luther Adams and Walter F. Bense. Minneapolis, MN: Fortress Press, 1991: 321–42.

Tzamalikos, Panayiotis. *Origen: Philosophy of History and Eschatology.* Leiden: Brill, 2007.

VanDrunen, David. *A Biblical Case for Natural Law.* Grand Rapids, MI: Acton Institute, 2006.

—— *Natural Law and the Two Kingdoms: A Study in the Development of Reformed Social Thought.* Grand Rapids, MI: Eerdmans, 2009.

Vatican Council II. Volume 1: *The Conciliar and Postconciliar Documents.* New revised edition. Edited by Austin Flannery, O.P. Northport, NY: Costello Publishing Company, 1996.

Velde, Rudi te. *Aquinas on God: The 'Divine Science' of the Summa Theologiae.* Aldershot: Ashgate, 2006.

Volf, Miroslav. *Allah: A Christian Response.* New York: Harper Collins, 2011.

Von Harnack, Adolf. *Marcion: the Gospel of the Alien God.* Translated by John E. Steely and Lyle D. Bierma. Eugene: OR: Wipf & Stock, 2007.

Welch, Lawrence J. "Christ, the Moral Law, and the Teaching Authority of the Magisterium." *Irish Theological Quarterly* 64 (1999): 16–28.

—— "Faith and Reason: The Unity of the Moral Law in Christ." *Irish Theological Quarterly* 66 (2001): 249–58.

Wilken, Robert Louis. *John Chrysostom and the Jews: Rhetoric and Reality in the 4th Century* (Eugene, OR: Wipf & Stock, 2004)

—— "Origen, Augustine, and Thomas: Interpreters of the Letter to the Romans." In *Reading Romans with St. Thomas Aquinas.* Edited by Matthew Levering and Michael Dauphinais. Washington, D.C.: Catholic University of America Press, 2012: 288–301.

—— *The Spirit of Early Christian Thought: Seeking the Face of God.* New Haven, CT: Yale University Press, 2003.

Winston, David. *The Wisdom of Solomon.* New York: Doubleday, 1979.

Classic Islamic Sources

al-Amidi, Sayf al-Din. *al-Ihkam fi Usul al-Ahkam*. Beirut: Dar al-Fikr, 1997.

al-Asfahani, Abu 'Abd Allah. *al-Kashif 'an al-Mahsul fi 'Ilm al-Usul*. Edited by 'Adil Ahmad 'Abd al-Mawjud and 'Ali Muhammad Mu'awwad. Beirut: Dar al-Kutub al-'Ilmiyya, 1998.

al-Basri, Abu al-Husayn. *al-Mu'tamad fi Usul al-Fiqh*. Beirut: Dar al-Kutub al-'Ilmiyya, n.d.

al-Ghazali, Abu Hamid. "al-Munqidh min al-dalal." In *Majmu'a rasa'il al-Imam al-Ghazali*. Edited by Ahmad Shams al-Din. Beirut: Dar al-Kutub al-'Ilmiyya, 1988.

—— *al-Mustasfa min 'Ilm al-Usul*. Edited by Ibrahim M. Ramadan. Beirut: Dar al-Arqam, n.d.

—— *The Incoherence of the Philosophers: A Parallel English-Arabic Text*. Translated by Michael Marmura. Salt Lake City: Brigham Young University Press, 1997.

—— *Shifa' al-Ghalil fi Bayan al-Shabh wa al-Mukhil wa Masalik al-Ta'lil*. Edited by Muhammad al-Kubaysi. Baghdad: Ra'asa Diwan al-Awqaf, 1971.

Ibn al-Farikan. *Sharh al-Waraqat*. Edited by Sarah Shafi al-Hajiri. Beirut: Dar al-Basha'ir al-Islamiyya, 2001.

Ibn Hazm. *al-Ihkam fi Usul al-Ahkam*. Cairo: Dar al-Hadith, 1984.

Ibn Manzur. *Lisan al-'Arab*. 6th edition. Beirut: Dar Sadir, 1997: 2:517;

Ibn Rushd. *Tahafut al-Tahafut*. Edited by Muhammad al-'Arabi. Beirut: Dar al-Fikr al-Libnani, 1993.

——. *Averroes' Tahafut al-Tahafut (The Incoherence of the Incoherence)*. Translated by Simon Van Den Bergh. Cambridge: EJW Gibb Memorial Trust, 1954.

al-Jassas, Abu Bakr. *Usul al-Jassas: al-Fusul fi al-Usul*. Edited by Muhammad Muhammad Tamir. 2 vols. Beirut: Dar al-Kutub al-'Ilmiyya, 2000.

al-Khatib al-Baghdadi. *Kitab al-Faqih wa'l-Mutafaqqih*. N.p.: Matba'at al-Imtiyaz, 1977.

al-Sam'ani, Abu al-Muzaffar. *Qawati' al-Adilla fi al-Usul*. Edited by Muhammad Hasan Isma'il al-Shafi'i. Beirut: Dar al-Kutub al-'Ilmiyya, 1997.

al-Sarakhsi, Abu Bakr. *al-Muharrar fi Usul al-Fiqh*. Edited by Abu 'Abd al-Rahman 'Awida. Beirut: Dar al-Kutub al-'Ilmiyya, 1996.

al-Shatibi, Abu Ishaq. *al-Muwafaqat fi Usul al-Shari'a*. Edited by 'Abd Allah Daraz et al. Beirut: Dar al-Kutub al-'Ilmiyya, n.d.

al-Shirazi, Abu Ishaq. *Sharh al-Lum'a*. Edited by 'Abd al-Majid Turki. Beirut: Dar al-Gharb al-Islami, 1988.

al-Subki, 'Ali b. 'Abd al-Kafi, and Taj al-Din al-Subki. *al-Ibhaj fi Sharh al-Minhaj*. Beirut: Dar al-Kutub al-'Ilmiyya, n.d.

al-Zabidi, Muhibb al-Din. *Taj al-'Urus min Jawahir al-Qamus*. Edited by Ali Shiri. Beirut: Dar al-Fikr, 1994.

Secondary Islamic Sources

Abou El Fadl, Khaled. *Speaking in God's Name: Islamic Law, Authority and Women*. Oxford: One World Publications, 2001.

Abu Zayd, Nasr Hamid, with Ester R. Nelso. *Voice of an Exile: Reflections on Islam*. Westport, CT: Praeger, 2004.

Ahmad, Ahmad Atif. *Structural Interrelations of Theory and Practice in Islamic Law: A Study of Six Works of Medieval Islamic Jurisprudence*. Leiden: Brill, 2006.

Ahmed, Rumee. *Narratives of Islamic Legal Theory*. Oxford: Oxford University Press, 2012.

—— "[Review] *Islamic Natural Law Theories*." *Review of Middle East Studies* 45 (2011): 100–102.

Ali-Karamali, Shaista P. and F. Dunne. "The Ijtihad Controversy." *Arab Law Quarterly* 9 (1994): 238–57.

Bender, Courtney and Pamela Klassen, editors. *After Pluralism: Reimagining Religious Engagement*. New York: Columbia University Press, 2010.

Bertolacci, Amos. "The Doctrine of Material and Formal Causality in the 'Ilahiyyat' of Avicenna's 'Kitab al-Šifa'." *Quaestio* 2 (2002): 125–54.

Casanova, José. *Public Religions in the Modern World*. Chicago: University of Chicago Press, 994.

Chakrabarty, Dipesh. *Provincializing Europe: Postcolonial Thought and Historical Difference*. Princeton: Princeton University Press, 2000.

Cooperson, Michael. *Al Ma'mun*. Oxford: Oneworld Publications, 2005.

Emon, Anver M. *Islamic Natural Law Theories*. Oxford: Oxford University Press, 2010.

—— *Religious Pluralism and Islamic Law: Dhimmis and Others in the Empire of Law*. Oxford: Oxford University Press, 2012.

—— "To Most Likely Know the Law: Objectivity, Authority and Interpretation in Islamic Law." *Hebraic Political Studies* 4 (2009): 415–40.

—— "The Paradox of Equality and the Politics of Difference: Gender, Equality, Islamic Law and the Modern Muslim State." In *Gender and Equality in Islamic Law: Justice and Ethics in the Islamic Legal Tradition*. Edited by Ziba Mir-Hosseini, Kari Vogt, Lena Larson, and Christian Moe. London: IB Tauris, 2013: 237–58.

Emon, Anver, and Mark Ellis, Benhamin Glahn, editors. *Islamic Law and International Human Rights Law: Searching for Common Ground?* Oxford: Oxford University Press, 2012.

Fadel, Mohammad. "A Tragedy of Politics or an Apolitical Tragedy?" *Journal of the American Oriental Society* 131 (2011): 109–27.

Frank, Richard M. *Al-Ghazali and the Ash'arite School*. Durham, NC: Duke University Press, 1994.

Griffel, Frank. *Al-Ghazali's Philosophical Theology*. Oxford: Oxford University Press, 2009.

Hallaq, Wael B. "Was the Gate of Ijtihad Closed?" *International Journal of Middle East Studies* 16 (1984): 3–41.

Hildebrandt, Thomas. "Between Muʿtazilism and Mysticism: How much of a Muʿtazilite is Nasr Hamid Abu Zayd?" In *A Common Rationality: Muʿtazilism in Islam and Judaism.* Edited by Camilla Adang, Sabine Schmidtke, and David Sklare. Würzburg: Ergon in Kommission, 2007: 495–512.

Janssens, Jules. "[Review] *Al-Ghazali's Philosophical Theology.*" *The Muslim World* 101 (2011): 115–19.

Johansen, Baber. "Apostasy as Objective and Depersonalized Fact: Two Recent Egyptian Court Judgments." *Social Research* 70 (2003): 687–710.

Kapur, Ratna. "Un-Veiling Equality: Disciplining the 'Other' Woman Through Human Rights Discourse." In *Islamic Law and International Human Rights Law: Searching for Common Ground?* Edited by Anver M. Emon, Mark Ellis, and Benjamin Glahn. 265–290. Oxford: Oxford University Press, 2012.

Khaliq, Urfan. "Freedom of Religion and Belief in International Law: A Comparative Analysis." In *Islamic Law and International Human Rights Law: Searching for Common Ground?* Edited by Anver M. Emon, Mark Ellis, and Benjamin Glahn. 183–225. Oxford: Oxford University Press, 2012.

Kukkonen, Taneli, "[Review of] *Islamic Natural Law Theories.*" *Philosophy in Review* 31 (2011): 26–28.

Levering, Matthew. "Providence and Predestination in Al-Ghazali." *New Blackfriars* 92 (2011): 55–70.

March, Andrew. *Islam and Liberal Citizenship: The Search for an Overlapping Consensus.* Oxford: Oxford University Press, 2009.

—— "[Review] *Islamic Natural Law Theories.*" *Journal of Law and Religion* 26 (2011): 101–109.

Marmura, Michael E. "al-Ghazali." In *The Cambridge Companion to Arabic Philosophy.* Edited by Peter Adamson and Richard C. Taylor. Cambridge: Cambridge University Press, 2005.

—— "Final and efficient causality in Avicenna's cosmology and theology." *Quaestio* 2 (2002): 97–123.

Martin, Richard C., Mark R. Woodward, and Dwi S. Atmaja. *Defenders of Reason in Islam: Muʿtazilism from Medieval School to Modern Symbol.* Oxford: Oneworld Publications, 1997.

Mernissi, Fatima. *The Veil and the Male Elite: A Feminist Interpretation of Women's Rights in Islam.* Reading, MA: Addison-Wesley Pub. Co., 1991.

Mir-Hosseini, Ziba. "The Construction of Gender in Islamic Legal Thought and Strategies for Reform." *Hawwa* 1 (2003): 1–31.

Mitha, Farouk. *Al-Ghazali and the Ismailis: A Debate on Reason and Authority in Medieval Islam.* London: The Institute of Ismaili Studies, 2001.

Moosa, Ebrahim. "The Debts and Burdens of Critical Islam." In *Progressive Muslims: On Justice, Gender, and Pluralism*. Edited by Omid Safi. 111–27. Oxford: Oneworld Publications, 2003.

Nawas, John A. "A Reexamination of Three Current Explanations for al-Ma'mun's Introduction of the *Mihna*." *International Journal of Middle East Studies* 26 (1994): 615–29.

—— "The *Mihna* of 218 AH/833 AD Revisited: An Empirical Study." *Journal of the American Oriental Society* 116 (1996): 698–708.

Novak, David. "The Treatment of Islam and Muslims in the Legal Writings of Maimonides." *Studies in Islamic and Judaic Traditions*. Edited by W. M. Brinner and S. D. Ricks. Atlanta, GA: Scholars Press, 1986.

Olsson, Susanne. "Apostasy in Egypt: Contemporary Cases of *Hisbah*." *The Muslim World* 98 (2008): 95–115.

Reinhart, Kevin. *Before Revelation: The Boundaries of Muslim Moral Thought*. Albany: SUNY Press, 1995.

Said, Edward. *Orientalism*. London: Routledge and Kegan Paul, 1978.

Scott, David. *Conscripts of Modernity: The Tragedy of Colonial Enlightenment*. Durham: Duke University Press, 2004.

Vishanoff, David R. *The Formation of Islamic Hermeneutics: How Sunni Legal Theorists Imagined a Revealed Law*. New Haven: American Oriental Society, 2011.

Warren, David. "[Review] *Islamic natural law theories*." *Islam and Christian-Muslim Relations* 22 (2011): 495–96.

Wensinck, A. J. "Mu'djiza." *Encyclopaedia of Islam, Second Edition*. Edited by P. Bearman, Th. Bianquis, C. E. Bosworth, E. van Donzel, and W.P. Heinrichs (Leiden: Brill Publications,, 6 September 2011. *Brill Online*)

Wisnovsky, Robert. "Avicenna and the Avicennian Tradition." In *The Cambridge Companion to Arabic Philosophy*. Edited by Peter Adamson and Richard C. Taylor. Cambridge: Cambridge University Press, 2005: 92–136.

Wolfson, Harry Austryn. *The Philosophy of the Kalam*. Cambridge: Harvard University Press, 1976.

Legal and Philosophical Sources

Alonso, Fernando Llano. "Cosmopolitanism and Natural Law in Cicero." In *The Threads of Natural Law: Unravelling a Philosophical Tradition*. Edited by F. J. Contreras. New York: Springer, 2013: 27–36.

Anghie, Antony. *Imperialism, Sovereignty and the Making of International Law*. Cambridge: Cambridge University Press, 2009.

Arkes, Hadley. *Constitutional Illusions and Anchoring Truths: The Touchstone of the Natural Law*. Cambridge: Cambridge University Press, 2010.

—— *First Things: An Inquiry into the First Principles of Morals and Justice*. Princeton: Princeton University Press, 1986.

Assmann, Jan. *The Price of Monotheism*. Translated by Robert Savage. Stanford, CA: Stanford University Press, 2010.

Belo, Catarina. *Chance and Determinism in Avicenna and Averroes*. Leiden: Brill, 2007.

Bodnar, Istvan. "Aristotle's Natural Philosophy." In *The Stanford Encyclopedia of Philosophy*. <http://plato.stanford.edu/entries/aristotle-natphil/>.

Brague, Rémi. *The Law of God*. Translated by L. G. Cochrane. Chicago: University of Chicago Press, 2007.

Cicero, Marcus Tullius. *De natura deorum, academica*. Translated by H. Rackham. Cambridge, MA: Harvard University Press, 1951.

—— *De officiis*. Translated by Walter Miller. Cambridge, MA: Harvard University Press, 1913.

Cover, Robert. "Foreword: *Nomos* and Narrative." *Harvard Law Review* 97 (1983): 4–68.

D'Entreves, A. P. *Natural Law*. New York: Harper and Row, 1965.

Falcon, Andrea. "Aristotle on Causality." In *The Stanford Encyclopedia of Philosophy*. <http://plato.stanford.edu/entries/aristotle-causality/>.

Finnis, John. *Natural Law and Natural Rights*. Oxford: Clarendon Press, 1980.

Fox, Marvin. *Interpreting Maimonides*. Chicago: University of Chicago Press, 1990.

Gadamer, Hans-Georg. *Truth and Method*. Translated by Joel Weinsheimer and Donald G. Marshall. 2nd ed. New York: Continuum, 1989.

Gierke, Otto. *Natural Law and the Theory of Society*. Translated by E. Barker. Boston: Beacon Press, 1957.

Glasner, Ruth. *Averroes' Physics: A Turning Point in Medieval Natural Philosophy*. Oxford: Oxford University Press, 2009.

Heidegger, Martin. *Identity and Difference*. Translated by J. Stambaugh. Chicago: University of Chicago Press, 2002.

—— "On the Essence of Truth." Translated by J. Sallis. In *Martin Heidegger: Basic Writings*. Edited by D. F. Krell. New York: Harper and Row, 1977.

Hingorani, G. *Modern International Law*. 2nd ed. Dobbs Ferry, NY: Oceana Publications, 1984.

Holowicz, H. F. *Historical Introduction to Roman Law*. 2nd ed. Cambridge: Cambridge University Press, 1952.

Jaffa, Harry V. "Natural Law." In *The International Encyclopedia of the Social Sciences*. <http://www.encyclopedia.com/topic/natural_law.aspx>.

Kant, Immanuel. *Critique of Practical Reason*. Translated by W. S. Pluhar. Indianapolis, IN: Hackett, 2002.

—— *Groundwork for the Metaphysics of Morals*. Translated by H. J. Paton. New York: Harper and Row, 1964.

—— *Religion Within the Boundaries of Mere Reason*. Translated by A. Wood and G. di Giovanni. Cambridge: Cambridge University Press, 1998.

Kymlicka, Will. *Multicultural Citizenship: A Liberal Theory of Minority Rights.* Oxford: Clarendon Press, 1995.

Koester, Helmut. "νόμος φύσεως: The concept of Natural Law in Greek Thought." In *Religions in Antiquity: Essays in Memory of Erwin Ramsdell Goodenough.* Edited by J. Neusner. Leiden: Brill, 1968.

Levinas, Emmanuel. *Totality and Infinity.* Translated by A. Lingis. Pittsburgh: Duquesne University Press, 1969.

MacIntyre, Alasdair. *After Virtue.* Notre Dame, IN: University of Notre Dame Press, 1981.

—— *Dependent Rational Animals: Why Human Beings Need the Virtues.* Chicago: Open Court, 1999.

—— *First Principles, Final Ends and Contemporary Philosophical Issues.* Milwaukee, WI: Marquette University Press, 1990.

—— "Intractable Moral Disagreements." In *Intractable Disputes about the Natural Law: Alasdair MacIntyre and Critics.* Edited by Lawrence S. Cunningham. Notre Dame, University of Notre Dame Press, 2009: 1–52.

—— *Three Rival Versions of Moral Enquiry: Encyclopedia, Genealogy, and Tradition.* Notre Dame: University of Notre Dame Press, 1991.

Martens, John W. *One God, One Law: Philo of Alexandria on the Mosaic and Greco-Roman Law.* Leiden: Brill, 2003.

Mazower, Mark. *No Enchanted Palace: The End of Empire and the Ideological Origins of the United Nations.* Princeton: Princeton University Press, 2009.

Moran, Mayo. *Rethinking the Reasonable Person: An Egalitarian Reconstruction of the Objective Standard.* New York: Oxford University Press, 2003.

Moyn, Samuel. *The Last Utopia: Human Rights in History.* Cambridge, MA: Belknap Press, 2010.

Novak, David. *Suicide and Morality: The Theories of Plato, Aquinas and Kant and Their Relevance for Theology.* Revised edition. New York: Scholars Studies Press, 1975.

Rachels, James. "God and Human Attitudes." In *Divine Commands and Morality.* Edited by P. Helm. Oxford: Oxford University Press, 1981.

Rawls, John. *A Theory of Justice.* Cambridge, MA: Harvard University Press, 1971.

—— *Political Liberalism.* New York: Columbia University Press, 1993.

Rommen, Heinrich A. *The Natural Law.* Translated by T. R. Hanley. Indianapolis, IN: Liberty Fund, 1998.

Ross, W. D. *Aristotle.* New York: Meridian Books, 1959.

Schneewind, J. B. *The Invention of Autonomy.* Cambridge: Cambridge University Press, 1998.

Sorabji, Richard. *Necessity, Cause and Blame: Perspectives on Aristotle's Theory.* Chicago: Chicago University Press, 1980.

Spinoza, Baruch. *Tractatus Theologico-Politicus.* Translated by M. Silverthorne and J. Israel. Cambridge: Cambridge University Press, 2007.

Strauss, Leo. *Natural Right and History*. Chicago, University of Chicago Press, 1953.

—— *Philosophy and Law*. Translated by E. Adler. Albany: State University of New York Press, 1995.

—— *The Rebirth of Classical Political Rationalism*. Edited by T. L. Pangle. Chicago: University of Chicago Press, 2007.

Taylor, Charles. *A Secular Age*. Cambridge, MA: Harvard University Press, 2007.

—— *Sources of the Self: The Making of the Modern Identity*. Cambridge, MA: Harvard University Press 1989.

Tierney, Brian. *The Idea of Natural Rights*. Atlanta, GA: Scholars Press, 1997.

Wittgenstein, Ludwig. *Philosophical Investigations*. Translated by G. E. M. Anscombe. New York: Macmillan, 1958.

Index

Abel 64, 142
Abou El Fadl, Khaled, 183 n90
Abraham 106 n105, 139, 203
Adam 78
Ahmad, Ahmad Atif 144 n2
Ahmed, Rumee 48, 48 n9, 49,
  49 n12, 144 n2
Akiba ben Joseph 130–131
Albo, Joseph 17 n37
Ali-Karamali, Shaista P. 148 n9
Alonso, Fernando Llano 76 n26
Ambrosiaster 66, 68, 92, 92 n67–68,
  93, 93 n69–72, 94, 94 n73–76, 95,
  95 n77, 105, 115, 119
al-Amidi, Sayf al-Din 123, 123 n18–19
Amos 77
anthropology 83
analogy 173
antinomy 130
apologetics 18
Aquinas see Thomas Aquinas
Arabic 52, 158–159, 164, 169, 190,
  193 n13, 194
Archimedean Fulcrum 29
Aristotle 5, 7, 9 n18, 13 n31, 22 n46,
  29 n58, 42 n94, 44 n105, 45, 132,
  132 n15, 159–161, 163, 168, 173,
  174 n76, 188, 193
Arkes, Hadley 109 n111, 195, 195 n16
al-Asfahani, Abu 'Abd Allah 151 n14
Assmann, Jan 69 n7
Atmaja, Dwi S. 180 n88
Augustine of Hippo 62, 66, 67 n3, 68,
  71 n14, n15, 92, 92 n67, 96, 96 n79,
  99, 99 n87–88, 100, 100 n90–93,
  101, 101 n94–95, 102, 102 n96–98,
  103, 103 n99–102, 104, 104 n103,
  105, 113, 116
authentic 8
authority 16, 23–25, 53, 60, 146, 181
  epistemic 47, 148, 197
  interpretive 182
  ontological 47, 50, 148, 173, 176
    183–184, 190, 197–198
Averroes 174 n76

Avicenna see Ibn Sina
avodah zarah see idolatry

Babel, Tower of 30
bad inclination 10
bad 123
Bammel, Caroline Hammond 76 n24
Banner, William 76 n26
Barth, Karl 69–70, 70 n6, 72
Barr, James 74 n23
Basil the Great 68 n6
al-Basri, Abu al-Husayn 150 n11
berit see covenant
Bender, Courtney 145 n4
Bertolacci, Amos 162 n47
Bible, the 107
Biggar, Nigel 72, 72 n15
al-Baghdadi, Al-Khatib 151 n15
Bleich, J. David 16 n35,
Bodnar, Istvan 160, 160 n40–42,
  161 n43–44
Bonner, Gerald 96 n79
bonum commune see common good
Boyd, Craig A. 72, 72 n15
Boyle, Joseph 73 n17
Brague, Rémi 6 n15, 9 n17
Braaten, Carl 72, 72 n15
Bray, Gerald L. 92 n67
Brock, Stephen 73, 73 n19, 109 n110
Bruyn, Theodore De 96 n78
Buber, Martin 131
Budziszewski, J. 70 n10, 108
Burrell, David B. 193 n13
Bussieres, Marie-Pierre 92 n68

Cahn, Edmond 71 n12
Cain 64, 142
Campbell, Douglas A. 70 n9
Calvin, John 72
Casanova, José 145 n5
Cassiodorus 96 n78
Cessario, Romanus 73 n19
Chadwick, Henry 76 n26
charity 133
Charles, Daryl J. 72, 72 n15, 86

Printed and bound by CPI Group (UK) Ltd, Croydon, CR0 4YY